OP 15

The Films of
Montgomery
CLIFT

The Films of
Montgomery
CLIFT

by *Judith M. Kass*
Foreword by Brooks Clift

ITADEL PRESS
ecaucus
ew Jersey

Acknowledgments

My heartfelt thanks to Fred Davis and Carla Garcia of the Religious Society of Friends; Joseph Balian and Barbara J. Humphrys of the Library of Congress, Motion Picture Section; Monty Arnold, David Bartholomew, Richard Ryan, and Dorothy Swerdlove of the Library of Performing Arts at Lincoln Center; Movie Star News, Carol Carey; Mary Corliss, Emily Sieger, and Charles Silver of the Museum of Modern Art, Department of Film; Bettman Archive, Inc.; Kevin McCarthy; William K. Everson, Sara Fishko, and Alice Geyer of Universal Films; Elia Kazan, Howard Mandelbaum, and Paul Noble of WNEW-TV, Metromedia, Inc.; Mira Rostova, Frank Rowley, Mark Urman, Lou Valentino, Jerry Vermilye, and Pat and Brad Warner; and most especially to Lewis Archibald, Patricia Bosworth, and John Cocchi.

My greatest debt, for his extraordinary generosity, is to Stephen V. Russell.

First Edition
Copyright © 1979 by Judith M. Kass
All rights reserved
Published by Citadel Press
A division of Lyle Stuart Inc.
120 Enterprise Ave., Secaucus, N. J. 07094
Manufactured in the United States of America by
Halliday Lithograph, West Hanover, Mass.
Designed by Tim McKeen

Library of Congress Cataloging in Publication Data

Kass, Judith M
    The films of Montgomery Clift.

    1. Clift, Montgomery.   2.   Moving-picture actors
and actresses—United States—Biography.   I. Title.
PN2287.C545K3   791.43′028′0924 [B]   79-16345
ISBN 0-8065-0717-9

TO BROOKS CLIFT

FOREWORD

Probably the best reason for me to say anything by way of introduction is that I admire the research Judy Kass has put into compiling this book. It's visual as well as factual. She's collected such an incredible number of pictures showing the person as well as his work.

Monty was affected by everything—a man without skin. It's amazing to me how he was able to survive, despite all his mental, moral, physical and legal problems, to the ripe old age of forty-five. He used to say, looking down on mankind from the viewpoint of a top neurotic, "If one is not a troubled man, problems can be solved easily in one day, but life is too complicated for such glibness, particularly if you're an actor. You cannot play out your life as a middle-of-the-roader or you'll never learn anything about yourself or other people. Whatever hurt may happen, you've got to force yourself to keep on being able to be deeply involved and open to whatever happens—an innocent." Given that philosophy, the only way to survive was to have an incredible sense of humor, of irony, of the ridiculous. He said once, "What makes an actor great is the same thing that makes a person great, a sense of humor."

For me, one of the most memorable moments involving Monty occurred during my wedding, which was held at his house. The minister asked the assembled group—two mothers, a matron of honor, and my best man, Monty—if there were any objections to the marriage. Monty replied sarcastically, "He smokes." Another time we were having a drink in a bar on a summer's day. I'd just been to Cape Cod, and a girl I'd met there came swooping over from the other side of the room—obviously a Montgomery Clift fan, I thought. Monty slumped slowly under the table as she came over to us. And then she said, "Aren't you Brooks Clift?" whereupon he completely dissolved in hysterical laughter.

Monty told me that once when visiting friends in New York, before knocking on their door, he stripped to his shorts, socks, shoes and dark glasses. His remark on entering was, "I have to do something to keep people from recognizing me."

I think Monty would have been appalled and roared with laughter at his own funeral if he could have seen it: The pompous, empty, meaningless, perfunctory service, the extras hired by Campbell's funeral home as pallbearers instead of his brother and his friends, the gravediggers unceremoniously yanking away the grass mats once the coffin had been lowered into the grave.

How jealous he was of the rare people he considered really great: Olivier, Ella [Fitzgerald] and Sinatra. After *The Misfits*, he said about Marilyn Monroe, "She's the most, for me, rewarding

actress I've ever worked with. I could look into her eyes and whatever way I read what I read, she heard it all, so we were both listening.''

He talked about the problem of living the character one was playing, and said one really doesn't: "If you lived the part, you'd be shot before the picture was shot.'' Monty said, "If the hurdles in a part are only so high, a part's not worth doing, but if you can really raise the hurdles, then you've achieved something, I hope.''

Even as his older brother, because we could communicate, and felt many of the same moral convictions, I could always evaluate my thoughts or my decisions with the question, "OK, Monty, what about this decision, this remark or this love or this cruelty or this waste of time or this goal or this put-down?'' And he'd ask me the same things, which I naturally felt was a great compliment. And it's tough now not to really hear him answer or question or yell or cry. I miss that wavelength of understanding that we had.

I have a recurring dream in which my brother is alive. We meet in a bookstore and sit at a counter. We talk and he asks me how I feel about his resurrection, and I answer that I guess he must never have really died. And we talk about all the things that I can't discuss with him anymore.

Monty would laugh at the fact that I'm furious at him for not sending me a case of Pouilly-Fuissé on my birthday anymore.

BROOKS CLIFT

CONTENTS

INTRODUCTION

If one image from the movies dominates our memories of the fifties, it is of Montgomery Clift, Marlon Brando, and James Dean as *the* rebel heroes: the inarticulate romantics who both embodied female—and some male—fantasies and countered them. The three were not all cut from the same cloth.

Brando was the id—snarling, laconic. He was a brute; you could get in trouble with him. His screen career was only three years old when Brando verbalized the rebel hero's credo. Asked in *The Wild One* what he is against, Brando sneered, "What have you got?"

Dean was like a defenseless, innocent, but surly, puppy. If he was the super-ego, he was also childlike, and he was so neurotic, he was almost unable to speak. As much as Dean evoked teen-agers' romantic fantasies, he clearly needed a mother, too. He was sullen, resentful, and hurt, searching for a love and warmth forever denied him.

If Brando and Dean represented the lower and middle classes, respectively, Clift was upper class—the refined, thoughtful ego. His was an almost feminine sensitivity, described by that most overworked of definitions, "vulnerable." But if Clift lacked power, he was not always a victim. George Eastman in *A Place in the Sun* lives in a world dominated by women; he is unable to break free of their demands on him and shape his own destiny. It is inferred that George is without character, that longing for material advantages has weakened his moral fiber.

The individuals Clift portrayed were bent on accomplishing some formidable, but not impossible, task: getting John Wayne's cattle to Abilene in *Red River*, marrying Olivia de Havilland in *The Heiress*, or finding Ivan Jandl's mother in *The Search*. But the *image* goes beyond this.

Clift in repose is the recurring figure: Clift sitting or standing, meditating on some insoluble moral dilemma—whether or not to kill Shelley Winters in *Place*, or how to escape being tried for murder without betraying his priest's oath in *I Confess*. It is an image, summed up by his performance as Prewitt in *From Here to Eternity*, of a man pushing himself past the point of normal human endurance. He is a symbol of inner tension, the result of smothered defiance, and it explodes in *Eternity* in the killing of Fatso Judson.

It is for Prewitt and Matthew Garth in *Red River* that Clift is thought of as a rebel. In *River*, Clift took the role of The Kid from Wayne. Clift was the ambitious, fair-minded Mr. Christian to Wayne's Captain Bligh. Clift takes Wayne's cattle, in an act of open rebellion justified by the success of the drive. But Clift's insurgency must be punished, so Wayne beats the hell out of him, a physical victory that is quickly undercut by Joanne Dru's shooting the fight to an end.

Clift's attractiveness lay in his being a romantic figure, rather than, like Brando, a sexual one. He is cerebral, not physical, an instinctive intellectual rather than an educated one. His appeal stemmed from an excessive sensitivity tinged with neurosis. There is no real sex in any Clift film, just the suggestion of it, as in the seduction scene in *A Place in the Sun.* But there is romance in his relationship with Elizabeth Taylor in that film, with de Havilland in *The Heiress*, and with Joanne Dru in *Red River.* There is perhaps more implicit sex in *The Big Lift*—with Clift's intense yearning for female companionship sharply focused on Cornell Borchers—than in most other Clift films.

But no star ever had an easier time getting women on screen. Clift never had to compete with another man, or a woman's desire for a career. The women he wants, from de Havilland's heiress, through Taylor's Angela Vickers, to Lee Remick's Carol (in *Wild River*) are totally available. In spite of this, he seldom gets what he wants; his own neurosis, or the conflicts imposed by an unsympathetic social milieu, stand in the way.

Thus, Clift is emblematic of the beautiful loner who loses everything, the flawed hero who is not permitted to enjoy the results of his efforts. And this is an image that persists into the seventies. Today, audiences make heroes of rebels like Al Pacino in *Serpico*, the one honest cop in a world pervaded by corruption; of Jack Nicholson in *Five Easy Pieces*, the supremely sensitive man who is unable to connect on a meaningful level with other people; and of Warren Beatty in *Shampoo*, the handsome stud whose promiscuity costs him the woman he loves. These are the morally ambivalent, psychically assailable heroes who are the spiritual heirs of Montgomery Clift.

MONTY

He was born Edward Montgomery Clift in Omaha, Nebraska, on October 17, 1920. A twin sister, Roberta, had arrived several hours before. Monty's parents, William Brooks and Ethel "Sunny" Clift, already had a son, William Brooks (called Brooks), who had been born eighteen months earlier.

To understand Montgomery Clift's life, one has to know something of Sunny Clift's background, for it was her desire to be recognized by the families that had disowned her which influenced her behavior and the way in which her children grew up.

Sunny's mother, Maria Anderson, eloped with Woodbury Blair in defiance of her mother, Eliza Anderson, who harbored a grudge against Blair's father. Despite the fact that Maria was pregnant by Blair, Eliza had the marriage annulled. Eliza, Maria, and her sister Sophie journeyed from Washington, D.C., where they lived, to Philadelphia for Maria's confinement. They left Ethel, the child who was born there in the summer of 1888, in the care of Dr. Edward E. Montgomery, who had delivered her. Dr. Montgomery was under strict orders not to reveal her family's identity to the child, and "Sophie and Frank Adams" were named as parents on Ethel's birth certificate. For a year, the doctor cared for Ethel— whom he later nicknamed Sunny—then he arranged for her adoption by Mr. and Mrs. Charles Fogg of Germantown.

Sunny's childhood with the Foggs was not a happy one. When she was about to leave for Cornell University, Dr. Montgomery finally revealed the story of her adoption to her.

At Cornell, Sunny met Bill Clift. He was a quiet, amiable young man who had deferred his ambition to go into banking in favor of his parents' wishes that he study engineering.

As Bill told it, the first Clifts had emigrated from England around 1695, settling first in Maryland and later in Tennessee. Bill's father, Colonel Moses Clift, had fought for the Confederacy in the Civil War, then settled in Chattanooga where he raised four sons and two daughters—by two successive wives.

Bill and Sunny were married in 1914, and his family's refusal to accept her—she had neither money nor family—may have fueled Sunny's desire to be recognized by the Andersons.

Bill had always hated engineering and wanted to study investments, which he did in night school with an eye to leaving engineering and becoming a banker. In 1918, the couple moved from Mississippi, where Bill was employed building dams, to Omaha.

Sunny had gradually disclosed her background to Bill and, when she was pregnant in 1919, made him swear to keep her secret from

Monty, age one, Omaha, Nebraska.

their children until the Andersons recognized her. Sunny also announced her intention of raising their progeny in the style she felt the Andersons would expect. Bill, who loved Sunny intensely (Brooks would later say, ''My mother could do wrong in Pa's eyes''), apparently did not question the reasoning behind her attitude.

Sunny and her three children—accompanied by Emma Wilke, the children's nurse—embarked on a series of extended journeys: first to New England for summer vacations, later to Bermuda, Yorktown Heights and Manhasset. ''Wilke,'' as the kids called her, was the family disciplinarian; she was stern, spinsterish and—sadly—hated by her charges.

In 1925, Sunny learned that her mother had died so she stepped up her efforts to locate her family. Bill had left his position as a vice-president of the Omaha National Bank and moved his family to Highland Park outside Chicago, where he become sales manager for the Ames Emmerich Investment Company. He conducted some of his business in the East and—at Sunny's behest—searched Washington, D.C., and Virginia, eventually locating Sophie Anderson in Washington.

Sophie was by then an elderly woman, unwell and eccentric, but once contact was made, Sunny accepted her every word as law.

Sunny Clift in Pau, France, May 1929.

Sunny had decided that her children would be raised as royalty, as befitted descendants of the Andersons and the Blairs; tutored by herself and professionals until they went to college; and segregated from the contaminating influence of "ordinary" children. To ensure their good behavior, the three were bribed. Brooks, Roberta (She had been named after Bill's sister, but when the rift between the two branches of the family—over Bill's marriage to Sunny—worsened, Sunny declared that thereafter her daughter would be called Ethel. Monty was named after his greatgrandfather, Montgomery Blair.), and Monty were dressed identically—that is, Ethel was dressed as a boy—and their hair was cut in bangs.

Sophie decreed that before Sunny and her children could be recognized by the Andersons, or by Sunny's father, Woodbury Blair, who was still alive, they must go abroad, absorb European culture, learn French and German, and perfect their manners. Bill agreed to this enforced separation, by now only one of many, without demur. He wanted Sunny to be happy.

In May 1928, the four Clifts—plus Wilke—departed for the Continent on the *Ile de France*. While swimming in the ship's pool, Monty was held under water by another boy and nearly drowned. Trying to catch his breath, he burst a gland in his neck and developed a temperature of 104° and an abscessed ear. Learning of a gland specialist who had treated the Kaiser, Sunny rushed her charges to Munich. There Monty underwent a lengthy operation. It was successful in that he survived, but the surgery left the long scar which is visible on the right side of Monty's neck whenever one sees him on screen.

When Monty recovered, Sunny took everyone to Paris where the three youngsters were tutored in French; they went to the Louvre, the Tuileries, and the theater. Monty was first drawn to the stage that summer in Paris. Later that year, in St. Moritz, after sojourns in Montreux and Geneva, Switzerland, Monty performed *The Conversion of King Clovis*, a play he had fabricated out of a French history book. He, Brooks, and Ethel acted in it for an audience composed of their tutor, M. Helman, Sunny, and Wilke.

That trip lasted nine months; there was another starting in the fall of 1929, when they went back to St. Moritz. There, under the tutelage of M. Quiot, they studied French grammar and history, penmanship, and metric math. In the interim, Sunny enrolled the children in public school in Highland Park, but with their European manners and clothes, and their fluent French, they were anathema to their fellow students, who gibed at them mercilessly. Once more Brooks, Ethel, and Monty were tutored at home.

In October 1929, of course, came the stock market crash and by January 1930 the family was reunited in Highland Park. Although

Monty and his sister Ethel,
Fort Lauderdale, winter, 1933.

Bill was in serious financial difficulty, Sunny, acceding to her aunt's dictum that the children were still socially unacceptable, scrounged up enough money for still another trip—this time to France and Germany where they stayed from June to November, 1930. Before the end of 1931, Bill Clift was broke, the house in Highland Park and most of its furnishings were sold, and the family was living in a furnished room in Greenwich Village, New York. Although Bill was unable to find work, Sunny had two jobs: one at Mt. Sinai Hospital writing up patients' histories, and a second scrubbing floors at the 42nd Street library.

Through it all, Bill and Sunny never discussed their financial predicaments with their children. What had happened to them was obvious to Brooks, but it was never acknowledged verbally. Instead, Sunny behaved as though they still had money, setting the table with silver, and even scraping together enough money so that her brood could go on being tutored.

Without being specific, Bill and Sunny made them feel they had martyred themselves to give the children the best of everything. Brooks had the impression they were in "protective custody," cross-examined as they were about where they went, who they met, and what they did and said. They were prevented from having normal children's reactions—like hostility—or, as Brooks said, from experiencing "the joy of being right, or wrong." They enjoyed the traveling, but hated the readjustment to the United States.

In a 1957 article for *McCall's*, Eleanor Harris quoted Monty as saying, "I call all that traveling a hobgoblin existence for children. Why weren't roots established?" The same year he told Jesse Zunser of *Cue:* "My formal education was a mess. I even skipped high school. . . . If I want to know something, I've got to ask my brother who was a Harvard man, or my sister who went to Bryn Mawr." Monty asked, "On how many things could I be an authority? I've done nothing but act since I was fourteen." Harris quoted a friend of Monty's: "He's almost in a state of amnesia about his childhood. He never speaks of it, and if he's asked questions, he sidesteps."

*   *   *

Bill finally found employment, but the family was separated again—this time because it was cheaper to live in Florida. In Sarasota, from fall to fall, 1932 to 1933, the four Clifts and Wilke occupied a large house. The kids' tutor, Walter Hayward, lived across the street. Hayward, who had acted himself, was friendly with a local stock company producer who told him that he was looking for a twelve-year-old boy for a role in *As Husbands Go.* As their tutor, Hayward had helped the boys recite Shakespeare and, thinking Monty might enjoy this particular part, told Sunny about the play. Subsequently, Monty recollected his first dramatic experience: "I told a guy with an amateur theatrical company I'd like to act in one of his plays. It was my own idea; nobody in the family had ever thought of acting. I wouldn't know why I wanted to act, but someone said it had to do with competition with my sister and older brother."

Although Monty loved being in the spotlight, Sunny was unsure about a theatrical career for her son. It was too undignified. But once they were in Sharon, Connecticut, in the summer of 1934, Sunny reconsidered. Bill, as a fiscal and engineering expert, had departed for a gold mine in Salvador. Brooks went with him, Ethel left for camp, and Monty and his mother were staying in a rented house for the month of August. Not far away, at the Berkshire Playhouse in Stockbridge, Massachusetts, *Fly Away Home* was about to begin rehearsals for its pre-Broadway tryout. Sunny heard that producer Theron Bamberger was looking for a fourteen-year-old actor to play Harmer Masters, the younger of Thomas Mitchell's two obstreperous sons, in the play.

Although Bamberger was worried about Monty's lack of experience, he hired him, thinking, "Something may come of it." As he wrote in a *New York Times* article about the production: "The boy turned out to be both handsome and intelligent; he read for me and I liked him. The first day of rehearsal proved that Monty was an actor. [He had] a natural histrionic talent."

When *Fly Away Home* moved to Broadway, Monty moved with it. The play was harmless fluff about the children of a divorced couple trying to reunite their parents just before their mother marries another man. Reviewing the play, Whitney Boulton of the *Morning Telegraph* said: "This event is performed by four youngsters of exceptional value to the play and, probably to the profession of acting. . . ." Bamberger recalled that Monty "was very self-contained on opening night, while Thomas Mitchell, the star, had a bad attack of stage fright."

Phyllis Bamberger remembered Monty as charming, but smothered by his mother and trying intermittently to escape her influence. He was clearly well-bred and quiet, frequently staying in his dressing room reading plays when he wasn't on stage. Monty was also very much absorbed by the adventure of acting and studied Mitchell's performance closely.

For several months after *Fly Away Home* closed, Monty toured the Broadway producers' offices with Sunny. For a time, nothing happened, so Sunny enrolled Monty with the John Robert Powers model agency, believing one thing might lead to another and he would be spotted for a show. He wasn't. Instead, Monty found

Monty and Brooks, Sharon, Conn., summer, 1934.

Monty with his father, Bill Clift, at Ethel's wedding,
Milwaukee, 1945.

himself posing for photographers and hating it. Brooks still has an
advertisement which shows Monty leaning over a Steinway, smil-
ing and turning the pages for the pianist.

In October 1935, Monty was cast as Prince Peter in *Jubilee*, a
Cole Porter musical which is remembered today chiefly because
the score included "Begin the Beguine" and "Just One of Those
Things." The cast was immense; the stars were Mary Boland and
Melville Cooper; and scarcely anyone noticed that Montgomery
Clift played the good prince to Jackie Kelk's naughty one.

Sunny continued to see that Monty had all the advantages she
could provide for him—advantages usually given the children of
wealthier parents. They attended concerts and the theater, and
Sunny gave Monty expensive presents such as art books and clas-
sical records.

While he was modeling, Monty had become interested in photography. He not only took pictures, he developed and printed them at
home. When he was older, Monty said, "I was a camera bug.
Nobody in the family could take a bath on weekends because the
tub was full of negatives I was developing." Subsequently, he
gained modest recognition for his work; in 1937, Monty took a

picture of Thomas Benton's son that won an award and was reproduced in *Good Housekeeping*.

Just after *Jubilee* opened, Aunt Sophie ordered Sunny to Washington and, when she got there, demanded that she and Ethel move in with her as her companions. For once, Sunny was firm, declaring that she couldn't just leave the rest of her family in New York. Sophie teased her yet again with the idea of acknowledgment by the Andersons and the Blairs, but the meeting ended in a furious argument with Sophie yelling at Sunny to leave. Recognition for herself and her children was clearly impossible. The years of sacrifice, of shepherding her youngsters through Europe, and of separation from her husband had been in vain.

In 1948, when Brooks and his father were in Paris, Bill Clift finally told his older son his wife's story—a story he accepted as the tragedy she felt it to be. Brooks told Monty, who arrived subsequently in Paris, only to discover that, somehow, he already knew. They had lunch, went to see the Dior collection, and that evening saw Noel Coward in *Present Laughter*, but their minds were on their mother's quest. Monty couldn't have cared less about the Andersons or the Blairs, but at least this tale explained his mother's determination to turn himself, Brooks, and Ethel into "thoroughbreds." It was for them as well as for herself that Sunny had insisted on a privileged life separated from their peers. She apparently never understood what their so-called "specialness" had cost each of her three children.

*   *   *

In 1935, Brooks had boarded with the Ned Smith family while he attended the Friends School in Germantown, Pennsylvania. Monty spent the summer of 1937 with Ned, Jr. and his sister, who was married to Thomas Benton, the sculptor. With *Jubilee* closed, he had enrolled briefly at Ethel's school, Dalton, but Monty couldn't get used to being just one student among many—his experiences in the theater and his mother's attitude had conditioned him to think of himself as unique. Now he was in Newport, Rhode Island, where—with Ned's help—Monty learned to sail and fish. Smith later recalled how he had tried to bring out Monty's so-called masculine side by going hiking, camping, or boating with him, rather than letting him stay home with his nose in a book.

Bill Clift had never fully supported his son's acting career (In one of his earliest interviews, Monty stated, "My father simply told me acting was an insecure profession and could be a big embarrassment. He said an ordinary doctor or lawyer could get by respectably, but nobody had much use for an actor. How right he was!") and was undoubtedly pleased when Monty didn't find work until that fall. In January 1938, he opened in New York in *Yr.*

Monty gets instruction from Howard Hawks on how to fight with John Wayne on the Red River *set.*

Obedient Husband, a comedy starring Fredric March (as the eighteenth-century English essayist Richard Steele), Florence Eldridge, and Dame May Whitty. In Columbus, Ohio, during the long pre-Broadway tour, Monty fell ill with the flu, and director John Cromwell's wife, Kay Johnson, went on in his place. The play was generally panned, the critics finding it "indifferent" and "mild and monotonous," but Richard Watts, Jr. of the *New York Herald Tribune* singled Monty out, saying: "There is an excellent performance in the minor role of an eager young nobleman by Montgomery Clift, who plays with a surprisingly successful suggestion of shyness. . . ."

Eye on the Sparrow, Monty's next play, was also a failure, with one reviewer calling it an "aimless and uninviting comedy." But the Clift family's fortunes had changed for the better; they were by then living in a huge apartment at 116 East 53rd Street. With *Sparrow* closed, Monty was free to appear with Celeste Holm in *The Wind and The Rain*, a summer stock production in Millbrook, New York.

1938 was an important year in Monty's life. He was cast as the fifteen-year-old André Brisac in *Dame Nature*, and he made friends with Morgan James, who played Batton in the play. Monty had had few friends up until that time. He had spent some time with Anne Baxter when they were both auditioning for a movie neither was cast in, and he had befriended a theater apprentice in Millbrook, a girl who found him "unbelievably sympathetic."

Patricia Collinge—the actress who translated *Dame Nature* from

Every inch a cowboy. Monty during Red River.

André Birabeau's French comedy—also became friendly with Monty. During rehearsals, she observed him creating stage "business" which was different and original. Miss Collinge described him as "starting to make unorthodox acting choices even then."

In a memorial letter to the *Times*, actor Fitzroy Davis, who met Monty after a performance of the play, wrote: "I remember his dazzling beauty and talent in that first major appearance, but I also remember his hypersensitive quickness to misinterpret and mistrust, even at that age. . . ."

Dame Nature concerns two adolescents who become parents, a delicate premise at best, but one that Monty carried off. Sidney B. Whipple of the *New York World Telegram* noted that ". . . he has a role made for him, one which. . .he handles capably and surely," and Richard Watts, Jr., said, in the *Tribune:* "Young Mr. Clift has an enormously difficult characterization to manage, and on the whole he handles it excellently, although there are times when he makes the youthful father too neurotic for comfort."

Dame Nature was notable for other reasons. Brooks says that it was the first time that he seriously thought his brother had a future as an actor of real talent. And, for the first time, "Montgomery Clift" appeared above the title of a Broadway play.

Morgan James became Monty's principal companion during the run of the play. He was envious of James' comparative worldliness. Monty knew he had been overprotected and he was anxious to experience life for himself. Together they went out to eat after the show, or visited burlesque houses, or just roamed the Broadway area, enjoying whatever came their way.

Sunny tried to keep her son from dating, but Monty began a few hesitant relationships with girls, making dates with female admirers, and often standing them up when they waited for him after the show. He occasionally saw Anne Baxter or actress Louisa Horton, and attended socialite Brenda Frazier's debut at the Ritz Carlton Hotel (but never got up the nerve to ask her to dance).

On April 25, 1939, Monty opened (and closed three nights later) with the legendary Alla Nazimova in Karel Capek's *The Mother*. *Variety* said: ''Montgomery Clift is sincere and direct as the youngest son, but all others are constrained by the bad writing and direction.''

''*The Mother* was not the kind of play that would run very long,'' Brooks says now, ''but he was incredible. I don't think his part was all that sensational, but he did it to learn from this goddess, Nazimova.''

While photographing the dance rehearsals of *Everywhere I Roam* —for the fun of it—Monty met Lehman Engel, the composer-conductor, and a friend of the show's choreographer, Felicia Sorel. Monty and Engel became fast friends; they talked about music

Monty and Fred Zinnemann talk over a scene as Ivan Jandl listens during the filming of The Search.

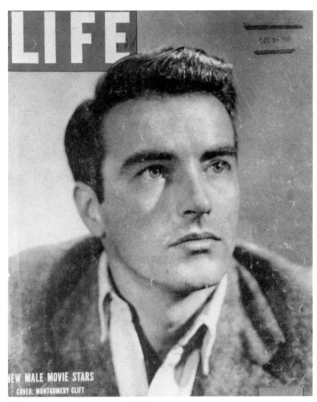

Monty on the cover of Life.

(Monty was taking piano lessons at the time) and they attended museums, concerts, and plays together.

Sunny encouraged Monty's friendship with Engel and, later that spring, when she found Engel was sailing to Mexico, she asked if Monty could go along. The two young men—Engel was ten years older than Monty—arrived in Vera Cruz, then entrained for Cuernavaca where they spent a lot of time sightseeing.

In Acapulco, Monty came down with dysentery, so Engel chartered a plane to take them to Mexico City. From there, Monty—seriously ill and in great pain—flew immediately to New York. He had amoebic dysentery and, although he was well a few months later, his body never fully recovered; Monty would have repeated bouts with the disease in the future.

To fight the bleeding and diarrhea caused by his illness, Monty started carrying a supply of pills around with him. He began studying drugs with the same zeal he applied to his acting, consulting with a pharmacist on the specifics of the painkillers and other drugs he was taking. From then on Monty was fascinated by medicine. Years later, his doctor in Hollywood, Rex Kennamer, would say: "He had an enormous knowledge of medicine. With Monty, it seemed like an extraordinary preoccupation." Another doctor remarked; "He has the greatest knowledge of various medications, their uses and effects of any nonmedical person I've ever known." Monty described his interest in the subject by saying: "Medicine to me is modern fiction, with just the same excitement." He also became preoccupied with his diet; to regulate his symptoms Monty had to rely primarily on milk and nearly-raw steak.

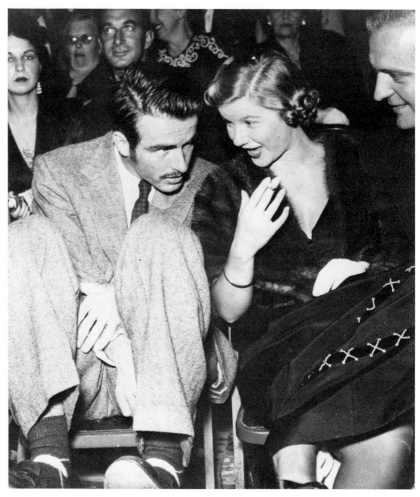

*Monty, Barbara Bel Geddes, and her husband at the
Ice Follies, 1948.*

Almost as soon as he had recuperated, Monty was cast as Clarence Day, Jr., in *Life with Father*. He was just as quickly dismissed, some say because of his method of breaking up his deliv-
ery so his voice would carry, others because he wasn't ordinary
enough for the part. Reportedly, Monty himself knew he wasn't
right for the role, but he wanted to work with director Bretaigne
Windust.

Disappointing as it was to be fired, Monty was nevertheless left
free to accept a leading role in Robert E. Sherwood's *There Shall
Be No Night*. After his first movies were released, Monty described meeting the Lunts on the stage of the Alvin Theater for the
Saturday Evening Post: "Lunt had me read some lines, then said I
must meet Lynnie. Fontanne swept across the stage, dragging her
eyelashes on the floor, and gave out with the customary, graceful,
empty phrases. Two days later they called me for the part I
wanted." Considering the kindly, parental manner in which the
Lunts treated Monty, this is a curiously unfriendly reaction for him
to have a mere nine years later.

Since Alfred Lunt and Lynn Fontanne would be playing his
parents, the part of Erik Valkonen was a gigantic step for Monty

Monty and Paul Douglas compare beards on the set of
The Big Lift.

professionally. Also in the cast was Sydney Greenstreet, with
whom Monty spent hours reading plays; later when he was in
Hollywood discussing movie deals, he would stop by Greenstreet's
house to renew their friendship. Bill Le Massena, who played
Frank Olmstead, also became a close friend.

But the most important relationship Monty developed was with
the Lunts themselves. From Alfred, he "borrowed" an almost
staccato manner of speaking, full of pauses for breath and unorthodox emphasis. Monty continued aping Lunt's speech patterns and
when, later on, he was criticized for this imitation, he protested
that at least he was mimicking the best actor in the world. Monty
also spoke appreciatively of the Lunts, telling an interviewer late in
1948: "I learned from the Lunts, first by watching them across the
footlights, later by working with them in *There Shall Be No Night*,
and by taking the advice they so kindly and helpfully gave me
when, and where, I needed it most."

Monty also borrowed the Lunts as his family. Occasionally they
invited him to their home for dinner; they encouraged him to
stretch himself as an actor, to take chances, to study. When they
presented Monty with a photograph of themselves, the Lunts auto-
graphed it "from your *real* mother and father."

Working with the Lunts was exhilarating, inspiring; Monty was
keyed up all the time with the discoveries he was making about
acting, experimentation, and most importantly, the dedication re-

George Seaton, Cornell Borchers, Monty, and
unidentified man on the set of The Big Lift.

quired to achieve perfection—the only goal Monty deemed worth aiming for. He always remembered Lunt admonishing him to work for quality, not for money or fame.

There Shall Be No Night was a polemic inspired by Sherwood's outrage at the Russian invasion of Finland. It suffered from being written too hastily (Russia attacked on November 30, 1939 and the play opened five months later) and from a didactic stress on the thesis that however much rational man abhors war, he must abandon his pacifism to fight on principle. Brooks Atkinson of the *Times* complained that *Night* was "no masterpiece," and criticized Sherwood's "uncertain craftsmanship," but praised the performers and noted: "Montgomery Clift has grown up to the part of the son and plays it well."

Night went on tour when it left Broadway, but closed on the road when Finland allied itself with the Axis powers. Via telegram, Sherwood ordered the company to close down "because the content of the plot is opposed to America's war interests." It was just after Pearl Harbor.

* * *

Some time before the middle of 1939, Monty had made his first tentative experiments with sex. Sunny realized that "he was ad-

Monty at Tempelhof Airbase, Berlin.

dicted to little boys,'' but Monty also liked girls, platonically and affectionately for the most part. Bill was outraged at the idea that his son might be homosexual, but Brooks took a more temperate view, saying that he didn't think it mattered to Monty which sex he went to bed with, ''I think he just liked a good lay.'' Brooks states that his brother was bisexual: ''I met two girls he got pregnant.'' According to Brooks, Monty objected to effeminacy in men, but sometimes, later on, Monty would become involved with someone who was very obviously gay.

Patricia Bosworth, in her thoughtful and incisive book, *Montgomery Clift, A Biography,* * describes his relationship with a would-be actor she calls ''Josh'' whom Monty met while both were working out at Klein's gym. ''Alone we could be emotional and passionate,'' Josh recalled, ''but outside we had to hide our feelings.''

Robert LaGuardia, whose biography, *Monty,*† appeared a year before Bosworth's, quotes Bill Le Massena as saying, ''Monty was secretive about it. I never felt that Monty was disturbed about the homosexuality itself. . . . it was just the fact of having to pretend that bothered him.'' Monty's carefully considered personal ethics rebelled against lying or even dissembling, but there was no way to avoid it. Where homosexuality was concerned, nothing like the relative tolerance currently in force was possible, not even among theater people.

Alfred Lunt suspected that Monty might be homosexual, but

*Harcourt Brace Jovanovich, New York, 1978
† Arbor House, New York, 1977

never mentioned it directly, and simply warned him that there were few men in the theater who could survive that particular stigma.

Phyllis Thaxter understudied the maid in *There Shall Be No Night*, and she and Monty developed a lasting bond. Later, when she had replaced Dorthy McGuire in *Claudia*, Thaxter referred to theirs as "a romantic kind of love—I never went to bed with him." They once discussed the idea of marriage, but soon after Monty told her, "It just wouldn't be right." Thaxter didn't ask questions and, although they continued to see each other in the ensuing years, the subject never came up again.

* * *

For a week in August 1941, Monty acted in *Out of the Frying Pan* at the County Theater in Suffern, New York. He played Tony Dennison who, with five other theatrical aspirants, takes a room above a Broadway producer's office in attempt to convince him to hire them. In reviewing the Broadway production, *Life* called the comedy by Francis Swann, "inconsequential and pretty funny."

March 1942 brought Monty an invitation from Robert Lewis, a founding member of the controversial and influential Group Theater of the thirties. Monty was to play a young man tormented by his sordid surroundings in Ramon Naya's *Mexican Mural*, a four-part play illustrating the poverty and superstition of the Mexican people.

Monty and German children on the set of The Big Lift.

Mexican Mural was a flop, lasting only four performances. The
reviews were mixed and in John Anderson's piece for the *New
York Journal American*, the specter of Alfred Lunt arose in what
was otherwise a rave for Monty: "Montgomery Clift plays the
young man with fine perception and great effectiveness. If his vocal inflection and gesture remind us too often of Mr. Lunt, so, too,
does the greater quality of concentration in a young actor of unu-
sual promise."

Despite the short run and negative reception, *Mexican Mural*
was, like *Dame Nature* and *There Shall be No Night*, a pivotal
event for Monty. He met four people who would substantially
affect his life. Libby Holman was backing the production and acting in one of the vignettes. Famous as a torch singer in the late
twenties, she had been implicated in the 1932 death of her husband,
tobacco millionaire Zachary Smith Reynolds, and the scandal had
ruined her career. Monty was fascinated by Holman and, as she
was customarily drawn to younger men (particularly those who
were homosexual or sexually ambivalent), Monty attracted her,
too. When questioned about his relationship with Holman, Monty
brushed people off with statements like: "We are the best of
friends and I hope this friendship continues. She is a woman of
infinite resources."

A Russian actress, Mira Rostova, always thought of as one of
the "older women" in Monty's life, was actually only five years his
senior. Their friendship evolved from their discussions into a complex and hard-to-define alliance. Not only did Mira become one of
Monty's closest friends, she became his unofficial acting coach.

The other two people were younger. Kevin McCarthy and Augusta Dabney—married, nonchalant, and wholesome—were so unlike Holman and Mira that they captivated Monty by virtue of their
very ordinariness.

Monty had endured other bouts of his recurrent dysentery, but a
particularly virulent attack knocked him off his feet in May 1942.
On the advice of the Lunts, Monty flew to New Orleans, to Tulane
Medical Center's Ochsnee Clinic. When he left there in June after
endless testing, he headed for Cape Cod to stay with Augusta who
was acting at the Monomoy Playhouse in Chatham. Monty's dysentery had kept him out of the service, but Kevin was in the Army
and visited them on furlough. Kevin remembers their feeling of
ease with one another. Augusta said that she looked back on that
summer "as the most joyous time in my life" and recalled "the
intense happiness I felt when we were all together." When they
returned to New York in the fall the three were still as close. They
wandered the city together, sampling its cultural offerings.

Once he had made a life and a name for himself apart from his
parents (although he was still living in their apartment), Monty
became more relaxed—and more demonstrative. He embraced

*Monty reads the G.I. paper on the
set of* The Big Lift.

people publicly and privately and, for a time, there were rumors that he and the McCarthys had formed a *ménage à trois*. Although Monty said that Augusta was the only girl he could see himself married to, he loved the McCarthys as good companions; besides he was too self-involved to commit himself to any permanent relationship.

*   *   *

"I don't give a shit what you think, I want to do that play." That was Monty telling his agent, Leland Hayward, he wanted to play Henry in *The Skin of Our Teeth*, written by Thornton Wilder, directed by Elia Kazan and starring Fredric March, Florence Eldridge, and Tallulah Bankhead. Monty did play Henry né Cain, the son with the scar on his forehead who symbolizes the enemy and bellows, "I want everyone to hate me!"

The play, which opened in November 1942, was an allegorical comedy chronicling the Antrobus family's struggle to escape extinction over a 5,000-year period. Bankhead as Sabina, the Eternal Temptress, with her pointed asides and intentionally insolent performance, captured most of the attention. Monty earned his share of the praise, though. George Freedley of the *Morning Telegraph* noted: "Montgomery Clift's Cain . . . was as brilliantly acted as you would expect from this rising young actor. His growth as a player has been steady with no backsliding." Other critics mentioned Monty's "subtlety" and "exceptionally high level of performance."

Looking back on the experience of working with the Marches and Bankhead, Monty said: "I learned from Fredric March. And *there's* a great actor. *Great*. Working with March in *The Skin of Our Teeth*, I learned more than I could have from any six consecutive one-night courses I might have been given, spoon-fed, at any School of the Dray-ma." He also recalled Bankhead: "Nobody in the cast ever showed up until curtain time. The play was anticlimactic to Tallulah's tantrums backstage."

Elia Kazan now remembers Bankhead as a "nuisance," and says that Monty, unlike the rest of the company, which was warring openly with the temperamental Tallulah, was "discreet and kept his own counsel." Recalling Monty, Kazan said: "I loved Monty Clift. He used to come to my house and tell me his problems, and my wife [Molly Day Thatcher] was sort of a mother-figure to him. He had a terrible set of neurotic problems." Kazan also gave Monty some good advice: "If you can turn down parts you know you can't do well, and take only parts you can do with integrity, success will come of its own accord."

Monty paid attention to the guidance he received from people

Monty in the Paramount screening room, 1949.

like Kazan and Alfred Lunt. In a notebook, found among his possessions after his death, he penciled: ''We have to profit by older people's experience—a young person can't know what is right or wrong.'' There were other notations, too: ''Consideration—if everyone would just take the time out to think of the other fellow—the world would get along much more smoothly.'' And: ''Lead a law-abiding life.'' Monty was trying to find his own path, separate from his mother's repressive influence.

The Skin of Our Teeth ended for Monty halfway through its run when his dysentery acted up and he left for the New Orleans clinic. When he had recuperated from this bout, Monty began to visit the home of Janet Cohn, who worked in agent Harold Freeman's office in Bedford Village, Connecticut. From the middle of 1943 to 1947, he spent many weekends in a renovated barn he leased not far from her property.

Monty would invite Mira or the McCarthys to stay with him at times, and Sunny finagled an invitation from her son sometime in mid–1944. She brought a gift of tulips which she planted near the door, but as soon as she had left, Monty pulled them out by the roots and tossed them in the garbage. Although he had seemed pleased while she was there, it was clear that this was *his* place, one where Sunny had no maternal rights. Sunny still hadn't learned, and never did, that if she wanted to control Monty, the best way was through indirection, rather than by being arbitrary and manipulative as was her custom.

There were other theater people at Janet Cohn's place, among them Tallulah Bankhead and Bobby Lewis, whom Monty had worked with—and Thornton Wilder. The first New York revival of Wilder's *Our Town* opened in January 1944 and starred Monty as George Gibbs opposite Martha Scott in the role she had originated in 1938. George Freedley of the *Morning Telegraph* wrote: "Montgomery Clift is excellent. His playing of the bashful George almost entirely erases the memory of John Craven, the original, which is no easy task. Mr. Clift is beginning to achieve variety as an actor and should reach real heights in a few years."

Monty started rehearsing Lillian Hellman's *The Searching Wind* in late February 1944. When Monty was appearing in *Skin*, Stephen Cole had pointed out to him that he sounded like Alfred Lunt, and now director Herman Shumlin did the same thing, but this time Monty took the warning seriously and made a conscious effort to erase Lunt's diction from his own method of speaking. Monty developed a slight limp, which he practiced carefully, with and without a cane, for his role as the wounded soldier, Sam Hazen.

Like Hellman's *Watch on the Rhine, Searching* is an anti-fascist treatise and, like its predecessor, it is dated now, and full of too-pointed avisos. But Hellman's forceful, apposite writing provided

Monty and Paramount projectionist, 1949.

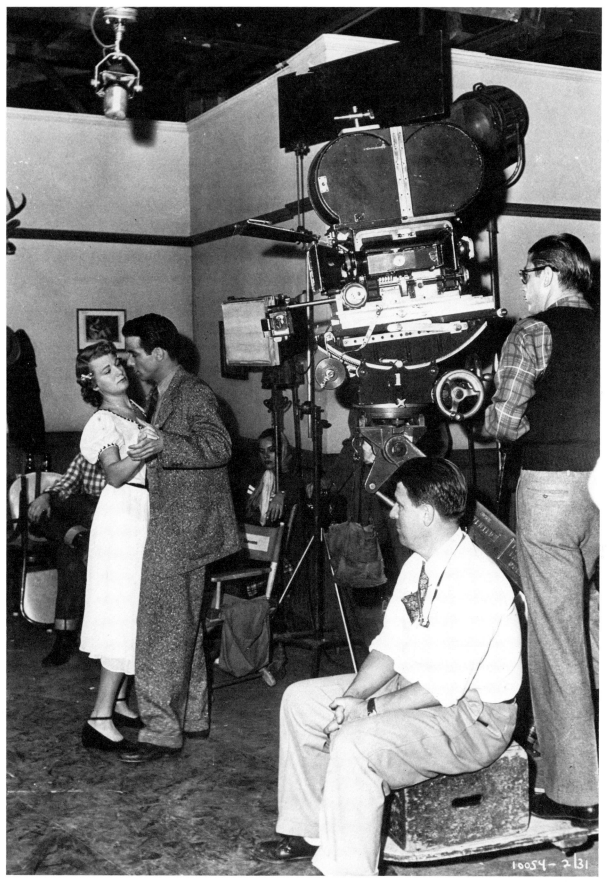

Monty and Shelley Winters rehearse as George Stevens watches.

Monty with one of his most effective roles. He was applauded in print by, among others, Howard Barnes of the *Tribune* ("With this performance in *The Searching Wind*, he serves notice that he is one of the finest youngsters on the stage") and Lewis Nichols of the *Times* ("As the young soldier . . . Montgomery Clift is offering one of the year's best acting jobs; he is intense and can play pathos and humor with equal facility").

In *Pentimento*,* Lillian Hellman writes of "a wonderful old actor, Dudley Digges, arriving at seven–thirty each night during the run of the play to meet Montgomery Clift, a gifted . . . young actor in his first large part. Together they would sit on the stage until the second curtain call and go through a scene from Shakespeare or Ibsen or Chekhov, or a series of poems, anything that Digges had chosen to teach Monty. I took to going to the theater several times a week just to stand in the wings and watch the delicate relationship between the dedicated old and the dedicated young."

Monty was aware of how much he owed Dudley Digges. He told Irving Drutman of the *Times*: "Doing a scene with Mr. Digges, you get the wonderful feeling of playing with an artist . . . an actor who instinctively gets to the root of a role. Once he is on the stage, Mr. Digges never steps out of the character he is playing. I've learned more from [him] than I ever expect to learn from anyone."

"Montgomery Clift gives the best performance of the season in *The Searching Wind*," said the caption under his photograph in *Vogue*; Brooks carried this picture and one of Monty in *The Skin of Our Teeth* folded in his wallet when he was in the Counter Intelligence Corps during World War II. Brooks was always extremely proud of Monty and has kept his huge scrapbooks on his brother's career. When Monty died, Sunny gave Brooks a watch she had given Monty when he was eight. It is inscribed "Montgomery Clift, 1928," and Brooks wears it now, exclaiming with pleasure that it still keeps perfect time.

In late 1945, Mira Rostova went to Germany to work on the Nuremberg trials and Monty, inspired by his brother's example (Brooks had defied his parents wishes to elope with Ann Pearmain) in leaving home, accepted Mira's offer of her apartment. He told Brooks: "If you hadn't done it first, I never could have."

Monty didn't go far, only two blocks away to East 55th Street and Lexington Avenue, and he visited his parents often. Furthermore, Monty accepted small sums of money from them when he wasn't in a play, rather than act in radio, which he detested.

Monty enjoyed his new-found independence; he could talk on the phone as much as he wanted and no longer felt obliged to behave like the "thoroughbred" his parents preferred him to be. He began dressing casually, even sloppily—an idiosyncrasy jour-

*Little, Brown and Company, Boston, 1973

Monty and makeup man Bill Woods on the set of A Place in the Sun.

nalists would pounce upon in a few years—as much in opposition
to his parents' oft-expressed preference for a more formal mode of
dress as out of personal choice.

Sunny, always critical of any activity that didn't include her,
railed at Monty as a "bum" for dressing inelegantly and for the
company he was keeping. When he reminded his mother that he
wasn't the only person who admired Mira's ability to dissect a role,
and offered as proof the fact that she was teaching acting at the
New School for Social Research, Sunny dismissed Mira as an
"opportunist." The McCarthys weren't in the same class as
Monty, and Libby Holman was "perverted." Ironically, it was
Ned Smith, one of the few friends Sunny approved of, who helped
him move out of the Clift apartment.

In May 1945, Monty, once again playing a soldier, opened in
Elsa Shelley's *Foxhole in the Parlor*, a turgid melodrama which
lasted only forty-five performances. It was entirely due to Monty's
talents that the play stayed on Broadway that long. His reviewers
called him "the hottest thing in town" (Ed Sullivan), "appealing
and sensitive" (John Chapman, *Daily News*), and an "exciting
young actor . . . a personal triumph" (Jack O'Brien, *Associated
Press*).

You Touched Me! Monty's next play, was adapted by Tennessee
Williams and Donald Windham from a D. H. Lawrence story and
opened at the Booth Theatre in September of the same year.
Monty played Hadrian, a pilot who is persuaded to marry the niece
(Marianne Stewart) of his foster father (Edmund Gwenn) and take
her away from the sheltered life she has led.

This was Monty's last play until he revived *The Sea Gull* in 1954.
Of the thirteen plays he had performed in New York, he had
played servicemen of varying types in six. Monty had begun his
career before World War II, stayed on the stage during the conflict

Monty and Elizabeth Taylor during filming.

and, when he went to California, would there become caught up in Hollywood's preoccupation with the war. In his second film, *The Search*, he played a soldier. Of his seventeen films, seven found Monty involved in various conflagrations, including the Civil War (*Raintree Country*), the Cold War (*The Defector*) and the aftermath of the Second World War (*Judgment at Nuremberg*). If Monty's health had prevented him from experiencing the real fighting, it hadn't kept him out of the war.

Monty had earlier begun to show signs of autocratic behavior (his demand that Leland Hayward get him the part in *The Skin of Our Teeth*, for example) and self-absorption (although the McCarthys saw all of his performances, he seldom reciprocated, and rarely discussed their work). Now he brought this streak of selfishness onto the stage. During the run of *Foxhole in the Parlor*, he had the air-conditioning turned off because its noise distracted him, leaving his fellow players and the audience to swelter. While acting in *You Touched Me!,* he deliberately spoke softly "so the audience listens more carefully," and arbitrarily changed the blocking, which threw some of the cast off during performances.

Montgomery Clift was no longer his mother's thoughtful, polite son. He was a man of twenty-five, using his extraordinary talent to create unforgettable characters, and in the process, forming a personality that was as unorthodox in its own way as those of the men he impersonated on stage. And he used the power those performances and his reviews gave him to order his life for his own, and few other's, convenience.

Although *You Touched Me!* enjoyed only a brief run, it too earned Monty enormous praise. Among these was a review by Louis Kronenberger of *PM*, which noted: "Montgomery Clift, one of the town's rising young actors, is fresh and invigorating as the Canadian bomber pilot, although at times he is quite inaudible." Yet another reviewer mentioned Monty's "indistinct diction."

Monty had flirted with the movies as early as 1941. During the tour of *There Shall Be No Night*, L.B. Mayer offered him a role in MGM's *Mrs. Miniver*. Monty would have agreed to it if Mayer had not insisted on the then-standard seven-year contract. This would have paid him $750 a week; his father urged him to sign, telling Monty, "You'll never get another chance like this." But Monty knew it was just a matter of time before the studios gave him what he wanted.

In January 1946, he flew to the coast to talk over a project with Leland Hayward. Monty told his agent he was "too snobbish" to stay in Hollywood, but Hayward demanded that he remain there a few months to meet with the chiefs of several studios. Hayward wangled a six month contract with Metro to pay Monty to stay in "Vomit, California" (as he termed Los Angeles in letters to his friends). The studio heads could not grasp Monty's desire to keep

George Stevens (back to camera), Shelley Winters,
Monty, and Herbert Heyes on the factory set shooting
A Place in the Sun.

his independence, telling him he would ''make mistakes'' if he did.
''You don't understand,'' Monty would reply. ''I want to be free to
do so.''

Monty was ambivalent about becoming a Hollywood star; there
was no doubt in his mind that he could be one if he wanted to. As
Mira Rostova put it: ''He was ambitious to do excellent work,'' but
not so sure he could acquiesce in all that would be necessary to
make his aspirations a reality. Monty hated the idea of drowning in
a press agent's dream of lotusland luxury; of the invasion of his
privacy; the premieres with starlets; and the autographs. His
equivocating impressed the studio chiefs as indifference, a non-
chalance that only increased their determination to sign him. And
that, in turn, made Monty still more elusive.

He had not changed his mind about Hollywood in 1960 when he
told columnist Joe Hyams: ''They try to put people into smart little
pigeonholes. It's the same way they like instant coffee [in New
York, Monty made his in an imported Italian espresso machine],
it's quick and easy—but I'm not coffee and I don't pigeonhole.''
He made other cracks about Hollywood: ''My home happens to be
New York. I like it there. I can hardly wait to get back to real
winter, not the kind you have here, where you have a cloudburst
and people drown in gutters.''

Monty's first screen test, an unsuccessful one, was for *Pursued*,
a Raoul Walsh film, which starred Robert Mitchum, Judith Anderson, and Teresa Wright, when Warners released it in 1947.

Elizabeth Taylor, Monty, and Shelley Winters on the set of A Place in the Sun.

When he was free of his brief contract, Monty drove east in "Beulah," the family's 1937 Buick his father had given him when he left the New Orleans clinic in the spring of 1943. He was accompanied by Fred and Jeanne Green, a young couple he had met through Augusta Dabney. Eventually Fred became a builder/designer and helped Monty redo the duplex on East 61st Street he had moved into in 1950.

But for now they were three young people taking ten days to motor from the Pacific to the Atlantic, stopping off in New Orleans, playing tennis, drinking brandy, and generally relaxing in a big way.

While in New Orleans, Monty would take off to explore the city's seedier districts. When Jeanne asked why he wanted to go there, Monty told her, "I need to."

Jeanne and Augusta had been, as Jeanne related to Patricia Bosworth, "half in love with him in a romantic and sentimental way," but—although the idea had occurred to them—they didn't, *couldn't* in 1943–44, talk about the possibility that their handsome and dear friend might be homosexual.

Ann Lincoln, who was Monty's leading lady in *Foxhole in the Parlor,* fell madly in love with him, and Kevin McCarthy noted that Monty really seemed to care about her. Their relationship was brief and intense, ending in a fight when Monty refused to marry her. Later they renewed their friendship, sometimes going away together on weekends to Monty's rented barn in Bedford Village.

Monty still had not made a decision about sex; as he could attract virtually anyone he wanted with his intellect, his physical beauty, and his enormous charm, he didn't need to make a decision. He wasn't grounded sexually, but followed his emotional

Monty and Elizabeth Taylor during filming.

inclinations. It didn't matter which sex the person was, as long as
Monty found that individual physically and emotionally attractive.

* * *

When Howard Hawks approached him to play Matthew Garth in
Red River, Monty hesitated. It was clear to him that holding out to
make a movie on his own terms had paid off. Hollywood *was*
coming to him as he had predicted, but first there were obstacles to
be overcome. John Wayne would play Tom Dunson, Matt's foster
father, and it took a free plane ticket and much persuasion on
Hawks' part to get Monty out to California just to talk about the
picture. Monty didn't see how he could out-act Wayne, and, in
fact, he didn't. But Hawks made Monty see that he could use the
resources he had developed on stage, the inner tension and still-
ness, and his penetrating expression to play *against* Wayne's more
bravura style.

Monty in Florence, Italy, February 1950.

As there are few interiors in *Red River*, the shooting schedule allowed for a long period of filming in Rain Valley in Arizona. Bad weather kept the company there from June to November of 1946, during which time Wayne and Monty grew to loathe and respect one another. Monty was polite, but hated the macho image both Hawks and Wayne were intent on projecting. For his part, Wayne told a *Life* editor that "Clift is an arrogant little bastard."

Right from the start, Monty establishes himself as an insidious force in *Red River*, rolling cigarettes to hand to Wayne, while watching the byplay between Wayne and Walter Brennan, who plays Groot, the grizzled, toothless old coot who is Wayne's only close friend.

An interesting, undeveloped rivalry between John Ireland—as Cherry Valance—and Monty, begins with a can-shooting contest at the start of the film and seems to be carried over to the Clift/Joanne Dru relationship explored toward the end of the movie. Ireland finds Dru first, but Monty takes over her affections after the Indian fight, without a word of protest from Ireland.

Dru and Hawks had been having an affair, but she left the director when she met Ireland. They were married from 1949 through 1956. Hawks could not drop Monty's romantic interest from the plot, but he could cut out some of Ireland's scenes, with the result that there are more conversations with Brennan, Noah Beery, Jr., and Monty, than between the two men who would most logically be concerned—in the script's terms—with Monty's opinions.

If Monty is Wayne's rival, Ireland is Monty's—both for power and sex—and as a result of their omitted scenes, the film has a slightly unbalanced, incomplete feeling, not wholly compensated for by the completion of the cattle drive nor the resolution of the central conflict.

Fred Zinnemann spoke to Monty about *The Search* when he was still shooting *Red River* and promised him, since he would make only $75,000 for the film, a six-week work schedule on location in Germany and Switzerland. Lazar Wechsler, the producer, also gave Monty verbal consent to working out changes in his own dialogue.

Monty valued Mira Rostova's advice about acting, so she accompanied him to Zurich for the start of filming. In describing his relationship with her to Hedda Hopper, Monty said: "She's helped me enormously with my work. She's simply a very dear friend whose judgment I respect tremendously. And I can depend on her for an honest opinion." Together they proceeded to rewrite not only Monty's lines, but at least half of the script. Monty prepared to play Steve—the Army engineer who finds a runaway boy in the bombed-out streets of Germany just after World War II—with the same thoroughness he had employed readying himself to play Matthew Garth. He spent ten days with Army engineers in the United

States Zone in Germany soaking up, not just enough technical lore to make his part believable, but details of the average soldier's life at that time. Monty outlined his complaints about *The Search* to the *Saturday Evening Post:* "The way the part was written, I was a boy-scout type spreading nobility and virtue all over the lot. I was so damned saintly. . . . I felt the soldier had to get mad at the kid and yell at him . . . just as any normal adult does with children."

Monty had loved working with Zinnemann, who was intelligent, courteous, and had listened to his suggestions. It had been all he wanted filmmaking to be and had feared it would not: exhilarating, fulfilling, and above all, instructive. Years later, Monty gave an interview in which he described his idea of the perfect collaboration:

"For me, acting is a kind of torture. I love the preparation—discussing with a writer and director who have the same ideas as I how the story should be developed, arguing over scenes."

* * *

In the spring of 1978, the Regency Theater in New York City ran a series called *Three Rebels*, seventeen films starring Monty, Marlon Brando, and James Dean. The program, which lasted twenty-eight days and included seven of Monty's films, provided the theater with its highest-grossing three days: those in which it played *The Search* and *A Place in the Sun.* The week of June 11–17, during which the Regency showed *Raintree County* and *Judgment at Nuremberg*, was the best week in the history of the theater.

In writing of the series for the *Times*, Janet Maslin characterized the way Monty functions vis-à-vis Wayne in *Red River* as being "an altogether subversive element in the film's very masculine scheme." Maslin also took note of Monty in *The Search*, saying: "The actor, at his most blindingly beautiful . . . in a performance for which he most painstakingly worked out every last glance and gesture" is an "absolute must for viewers unfamiliar with the Clift mystique."

* * *

The critical acclaim for both films assured Monty that he was going to be a star. When he completed *Red River*, he headed for the New Orleans clinic and his regular checkup, and to get "pissed out of my mind" anonymously, the last time he would be able to do so. He woke up in jail.

After he had finished *The Search*, Monty returned to New York to study singing, to work out at his gym, and to attend the newly formed Actors Studio. The Studio's credo, evolved from a Stanis-

Monty and the McCarthys' son Flip.

lavskian codification of acting techniques, via Bobby Lewis, Elia Kazan, and Lee Strasberg—the Studio's autocratic director—was "The Method." Although Monty attended classes, he was never at heart a Method actor. He did not believe he should enact a variation of himself, but rather use his intelligence and imagination to understand and embellish the character he was playing. That comprehension included psychological motivation, gestures, speech, and physical characteristics—anything that worked for him.

To publicize *The Search*, Monty and his co-star Jarmila Novotna, appeared on the Tex and Jinx show in March 1948. He joked about his newly-won stardom, asking which profile he should show to the radio audience, but he was very serious when discussing the film. Monty commented that Ivan Jandl (the little boy he adopts) had trouble keeping his balance while making the film (and it shows on screen, especially when the boy runs away from his adoptive home) because of malnutrition—the result of eating too much starch. Of himself, Monty said, "My part is strictly a plot business," the real story concerned Jarmila and Ivan, and mentioned that "half the outfits that were over there adopted children."

The Search opened in March 1948 and *Red River* six months later, but it had been nine months since Monty had worked and he needed the stimulation and sense of worth he got from slaving over a new part. In June, he returned to Hollywood to play Morris Townsend opposite Olivia de Havilland's Catherine Sloper in *The Heiress*. His price had risen to $100,000 for the role he took to avoid typecasting; Townsend was Monty's first and only heel.

Monty on the wharf.

Monty took Mira Rostova with him, stayed at a small hotel, and resisted Paramount's attempts to publicize their hot new star.

Although Monty criticized de Havilland for relying too much on director William Wyler to mold her performance, "Livvie" won her second Academy Award for her role. Monty complained that Ralph Richardson and Miriam Hopkins tried to steal scenes and he felt that Wyler was cold and dictatorial. He also knew that he was not at his best in *The Heiress.* The Montgomery Clift who plays the Morris Townsend of 1849 is not as convincing as the Montgomery Clift who plays the Matthew Garth of 1865 in *Red River.* His mannerisms and speech are too modern, as the critics suggested, and the familiar slouched posture is not what one expects of a penurious suitor for the hand of a wealthy nineteenth-century maiden.

Augustus and Ruth Goetz adapted their play for the screen and Goetz remembers his first meeting with Monty: "He was wearing a jacket full of holes, a pair of blue jeans and a T-shirt. He looked like a bum. But the transformation was startling when Monty got into costume. He suddenly *was* the fastidious Morris Townsend."

Monty argued his way into doing his own singing in a key love scene with de Havilland, saying: "I studied French and piano when I was a kid. My voice is lousy, but I can carry a tune. This guy doesn't figure to sound any better than I will."

A letter to Ned Smith dated October 20, 1948 (and quoted in Patricia Bosworth's biography), sums up Monty's frustration at being in Hollywood: "I have worked 10 months in the last three years and it might well have gone on like that. . . . Interesting things do not actually abound but they are here, they are for me and I can take them."

One of the "interesting things" was the deal his agent—Lew Wasserman of MCA (which had bought Leland Hayward's agency) —had consummated with Paramount for three pictures. Monty would have script approval and the services of either Billy Wilder, Norman Krasna, or George Stevens as his director, *and* the option to make movies outside Paramount if he chose to do so.

* * *

Monty left for Europe in the fall of 1948. He traveled alone—and light. He visited with Thornton Wilder and Wilder's sister Isabel who were in Paris at the same time. They had met while Monty was playing Henry in *The Skin of Our Teeth* and again at Janet Cohn's in Connecticut. Monty was impressed by Wilder's erudition and good humor and by the fact that Wilder was impressed by *him.* Over a ten-year period, Wilder worked intermittently on a play for Monty called *The Emporium,* based on Franz Kafka's *The Castle.* For a time, Wilder tried to write a play for Garbo called *The Alcestiad or A Life in the Sun.* Experimentally, Monty grew a beard and cut his hair in elfin bangs for a role in the play, but Wilder abandoned work on both plays sometime in 1949.

Monty saw Rome, his favorite city of that trip, and Israel, where he stayed for a few days at a kibbutz that was being attacked by the Arabs. When he got back, Monty said: "It's inconceivable to me that any young actor who had the fare didn't go to Palestine. There was one of the few really new countries being carved out since the American Revolution."

Upon arriving in St. Moritz he found he was on the cover of *Life* as one of Hollywood's *New Male Movie Stars.* Monty was also named Star of Tomorrow in an American theater exhibitors poll. "When I learned about this," Monty said, "I was really overwhelmed. I'm very happy they voted as they did. It gives me a lot of confidence."

Augusta Dabney remembered Monty as he appeared on his re-

Monty preparing to fish.

turn from Europe: "He struggled from the plane with an armful of unwrapped toys for all the kids he knows. His own luggage was in a beach bag. . . ."

* * *

Monty signed for two films to be made in rapid succession: first *The Big Lift* in Germany for 20th Century-Fox, then *A Place in the Sun* in Hollywood for Paramount. Before he started the first, Monty optioned *You Touched Me!* and announced that he and Kevin McCarthy had formed Kemont Productions to film the Williams/Windham play. They would adapt it together, and Monty would star and direct. Shortly after Kevin's and Monty's work on the script began, Kevin left for London to appear with Paul Muni in *Death of a Salesman*. Monty reminded Kevin that he would have to leave the play before it closed, to work on *Touched*. Kevin arrived in London in a quandary. He couldn't renege on his closest friend, but the role of Biff was the biggest break he had had. Kevin eventually told Muni he would have to quit and when the star refused to act with Kevin's understudy, Kevin had his out. He stayed with the production.

Monty and Vittorio de Sica at the 1952 Silver Ribbon award ceremonies, Rome.

Kevin had never examined his relationship with Monty before. He felt that, to all intents and purposes, Monty was "a member of my family." In 1950, while talking over film roles, Kevin was told that he performed like Monty and that many people thought they were lovers. Director Henry Hathaway advised him: "Do yourself a favor. You better stop shackin' up with him." Kevin understood that he had not paid attention to something that was apparent to others. His friendship with Monty was strictly platonic; therefore Monty could not be gay.

But after *The Search* had opened, Monty's lawyer squelched an incident involving Monty and a young man he had tried to solicit on 42nd Street. At about the same time, Hedda Hopper had a lead about Monty being arrested for pederasty in New Orleans, but it turned out he had been detained briefly for drunkenness.

Monty was drinking more—and more openly. "I love to drink!" he exclaimed, and friends would realize that where Monty used to drink milk, now he was drinking martinis. There was no one simple reason for his increased consumption. It was partly the pressure of being a star and his ambivalence about fame, and partly the deceptive life-style this newly-won prestige forced him to impose upon himself.

"Monty hated, loathed, and despised deception," Bill LeMassena said, "and here he was having to hide." "Monty never stopped being conflicted," Mira Rostova confirmed, "and he never stopped feeling guilty about being conflicted."

* * *

Although he professed hating to be interviewed, Monty knew it was better for the box-office if his name was before the public. Everything he said was news, so he talked about a number of things.

On acting: "I'm not afraid of being typed. The big danger is playing safe. The strongest motivating force in an actor is experimentation. Anything that stretches you is worth playing, even if it's a flop.

"In many respects, the screen is a more satisfying medium than the stage. Sincerity comes across better, and there is more chance for subtlety because the camera is on you all the time."

And he contradicted himself: "The challenge of acting on the stage is greater than in the movies. There's no coasting along on personality alone. If you have a long part, you have to sustain it. . . ."

He'd been teased about the sparsity of his wardrobe, so he talked about clothes: "I have one suit which I intend to keep as long as the Good Moth spares it to me."

Monty and Elizabeth Taylor at Camillo's restaurant in New York.

On girls: "I'm a bachelor, but if anyone writes that I don't like girls, I'll crown the gentleman."

And he guarded his privacy: "I keep my family out of my public life because it can be an awful nuisance to them. What's my mother going to tell strangers anyway? That I was a cute baby and that she's terribly proud of me? Nuts. Who cares?"

Paramount insisted that Monty cooperate with their publicity department. He spent some time at the studio being photographed in their various departments and, because they were building up Elizabeth Taylor and himself as a romantic couple for *A Place in the Sun*, they demanded that he take her to the premiere of *The Heiress* (also a Paramount picture). Sitting next to him in Grauman's Chinese Theater, Taylor told him how good he was, but Monty, in a rented tuxedo, kept slumping deeper into his seat and mumbling cracks about his acting. When the film was over, Monty grabbed her and pulled Elizabeth up the aisle, past a crowd intent on congratulating him. He kept calling her "Bessie Mae," which was his private name for her from then on. (Brooks was "Boof" and Mira was "Mupa.")

*   *   *

In many ways, Monty is more romantic in *The Big Lift* than in *A Place in the Sun*. Pairing him with Elizabeth Taylor and making them the American dream couple, removes him from the sphere of his audience. George Eastman may come from a humble background, but he quite rapidly gains social altitude and has begun his economic climb when his career is cut short. What Patricia Bosworth calls his "androgynous swagger" is most evident in *Place*, and during their big love scene, Monty's and Taylor's images seem to merge, intensifying the emotions they generate. It is this fusion, this incredible, unearthly passion, that lifts him right off the screen and *away* from, rather than toward, his female admirers.

In *The Big Lift*, the ideal of physical beauty is more real. Coupling him with an attractive, but unknown, German actress helps to keep Monty, the person, within the realm of possibility for his fans. And it was always that connection between the man in the fan magazines—sloppy, real, awkward—and the actor on the screen—desirable, remote, superhumanly handsome—that was Monty's most potent asset. Besides, a GI is easier to get than a young man on the make in society.

In *The Big Lift*, when Monty's eyes bore into Cornell Borchers', he is trying to break down her reticence, capture her. He doesn't have to do that with Taylor: she comes to him. But with Borchers, Monty has to *make* her fall in love with the same intensity he feels himself. And that intensity floods the screen, catching the audience too. As long as Monty is an *attainable* love object, as in *The Heiress*, *The Young Lions*, or *Wild River*, he can connect with his fans.

*   *   *

Nevertheless, *A Place in the Sun* is one of the two definitive Clift films (*From Here to Eternity* is the other), comprising, as it does, one of the performances upon which Monty's image as a tormented outsider is based. But, besides being Prewitt's story, *Eternity* is also Maggio's and Warden's. Prewitt is but one of three men, albeit the one most alone of the three. There is, too, the element of willfulness Prewitt possesses, most aptly expressed by his statement, "If a man don't go his own way he's nothin.' "

George Eastman is denied this opportunity of choice. He is propelled by society, by American materialism, by women, by whatever reasons one cares to indict for his behavior, into events he seems incapable of shaping through his own will. George is not without ambition. That impulse is the one which urges him on until his pregnant girlfriend is dead, the girl he loves is lost forever, and his own life is forfeit to the law. But George acts for motives he himself, unlike Prewitt, does not comprehend. On trial, he tries to make sense of his actions, but it is too late. Handsome, aloof, enigmatic, and as desirable for these reasons as Angela Vickers (Taylor) is for her wealth and beauty, George comes the closest to embodying the Clift screen persona.

Monty understood George very well and deliberately played him as even less sympathetic than the much-altered (from the Dreiser novel) screenplay represented him as being. His next concern was Elizabeth Taylor's Angela; his shaping of her performance has been much reported—among others, by Elizabeth herself: "I watched Monty. I watched how much time he spent on concentration—which has since become the key to my kind of acting, if you can call it acting."

She did more—she fell in love with Montgomery Clift. "I thought he was the most gorgeous thing in the world," she wrote in her book, "and easily one of the best actors. And he wasn't a bit snide about acting with a 'cheap movie star.' " From all accounts Monty loved Elizabeth almost as much as she did him, but their friendship was apparently never consummated sexually, and after a while, Elizabeth understood why.

Although Monty would gleefully chortle, "I've found my other half!" referring to Elizabeth, she knew very well that he was physically more attracted to men than women, and although it bothered her a great deal, she eventually took the wisest course. Elizabeth went to Monty and told him that she understood, that she would always be there for him whenever and for whatever reason he needed her.

Mira Rostova hovered on or near the set, running lines with Monty, and listening—with Monty—to Elizabeth's complaints about her mother. He would change the subject back to their work together; when he worked, it was *all* work. Later, that would change.

Mira says that she got along very well with George Stevens. "He actually came and thanked me" for working with Monty, Mira reported. Then, as always, her method of working with Monty was "to figure out exactly what it is one should be talking about, to zero in on the role with him."

In a letter to Brooks dated January 2, 1950, when work on *Place* was completed, Monty wrote: "At last tidings that are not of evil and of work. It is OVER. At last I can afford to collapse. Oy—I never thought this day would come.

"In this country the arts seem to be mixed up with a crock of people—none of whom are stretching themselves. A lot of craftsmen and no artists.

"I speak like Father Time—but then I feel like father Time—so what can I do."

*   *   *

After a brief stay with Libby Holman, Monty vacationed with Mira in Acapulco, then departed with the McCarthys from Paris for an extended trip. The three (There were actually four. Flip, the McCarthys' young son, accompanied his parents.) did what they had done earlier in New York: absorbed the local culture.

Monty was a star by then, as he and the McCarthys saw clearly when he was asked for his autograph or snapped by the *paparazzi* in Rome, their next stop. He loved the adulation but, as usual, ambivalently. He wanted the fame, but he knew what too much attention could do to his resolve to be an actor rather than a star, how easy it would be to let it all slip, and take easy roles for big money.

Monty sounded much more determined when he spoke to the press on the subject: "Luxury, swimming pools, expensive cars and all the rest just aren't very important to me. The big job in one's life is finding out what is important to you. It's a major tragedy to race after things that you neither want nor need."

Monty, Kevin, and Augusta met famous people (Tennessee Williams and Alberto Moravia) and were invited to a costume party at Luchino Visconti's. They ate and drank and had a fine time taking pictures, and they met Vittorio de Sica—the internationally known neo-realist director—who declared that he would like to make a film with this young American movie star. Shortly thereafter, he did.

The travelers sailed back to the States in March 1950. Monty described what happened when the ship ran into a hurricane:

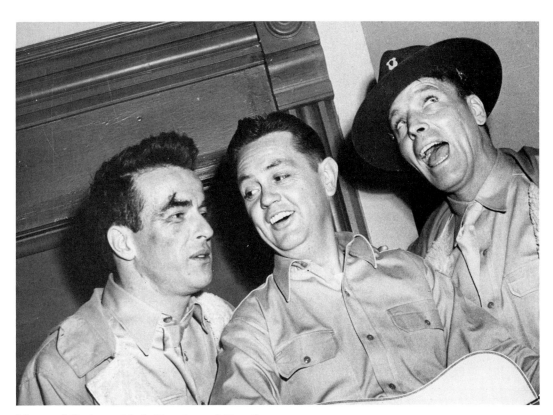

Monty, folk singer Merle Travis, and Burt Lancaster whoop it up on the set of From Here to Eternity.

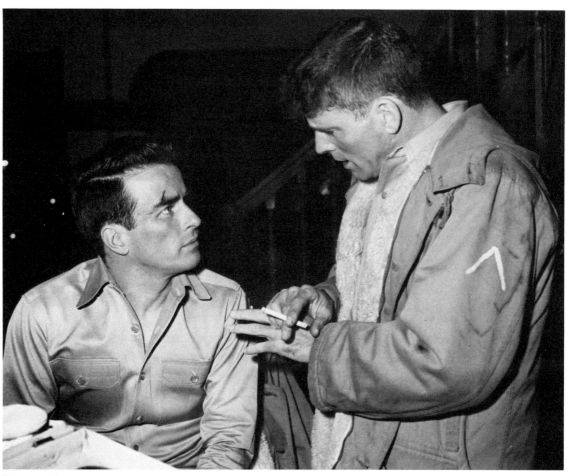

Monty takes some pointers from Burt Lancaster.

"Kevin McCarthy and I were on the *Queen Mary* and we wanted some photos of the trip. I put on my coat, grabbed a small suitcase, and lowered myself out the porthole. I hung onto a curtain rod, smiled, and when the picture was taken, pulled myself back in. I could have been arrested. The Cunard line doesn't like people walking around outside of their portholes."

Kevin had seen Monty hanging before: in Florence he almost fell into the Arno River fooling around outside his hotel window. And Mira reported that every so often she would look out of her window on the top floor of her apartment on East 55th Street to see Monty suspended, head hanging upside down, outside.

Later, Monty did his hanging from people. On the *Raintree County* set, he would grab assistant director Ridgeway Callow around the neck and let Callow pull him along the ground. He had taken other dangerous chances earlier. Janet Cohn noticed several years before, when he would drive her back from weekends in Connecticut, that Monty's driving had become erratic and frightening in its carelessness.

Monty had learned, very suddenly, how much he meant to people—as a friend, as a companion, and as an important young actor. He was now a "commodity," and he seemed to feel certain that people would look out for him, that he didn't have to spend so much time taking care of himself. Not only was Monty drinking a great deal, he was more or less indiscriminately taking pills. Not in the quantities he would consume after his near-fatal accident in 1956, but enough to worry his friends. In November 1950, he went to see Dr. Ruth Fox, a psychiatrist who treated many alcoholics. She saw him for a while, and even got Monty to a few Alcoholics Anonymous meetings. One morning he fell on her doorstep, dead drunk, and Dr. Fox had him admitted to the Neurological Center at Columbia-Presbyterian Hospital to have him detoxified.

Dr. Fox referred Monty to a colleague—her own former analyst, Dr. William Silverberg—who was known for the concept of "effective aggression," a method of channeling one's ability in overriding obstacles to achieve one's goals. Monty later discovered that Dr. Silverberg was himself a homosexual. As it developed, that was not much of a problem as far as their professional relationship went. "Billy," as Monty and everyone else called him, refused to acknowledge that Monty had a drinking problem of any kind. Subsequently, many of Monty's friends agreed that Dr. Silverberg was not helping Monty nearly enough; he might be helping him reach his subconscious, or get in touch with his repressed anger toward his mother, but analysis had no effect on Monty's drinking.

*   *   *

Monty had moved into a duplex on East 61st Street about half a block away from Libby Holman's apartment, and when Monty and Kevin returned to New York they went back to work on *You Touched Me!* By this time, Monty had a secretary, Arlene Cunningham, who proved to be much more than just another fan with a steno pad. She was indispensable to Monty; he valued her opinions and she brought order to his life. Now she was typing Kevin's and Monty's efforts.

You Touched Me! was dismissed by every producer who read it. Lew Wasserman told them to take out the first forty pages of dialogue and others had different advice—but the big problem was that they had no idea how to merchandise their "product," and were too innocent to realize that they should not be trying to sell it themselves.

*   *   *

Monty had attended the Command Performance of *The Heiress* in August of that year. He was accompanied by Linda Christian and presented to the Queen with Tyrone Power and James Stewart. There was a dinner with the Laurence Oliviers and Monty's former agent, Leland Hayward, arranged for Monty to meet his new wife.

Monty flew on to Rome for more publicity and met Giuseppe

Frank Sinatra, Monty, and Gary Merrill.

Perrone, a journalist for *Il Progresso.* They had something in common; they liked the same films, and they liked each other. Monty invited Perrone back to his hotel after they had dinner together, and they were talking when there was a knock on the door. Someone delivered roses to Monty, and then a blonde appeared wearing only a robe and offering herself to Monty. He was extremely embarrassed, shoved her out of the room, and made a fast phone call. It had been a Paramount publicity gimmick to build up Monty's masculine romantic image and his box office appeal, neither of which needed enhancement at that time. And he was furious!

Back in New York Monty would talk on the phone for hours (one of his favorite pastimes) and visit MCA's offices to talk to his agent, Jay Kantor, about the scripts he had been offered. And he was offered *everything.* "But everything is crap!" Monty would yell, and he refused to do anything that came along just to keep his name before the public and on the screen.

He met James Jones at a party at Vance Bourjaily's and got involved in a long discussion about *From Here to Eternity,* in which Jones thought Monty should play Prewitt. Jones warned him that

Harry Cohn, the head of Columbia Pictures (which owned the screen rights), wanted a contract player, John Derek, to have the role. Monty was worried about whether or not he could play a fighter, but "I told him he sure as hell could!" Jones declared.

Monty recalled for reporter Anthony Haden-Guest: "My problem is that I lack initiative. Do you know that I had the galleys of *From Here to Eternity* lying around in my room for three-quarters of a year! They were *so high.* But I didn't buy an option or commission a treatment. I didn't even read it. The *size.* But a treatment was done for Fred Zinnemann, and he sent it to me, so the ball started rolling."

Eternity was a long time getting to the screen. There were many treatments and several scripts. In the meantime, Monty made *I Confess* with Alfred Hitchcock and *Indiscretion of an American Wife* with Vittorio de Sica.

I Confess is a film that Hitchcock himself believes should never have been made, partly because the central theme is the idea that a priest would allow his vows of silence to protect a murderer—who had confessed his crime to him—to the point of going to the gallows in the place of the real killer. That was the original ending of the film. A plausible, but unsatisfactory, ending was appended during shooting, exculpating the priest and eliminating the real murderer in the same stroke.

Hitchcock derides the film today for its dominating sobriety and the casting of Anne Baxter in place of Anita Bjork, a Swedish actress who played Strindberg's *Miss Julie* for Alf Sjoberg.

Before accepting the role in *I Confess,* Monty had befriended a priest, a man Patricia Bosworth identifies in her biography of Monty as Brother Thomas. They had corresponded since their first meeting in 1945 and Monty stayed with Brother Thomas's order in Quebec for five days—observing services, learning the stations of the cross and how to genuflect, and attending mass at four A.M.

Before location filming began (coincidentally in Quebec), Monty began shooting in Hollywood, where he stayed with Fred and Jeanne Green, as he often did. Monty was unhappy about Hitchcock's telling him how to act and not allowing enough room for Monty's own interpretation to come through.

Karl Malden played the police inspector who tries to make Monty's character, Father Michael Logan, confess to a crime he did not commit. The two men had been friendly off and on for years in New York and, although Malden describes himself as a "very competitive" actor, he and Monty picked up their acquaintance as it had been previously. In Quebec they ran lines together at their hotel with Mira Rostova, whom Malden admired for her acute perceptions and ability to dissect a role. But when they got on the set and Malden felt their chemistry was working well together, he

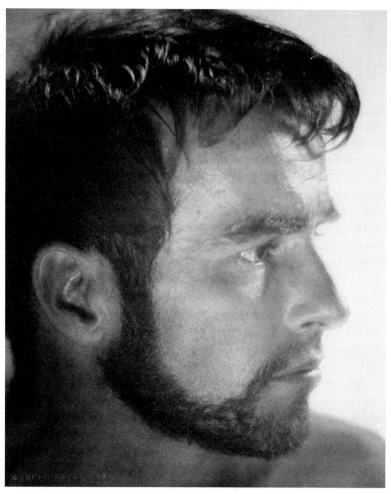

*Monty in the beard he grew experimentally for
Thornton Wilder's* The Alcestiad, or A Life in the Sun.

was dismayed to see Monty turn to Mira for her reaction, rather
than to himself, the man who had played the scene with him. "It
was like a conspiracy behind your back," Malden decided.

Hitchcock felt that Monty did not need Mira, but he did not try
to ban her from the set, because, as he said: "I know bloody well
more than she does."

Back in New York, Monty prepared to speak at a Madison
Square Garden rally for presidential candidate Adlai E. Stevenson.
Brooks went with Monty to the Garden, but Bill Clift was bitterly
opposed to Monty's coming out publicly for Stevenson. Brooks
remembers: "Dad was livid. He really felt that Monty was a trai-
tor. Dad said to me, 'What are they going to say on Wall Street
when I have a son who can be on the same platform as Stevenson?
It's like having a son who's a communist.' "

Monty had never taken his father's advice about anything: living
at home, his choice of friends, or taking contracts offered by Hollywood studios. He had politely refused his father's advice on how
to invest his money—and now this, the final filial slap in the face.
The fight ended with Bill telling Monty: "When I die, I don't want
you at my funeral."

After Monty departed for Rome to make *Indiscretion*, he wrote

Brooks about the rally, saying, "I hope that my appearance there that night in no way contributed to the overwhelming victory of the other candidate. Anyway it was a wonderful feeling to feel a part of something world-wide which was going on in one's lifetime."

* * *

Monty arrived in Rome to start *Terminal Station* (there is a double entendre in the discarded title since the lovers end their romance there) to find the film in total disarray. Paul Gallico, Carson McCullers, Alberto Moravia, Truman Capote, Cesare Zavattini, Luigi Chiarini and Giorgio Prosperi had all worked on the script at one time or another, and David O. Selznick, who was financing the film, had already begun to bombard de Sica with the memos for which he was legendary.

In November 1952, Monty wrote to Brooks from the Hotel Hassler in Rome, describing the physical circumstances of his work: "It's hell over here. We shoot out of doors in the station from 10:30 to 7 A.M. By one o'clock everybody is numb from the cold and by three the hacking and coughing and spitting and general wheezing is so all-pervasive that it is almost impossible to shoot a

Kevin McCarthy (far right) explains Monty's accident to the police, May 13, 1956.

scene with sound. . . . I . . . won't get a day off until Xmas, so I have no time to recover. I'm not praying to be healthy but only to live until 1953—Please God! My fond best to you, Monty.''

Monty fought with de Sica, who spoke no English, and with Selznick, who wanted the film to be a Hollywood-style romance. Selznick changed the title to *Indiscretion of an American Wife*, which aptly suggests his conception of de Sica's film. Monty himself was no angel. He was manipulative and, although it was a side of his personality he hid as carefully as possible, deceptive and insensitive. Although they had gotten along quite well in Rome, back in New York Monty made cracks about Jennifer Jones's performance.

Brooks summed up Monty's reaction to the experience: "That whole film was such a huge disappointment for him. He'd loved whatever de Sica had done before that. According to Monty, de Sica was sucking up to Selznick, and it was made for no money, so it was one of *the* big tragedies of Monty's life.''

* * *

Monty, James Jones, and Frank Sinatra became close friends during the shooting of *From Here to Eternity*. In Hollywood, they all stayed at the Roosevelt Hotel, ate dinner together, got royally drunk, and had deep philosophical conversations which Jones characterized as "nonsense," then they would retire to the Roosevelt where they would talk some more. Monty would often hang out the window to practice playing his horn for the role of Prewitt.

Monty brought Mira Rostova out to help him with his part, and when she departed Monty worked not only on his own part but with Sinatra on the role of Maggio. Subsequently, Monty denied that he had helped Sinatra, insisting, "He's a natural born actor. I couldn't help him, but he helped me, with the trumpet business and marching properly. Sinatra can do anything. . . .'' Nevertheless, Sinatra was very grateful; he knew how much he owed Monty and they remained friends for some time after *Eternity* was finished, calling each other and drinking together when they were in the same city.

But, on one occasion, Sinatra saw Monty make a pass at a man at a Bel Air party. Sinatra's bodyguards threw Monty out and that was the end of their relationship.

Monty put everything he had into portraying Prew, and when he was nominated for the third time for an Academy Award, he finally admitted that he wanted to win. He lost to William Holden, for a role (in *Stalag 17*) that also owed its genesis to World War II.

Holden's and Monty's paths had crossed before, first when Holden had the George Gibbs part in the screen version of *Our Town*, a role Monty had played on the stage, and second when Holden was in the film *Young and Willing*, as one of the same group of

Mike Kellin, Vincent Donehue (back to camera), and Monty on the Lonelyhearts *set.*

young men Monty was part of on stage in *Out of the Frying Pan*.
More recently, and far more importantly, Monty had turned down
the lead in *Sunset Boulevard* (1950), the role that made Holden a
star, because he felt that the young writer/older star relationship
was too close for comfort to his real-life associations to Libby
Holman and Mira. As Holden told it: ''I didn't get *Sunset Boulevard* because Billy Wilder was crazy to cast me. I got it because
Montgomery Clift turned it down.''

Billy Wilder, the director, gave his recollection of the events to
an American Film Institute seminar: ''The part of the writer, Joe
Gillis, who becomes a gigolo, was written for Montgomery Clift.
But about two weeks before we started shooting, he sent his agent
in, who said, 'Mr. Montgomery Clift, the great New York actor,
will not do the picture, because what would his fans think if he had
an affair with a woman twice his age?' You would expect that from
a Hollywood actor but not a serious actor. So we took William
Holden, who was playing second lieutenants in comedies at that
time.''

Several writers have theorized that Monty never won an Oscar
because he was never an actor acting on the screen, he *was* the
character (therefore he was playing himself and did not deserve the
award), so perfectly did he fuse body and soul with the part he was
playing. His final nomination, for supporting actor, was for *Judgment at Nuremberg,* in a role in which he does, in fact, in a brief
and terrifyingly real portrayal of the mental incompetent, Rudolf
Petersen, stick out of the picture. But in *Eternity,* Monty *is* Prew-

itt, from his carefully pared down dialogue, to his almost mystical attachment to his bugle, and finally, more important than any emotional or physical relationship to a woman, to his faith in, and need for, the Army.

As a favor to Fred Zinnemann, Monty attended the annual Reno Chamber of Commerce Silver Spurs awards. Zinnemann was given a plaque for the "Outstanding Western Film of 1952," *High Noon*, and Monty accepted Gary Cooper's award as best actor in the film. Monty, Zinnemann, and Ronald Reagan were sworn in as honorary colonels in the Nevada National Guard during the ceremony.

* * *

When Monty, Mira Rostova, and Kevin McCarthy wanted to work on a project, they picked Anton Chekov's *The Sea Gull*. They read all the translations, then did their own, fighting over every implication and syllable. Robert Lewis, their old friend from *Mexican Mural*, wanted to direct a workshop production of their adaptation. Kevin said that they did not want "a strong director like Bobby. We thought we could direct ourselves."

After much persuasion on the part of T. Edward Hambleton and Norris Houghton, Monty agreed to a limited run at the Phoenix Theatre on Second Avenue. The cast they decided on was not only studded with accomplished character actors (Maureen Stapleton, Sam Jaffe, George Voskovec and Will Geer), it starred Monty, Kevin, Mira, and Judith Evelyn, who had played *The Shrike* on Broadway. Although everyone who saw Mira act in workshop scenes or worked with her as their acting coach, described her ability to dissect scenes and discover hidden nuances in a role as uncanny, she was inappropriately cast as Nina, a forty-year-old woman playing a seventeen-year-old virgin. Monty said he wanted to do the play to give everyone a chance to see "what a rare and gifted actress she is."

Norris Houghton was directing, more or less informally. The cast floundered around on stage, exhibiting various acting styles and wondering what the motivation for their characters was until Kevin called on Arthur Miller for help.

John Fiedler, who played Medvedenko, recalled that "Arthur really pulled it together." His direction was specific, his suggestions pertinent, and he understood *The Sea Gull* so perfectly that he easily explained the missing motivations. It was too late to bring coherence to the dissimilar acting methodologies, and Mira, who had not been on the stage for years, spoke so softly she could not be heard beyond the first few rows.

The reviews were mixed. Walter Kerr of the *Herald Tribune* said: "Miss Rostova is waif-like and appealing; her hands and her body are enormously expressive." Brooks Atkinson of the *Times* said: "Montgomery Clift's lonely, brooding Constantin is beautifully expressed," and noted that Mira's and Kevin's "parts are inadequately played."

The reviews could not keep the audiences from flocking to the Phoenix to see Monty in his first stage appearance in nine years; the run, originally scheduled to last thirty-two performances was extended to include an additional eight.

The audience occasionally yelled, "We can't hear you, Mira!" and Monty felt that Mira had let him down, but he never displayed much sympathy for the embarrassment his dear friend must have felt. Mira explains his attitude by saying: "Monty had a hard time because of his drinking and acted very strangely." During the course of their work on the script, "Monty changed. He was no longer reliable and we [she and Kevin] couldn't count on him for support." A measure of Mira's feeling for Monty was expressed by her willingness to work with him twelve years later on *The Defector*. (She also consulted with him on the scripts of *Raintree County* and *The Young Lions*, but she did not accompany him to the locations.)

*   *   *

Joseph L. Mankiewicz talks with Elizabeth Taylor and Monty during Suddenly, Last Summer.

On The Misfits set. *Front row: Monty mimics Marilyn Monroe, with Clark Gable. Back row: Producer Frank Taylor, Eli Wallach, Arthur Miller and John Huston.*

Another view. Front row: Monty, Marilyn Monroe,
and Clark Gable. Back row: Frank Taylor, Arthur
Miller, Eli Wallach, and John Huston.

Although it was clear to all who knew him that Monty relied far
too heavily on liquor to get him through difficult situations, what
was not appreciated until some time later was the fact that he was
mixing it with pills, all kinds of pills, indiscriminately taken and
washed down with whatever was handy. Augusta Dabney reported
that when he dosed himself, Monty did not even bother to look at
what he was taking. Later, Monty's "little black bag," the satchel
he carried drugs in, and his thermos, containing a potent mixture of
vodka and grapefruit juice, would become widely known.

In any event, Monty was behaving very strangely when he vacationed in Mary McCarthy's (Kevin's sister's) house in Wellfleet on
Cape Cod. He left cigarette burns all over the woodwork, and once
he carved a steak on Miss McCarthy's rug and—despite the surprise of his guests—served it from the floor.

In April 1954, once more on the West coast for film talks, Monty
stayed at Elizabeth Taylor's house while Michael Wilding was

away making a film. Elizabeth phoned Fred and Jeanne Green one night when Monty's drinking drove her into action. The Greens arrived to find Monty in a state of advanced intoxication. They tried to cook dinner, but he kept butting in, and, since this was by now a long-standing behavior pattern, the Greens decided to stop seeing Monty. They had cared for him deeply and had been very close, but now, not only was Monty taking advantage of their friendship, he was destroying it.

Friends gave up on Monty *en masse*; he was violent, unpredictable, manic, and sad by turns. The McCarthys would not let him in their house since the time he had dropped Flip on the floor, although Kevin sometimes came by the East 61st Street duplex. The Lunts disapproved of drinking in general and, since Monty was no longer a "social" drinker, they had stopped extending dinner invitations to him some time ago.

After Libby Holman's one-woman show, *Blues, Ballads and Sin Songs*, played its allotted one week in New York, she and Monty took off for Cuba where they basked in the sun and always gave "the impression of being slightly high—perhaps on dope," in the opinion of an observer who saw them almost daily near their hotel.

Monty could be charming and interested in other people, showering gifts on them, and then burst out with an incredibly cruel diatribe, or a devastating imitation of their behavior.

He had read, or was reading—and rejecting—every sort of script, including *The Devil's Disciple, On the Waterfront, East of Eden, Moby Dick* and *Bus Stop*—and those were the best of what he was offered. It was announced in July 1955 that Monty would co-star with Irene Worth in Thornton Wilder's *A Life in The Sun* at the Edinburgh Festival under Tyrone Guthrie's direction. Monty got as far as Paris and cancelled.

In 1959, Monty told a reporter from the *Enquirer*: "If I'd played the James Dean character in *East of Eden*, the part would have come out as a maladjusted neurotic instead of a mixed-up boy."

Monty told another reporter: "As to *On the Waterfront*, I just felt that I was physically wrong for the part. At no point could I envisage myself as a fighter. I haven't the physique for it." Although he believed director Elia Kazan wanted him for Terry Malloy, Kazan now says he thinks it was producer Sam Spiegel who offered Monty the Brando role.

Bill Gunn, a black actor who knew Monty in the fifties, said that he should not have been so choosy; if he had found a role that suited him halfway, rather than settling only for his idea of perfection, "His life might not have turned in on itself."

Although he would yell at his mother and call her a "cunt" when she came to dinner at his place, Monty was still extremely close to Sunny. They shared their most intimate secrets, but when they were apart, they made catty remarks behind one another's backs.

The principals: Monty, Marilyn Monroe, and Clark Gable.

Sunny believed that "He had a very hard time saying no" to his friends and to people who wanted things from him—advice, money, or to share his star aura. "He'd go along with what others said simply not to hurt feelings."

Many of Monty's friends were appalled at Dr. Silverberg's continued denial that his patient was an alcoholic. Actor Jack Larson, who had met Monty in Hollywood during the filming of *I Confess* (he played Jimmy Olsen in the *Superman* television series), felt that Billy was "taking Monty's money, his time, fucking him over and letting him kill himself by inches. . . ." No one, not even the evidence of his own eyes when Monty turned up drunk at his office, could convince Silverberg that Monty could not tolerate liquor. He would dry out at Libby Holman's estate, Treetops, for a while, then return to New York to hole up in the duplex and read (and refuse) more scripts, making sporadic trips to several East Side haunts that still appealed to him. One reason he feared going out was that sooner or later he would be recognized. Even if the occasion passed without incident, or with merely an autograph book to sign, Monty couldn't be sure he would not be mobbed, as had happened, and have pieces of clothing ripped from his body.

Monty commented on the fans' reaction to his presence to Anthony Hadden-Guest: "Why do they act like this? All sorts of reasons, I guess. Mass hysteria. And a proxy sexuality." He imitated a worshipper: "You—are—Montgomery Clift. *Aren't you?*" —spitting it out.

Bill Gunn remembers sneaking into movie theaters after the lights went down so Monty would not be recognized. He also re-

Monty practices his roping.

calls Monty's insistence on helping him because he felt Bill was an "underprivileged Negro," despite the fact that Bill's background was as middle-class as Monty's. Monty took a genuine interest in Bill's career, coaching him, watching him from the wings in his first Broadway play, *Take a Giant Step,* and attending the first play Bill wrote, *Marcus in the High Grass,* at a tryout in Westport.

Ned Smith stopped by and, although the two old friends did not fight, their meeting ended on a sad note, with Ned asking Monty— since he felt Monty was no longer interested in him—to destroy his letters. He thought Monty would not want to have them as a reminder of their friendship. Monty was hurt; he left the room, apparently to take some pills, and when he returned, Ned asked if he were sick. Monty replied, "Yes, I am."

*   *   *

Elizabeth Taylor and Monty were still close, close enough so that when she came to town with her two sons by her second husband, Michael Wilding, Monty turned the duplex over to her and the children and moved in with Libby Holman down the block. "For Elizabeth I always put out all the St. Regis and Plaza Hotel towels I stole when she used to stay at those places," Monty joked.

Monty and Elizabeth had always wanted to work together again and when MGM put the best seller, *Raintree County,* into production, it seemed a good opportunity, despite the fact that both knew it was not the successor to *Gone With the Wind* the studio thought it was.

An MGM press release dated December 10, 1955 stated that Monty had signed a three picture contract with the studio and his first film would be *Raintree County.* In September 1954, the same studio's press department had announced that Monty was set to star with Spencer Tracy in *Bannon,* a film about the conflict between older and younger labor leaders in the same union. It would be written by Millard Kaufman, who was indirectly responsible for turning Ross Lockridge, Jr.'s sprawling novel (*Raintree*) into a screenplay. The studio's writers had been unable to lick either its size or its content and had left various scripts to gather dust, when Kaufman, angry at being removed from a picture, had been given the novel to pacify him until he could be assigned to another project. He was crazy about the book, although even then it had a doomed aura around it. Lockridge, an English teacher in Indiana, the state where *Raintree* takes place, was unable to deal with his success, and after MGM had bought the rights to his book for $150,000, he committed suicide.

After *Raintree County* was released, Monty explained his three-year absence from the screen to *Cue*'s Jesse Zunser. After *From*

Here to Eternity "I looked over many scripts and never found anything I wanted to do. . . . I do not have a neurotic ambition to act. As for money, I don't want any more. . . . I understand actors who take many parts. They want Cadillacs and swimming pools. I don't care especially for them. I got $250,000 for *Raintree County* and could have gotten more."

By the time Monty signed to make the film, he was in debt to his agents at MCA. When he was offered $300,000 for *Raintree*, he took only $250,000, saying, "Use the $50,000 to make the film better." Whether or not that money found its way into the film is irrelevant; by its very nature *Raintree* was destined to be a critical failure, if not a financial one. Sprawling, episodic, the story of a nineteenth-century Candide (Monty) in search of a so-called tree of life was doomed by the novel from which it was taken and the pedestrian realization Kaufman derived from it.

Monty was in every scene of the movie, so from the beginning the pressures on him were enormous. He and Elizabeth worried over the script and, although she had grown in confidence and expertise since *A Place in the Sun*, Monty helped her with her part and tried to do something with his own dreary role.

The Wilding/Taylor marriage was gradually coming apart, although neither of them was ready to admit it yet. Both used Monty as a sounding board. Elizabeth would tell him she was tired of supporting Wilding, who had a hard time getting work away from his native England. Wilding would say that the twenty-year difference in their ages did not matter, and he still loved her. Monty was getting sick of the whole thing. "Bessie Mae" would always be special to him, perhaps the one woman he would ever completely adore, but they had already defined the limits of their relationship and there was little more he could do.

On the evening of May 12, 1956, Elizabeth called repeatedly to ask Monty over for dinner. Kevin McCarthy would be there and Rock Hudson, with his secretary, Phyllis Gates. Jack Larson dropped in to see Monty, and he remembers at least three phone calls, with Wilding chiming in occasionally to add his invitation.

Finally Monty gave in. When he had arrived in Los Angeles this time, he had resolved not to drive; his behavior behind the wheel was beginning to scare even himself, and he had hired a chauffeur. He was tired and so determined to stay in that he had given the driver the night off. He had not driven for months, but after the fifth or sixth call, he drove over to Elizabeth's house.

Kevin recalls the meal as "subdued," and not too good. Monty hung around the door, drinking only a little wine the whole evening. The two men left together so Monty could follow Kevin down the steep hill; he was too tired to navigate by himself. They talked for a few minutes before getting into their cars. Monty, Kevin said, felt he had no control over the film or anything that happened in Hollywood. He was depressed and "God, how he hated that place!"

As they were driving down the hill, Kevin realized Monty's car was too close to his. He wondered if he was having a blackout, or playing a trick as he would have done in the old days, like bumping the rear of Kevin's car. Kevin accelerated, but Monty kept pace with him, screeching and careening through the darkness. He could see the headlights of Monty's car weaving from side to side. "Suddenly, I heard a terrible crash," Kevin related. He stopped and ran back through the night to find Monty's car crumpled against a telephone pole. He could smell gas and reached in to turn off the ignition, but it was so dark he could see nothing, not even Monty.

Kevin drove back to the Wildings' in terror, pounded on the door, and yelled for them to call an ambulance. He did not know if Monty was alive or dead.

Although Elizabeth told Eleanor Harris of *McCall's:* "Monty had only one drink before dinner," she later recalled for a Truman Capote article which appeared in *Playboy*, "He'd had a lot to drink, and he lost control of his car. He was really all right before the accident. Well, he always drank too much. . . ." The Harris story continues with Elizabeth saying, "At 12:30 he left to go home. He lived just four-and-a-half minutes from us, in a rented house on the next hilltop. He was completely exhausted and he'd promised to follow Kevin's car down the hill. . . . Ten minutes after they left Kevin was back at our house white and shaking. 'Monty's had an accident and I can't get him out of the car,' he said."

Both Kevin and Michael Wilding tried to prevent Elizabeth from going down the hill to Monty with them, but "she fought us off like a tiger, and raced down the hill," Kevin stated.

"His face was gushing blood—I couldn't see Monty at all," Elizabeth went on. "But I crawled into the car and put his head in my lap. Finally he came to, and he began to try to pull out a loose tooth. He asked me to pull out that one and another, and I did. I had to use control not to get sick."

Dr. Rex Kennamer arrived, and, working with Rock Hudson, managed to extricate Monty from the car. Elizabeth restrained herself during the ride in the ambulance with Monty to Cedars of Lebanon Hospital; then, when he was taken into the operating room, she went into hysterics.

Dr. Kennamer detailed the damage to Monty's face and body: lacerations of the left side of his face; a broken nose and crushed sinus cavity; both sides of his jaw broken; two front teeth lost; severe cerebral concussion; and whiplash.

Monty recuperated for a while in the hospital where, after three

Monty and Marilyn Monroe on The Misfits *set.*

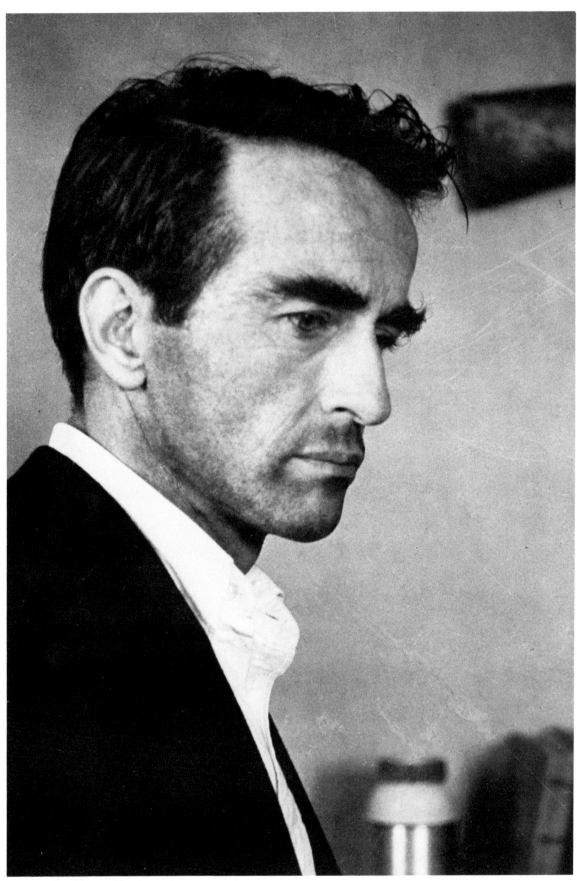

Monty after his accident.

weeks, the doctors discovered that his jaw had been wired incorrectly. It had to be broken and reset.

Hank Moomjian, a member of the *Raintree* company, collected money from the crew for flowers. As soon as they arrived, Monty called to say that they "were the nicest thing that could have happened to him," as Moomjian told Harris. "He said he'd leave the flowers on his dresser till they rotted. He did, too."

Back at his rented house, Monty continued his recovery. Libby Holman, Bill Clift, and Marge Stengel (Monty's secretary), flew out from New York. (UPI's Aline Mosby reported that Libby Holman "flew immediately to his side from New York. She spent much time in the hospital with him. The former singer and the actor have been friends for years and pals say, 'He doesn't make a move without her.' But they add, 'It's doubtful they'll marry.' ") All three were dead set against Monty's returning to work, and Holman was so adamant that, when Monty informed her he was determined to finish the picture, she got angry and returned to the East immediately. Monty made his father promise not to let Sunny see him, and Brooks stayed away, too, because, as he put it, "I was sure Monty didn't want me to see him in that condition." His face "was swollen out to here," as he told his brother in a letter. "It's been a long painful process."

To suppress the pain, Monty was drinking—a practice expressly forbidden by his doctors as it interfered with the healing process—and dosing himself with painkillers. His friends would come and tell him to take it easy, not to think of returning to work before he was fully recuperated. Then the MGM executives would turn up, saying how well Monty looked. Of course he looked well to them. There was a great deal of money involved in getting Monty back to the set as quickly as possible. And Monty was anxious not to let the film down. He wanted to go back to work, to prove that he could, and because he knew it was costing the studio a fortune to keep everyone on salary during the almost ten weeks he was out.

Monty's face was still swollen, but the biggest changes in his looks were due to the slight scar on the bridge of his nose and his torn upper lip. The doctors had decided against plastic surgery and had tried to maintain his appearance. A slight thickening of his facial characteristics and immobility in the left side of his face, the after-effects of his wired jaw and the nerves that had been severed, were the most noticeable results. Age accounted for the rest. He was a thirty-six-year-old man who had abused his health and suffered a severe accident. *And* he had to play a twenty-year-old.

Although Monty resumed filming *Raintree County* in Danville, Kentucky, under his own steam, he had misjudged his capacities. He was still in great pain, medicating himself, and under enormous tension to keep going for the sake of the film. His face was still slightly swollen, and his eyes—always his best feature—were not always clear. He put drops in them, but since he was drinking part of the time, he could not control the redness.

Monty had several minor accidents while on location; whether they were the result of poor coordination or the various combinations of pills he subsisted on is not clear. Elizabeth Taylor came down with heat exhaustion and Monty, who made sure he was present while a physician examined her, went through the doctor's bag, naming every medication it contained.

The doctor had prescribed chloral hydrates to help Elizabeth sleep. When she noticed some were missing, director Edward Dmytryk and Kaufman found them in Monty's satchel, along with "about 200 different kinds of pills—barbiturates, tranquilizers, painkillers," Dmytryk said. He and Kaufman had the chloral hydrates replaced with similar-looking vitamins by a local druggist, but they were sure Monty knew what they had done.

Monty was getting regular deliveries of medication from "Bird," his New York dealer, and doubtlessly he needed many of the drugs he took, not only because of the pain. MGM had promised him a closed set but, instead, fans from the area and journalists from all over appeared—taking pictures, trying to get interviews, and generally being a nuisance.

Far from maintaining a closed set, the studio turned its publicity men loose to tout the location shooting in the nation's press. A typical method of garnering advance publicity for the film, it was designed to keep *Raintree County* in the forefront of the public's consciousness until it was released. Southern belles and a high-school band met Monty, Elizabeth, and Dmytryk at the Lexington airport. In a news photo taken there, Monty looks stiff and resigned while Elizabeth smiles. There was a parade in Danville to welcome the company, and although the pictures taken along Main Street show Elizabeth waving to the crowds, her co-star is nowhere to be seen.

Cameron Shipp wrote in *Redbook* that Monty was "bellowing drunk" when he went into a laughing spell after he fell into a carriage he was trying to enter for a scene. In Lexington, Governor "Happy" Chandler, who was supposed to make Monty an honorary colonel, gave up and turned his duties over to Mrs. Chandler, who was told Monty's and Elizabeth's arrival had been delayed because she was "indisposed." The two stepped from their plane to find a crowd of 2,000 ready to greet them. Monty accepted his colonelship from Mrs. Chandler, mumbled, "Thank you very much," ignored the crowd, and disappeared.

In Danville, Shipp reported, Monty avoided the fans, who came laden with cameras and autograph books, "as if they were spear-carrying natives," and looked on reporters "as if they were Borgias." This was the atmosphere in which Monty was supposed to not only recover from his accident, but give a star performance.

Monty and Edward Dmytryk confer during Raintree County.

Once shooting was over, Monty returned to a rented house in
Brentwood. He seemed to be in a state of permanent despondency
not only over his injuries—which were healing well by this time—
but over *Raintree*, which Monty knew was a "monumental bore."
He was sure that audiences would go to see it chiefly to compare
the scenes made before and after his accident. In both cases he was
right.

Monty was also furious when MGM was exhibiting *Raintree* on a
hard ticket basis for its initial run. "Can you imagine charging $16
for four people to see *Raintree County*? I mean isn't that absolutely
ridiculous?" he fumed.

Jack Larson kept Monty company some of the time. One day,
after crying by himself for a while, he told Larson that he had
really looked at his face for the first time since the accident. He had
finished *Raintree* believing it was his last picture, but now he realized, as he told Larson, "I can still have a career."

Late in November, Larson recalls, Marlon Brando came to see
Monty. He did not hear their conversation, but when Brando had
left, Monty said that he had come to talk him out of destroying
himself. He had heard stories about Monty and pills, Monty and
booze, and since Monty was a sort of professional touchstone for
Brando, his major competition, Monty must stop. They had always
challenged each other, admired and envied one another professionally, and this kind of healthy competition should continue for both
their sakes. But it couldn't if Monty wrecked himself physically.

Larson reported that Monty was moved by Brando's effort, he
knew it was done as a gesture of friendship, that "we respect each

The check Monty gave his nephew Eddie.

other.'' After he and Monty made *The Young Lions*, Brando told Maureen Stapleton about his visit. He had offered to go with Monty to Alcoholics Anonymous to help him dry out. While consuming double vodkas, Monty informed Brando: ''I'll be all right.'' He repeated his gratitude for Brando's concern, insisting he had no problem with liquor. At that point, Brando told Stapleton, he had given up on Monty.

Some people were embarrassed by Monty's new face and he grew used to re-identifying himself to friends and acquaintances. He was still a good-looking man; he just was not as spectacularly handsome as he had been. And it bothered him.

In 1961, Monty was still justifying his appearance, this time to Wanda Hale of the *Daily News:* ''I have exactly the same face as I had before the accident. The only difference in my appearance is that I have some new teeth. I gave the old ones to Elizabeth Taylor and asked her to keep them for me in case I might need them again.''

He worried about his new face preventing him from getting roles, but he need not have. Monty was not without work for long. He signed to do *The Young Lions*, again working with director Edward Dmytryk, and starring with Brando and Dean Martin.

One must surmise that Monty agreed to make *Lions* with Dmytryk partly because Dmytryk had directed his last film; even if *Raintree County* was a disappointment, Dmytryk had gotten him through it after his accident, despite the many problems filming had presented. Dmytryk was only slightly better suited to direct *Lions*. Like *Raintree*, it is ponderous, unyielding material. It involved the kinds of logistical difficulties *Raintree* had presented, with shooting taking place in several locations.

The important aspect of the film for Monty, especially after the disaster of *Raintree County*, was that he liked the film and his own performance. In fact, after a time, he concluded that Noah was his favorite of all the men he had played. ''Noah was the best performance of my life,'' he said. When his next film, *Lonelyhearts*, was finished, Monty said: "I think I was prouder of *The Young Lions* and *Lonelyhearts* than any other two films I've ever made. I was happy because they were a development for me. I discovered in those films that my reactions were much quicker. . . . It wasn't such hard work for me to grasp a mood in a scene as it had been before."

Monty also talked about his acting philosophy: "When I play a role I pour all my energy and emotion into it. My body doesn't know I'm only an actor. The adrenalin rushes around just like in a real emotional crisis when you throw yourself into an emotional ‚scene. Your body doesn't know you're kidding when you become angry, tearful or violent for a part. It takes a tremendous toll of the performer emotionally and physically. I delve as deeply as possible into the characterization. I can't pace myself the way some other actors can. I either go all out or I don't accept the picture. I have to dredge it out of me. I'm exhausted at the end of a picture."

Edward Dmytryk confirmed Monty's view of himself as an actor: "He's tireless. He probes, tests, tries and retries the tiniest bit of business for a scene until he's convinced he's doing it the honest way to tell the most, and his instincts are uncannily right. Monty can't play something he's not. He thinks actors should wait for characters that truly represent themselves. The parts are more important to this boy than the money."

Dmytryk's description of Monty's attitude toward acting is an apt description of a "Method" actor. Monty never was one, but he had opinions on the subject: "The Method as such—I don't know really—I must say I'm baffled myself—because *any* good actor uses the principles of Stanislavsky no matter what they do. It's a marvelous thing for some poor slob who's in a hit—because he's playing that role every night—and he's not expanding. Every time you find a truthful actor, you find someone who bears out a little, not theories, but somehow the realism that Stanislavsky bothered to put on paper."

After the premiere at the Paramount in New York, there was a party for the picture at the Waldorf. Monty attended with publicist John Springer, Hope Lange, and her then-husband, Don Murray. Although the other critics praised the film and Monty's acting, everyone tried to prevent Monty from seeing Bosley Crowther's review in the *Times*. (He wrote that Monty was "strangely hollow and lackluster as the sensitive Jew. He acts throughout the picture as if he were in a glassy-eyed daze.") Everyone tried to protect Monty: from the world, from other people, from himself.

One friend who differed in her attitude was Nancy Walker. She and Monty had a "special" relationship, not unlike those he had formed with Libby Holman, Mira Rostova, and Elizabeth Taylor, but Nancy refused to mother him. If his secretary told her "Make sure Monty eats'' when they dined together, Nancy would growl, ''Isn't that what you're supposed to do when you go out to dinner?''

Along with other odd traits (perching on the back of furniture, eating with his fingers or rubbing his steak on his cheek, for example), Monty had developed an annoying habit of grabbing the food off other people's plates. Once, when he insisted on taking Nancy's food against her wishes, she threw her plate in his lap, and stormed out of the restaurant. Nancy refused to let Monty act like a child around her.

Others were not as successful in achieving their wishes for Monty. Most of his friends still felt that Dr. Silverberg was the worst analyst Monty could have. Not only was the psychoanalyst taking Monty's money for sessions Monty did not attend (when he was away working on a picture, Monty's hour was reserved anyway), he was not helping Monty deal with his two greatest problems—his drinking, and the guilt he felt about being a homosexual. Many of Monty's friends realized what Monty did not, that Dr. Silverberg was himself gay, although all agree that probably nothing physical ever happened between the two men. Dr. Silverberg admired Monty as an artist and Monty worshipped his analyst as an erudite, charming human being, as well as believing that his treatment was effective.

But how could it be effective if Monty was addicted, not only to liquor, but to a wide spectrum of drugs? While making *The Young Lions*, Monty was drinking from a thermos containing crushed Demerol, fruit juice, and bourbon. He took vast quantities of pills: depressants and painkillers, many for the very good reason that he was in pain. He still suffered from the effects of dysentery, he was a chronic insomniac, and the accident had caused head pains that were still with him. He also took what are now called mood enhancers, ''uppers'' to make one cheerful—and they made Monty positively hyperactive—or ''downers'' to help him sleep or bring him out of a manic phase.

Doctors gave him drugs seemingly with open hands. When Monty returned to Hollywood to finish *Lions*, he was given Benadryl to help him with the phlebitis he had developed preparing for the fight scenes in which he takes on the three soldiers who have been tormenting Noah. The same physician gave him Miltown to help him with his hung-over condition in the mornings, and belladonna for a ''stuffy nose.'' At one time or another, Monty was reportedly taking Seconal, phenobarbital, Nembutal, Luminal, and Doriden.

Like the rest of Monty's friends, Marge Stengel, Monty's secretary since 1954, worried about his pill-taking. She was amazed at the ease with which he was able to get drugs. Not from his regular doctor in California, Rex Kennamer, nor from Dr. Arthur Ludwig, whom Monty saw in New York, but there were many others (and these included pharmacists who sold him medication without a prescription) who were impressed by the status of their patient and saw how easy it was to gouge him for money. Despite Marge's efforts to stop the flow of pills, Monty could always find a doctor who would supply him without asking too many questions.

Late in 1958, Monty began work on Dore Schary's production of *Lonelyhearts*, which Schary himself adapted from Nathanael West's *Miss Lonelyhearts*. The cast was headed by three hard drinkers: Monty, Robert Ryan, and Myrna Loy. (Ironically, in the film, Monty's character can't drink and remarks, ''It always makes me sick,'' while sticking to ginger ale.) Predictably, the problems stemmed from Monty's behavior. He was at his best before lunch; afterward Monty was influenced by the drugs he was taking: they affected his memory and he often could not remember his lines.

Clarence Eurist, the assistant director, said that around two P.M., ''He would lose all energy and spontaneity . . . we'd work it out diplomatically. . . .'' and Monty would be told that he was not needed for the rest of the day's shooting. Off the set, Monty was seen dashing naked from his cottage at the Bel Air Hotel.

Myrna Loy became Monty's loyal friend during the filming and quit drinking herself in an effort to help him stop. It was rumored at the time that she was in love with Monty and, despite the fact that she was fifteen years his senior, wanted to marry him. She joined Maureen Stapleton, Dolores Hart, and Nancy Walker, who spent several weeks in Hollywood with Monty, in Monty's dressing room, sharing their lunch time. Miss Loy and Monty talked about adapting *Cheri*, the Colette novel, for the screen with Loy as the prostitute, but nothing came of the idea.

Lonelyhearts opened to mixed reviews and almost no business. Paul V. Beckley of the *Herald Tribune* called *Lonelyhearts* ''a strong, serious effort to deal with a mordant and difficult story.''

* * *

David O. Selznick was helping to cast the film version of the F. Scott Fitzgerald novel *Tender is the Night*, which would star his wife, Jennifer Jones. In a letter* to Jones, dated January 27, 1959, he discusses his opposition to casting Monty as Dick Diver: ''Monty Clift has become so impossible to work with that I am afraid he would throw you higher than a kite, although there are

Monty waiting to film The Defector.

*Memo from David O. Selznick, edited by Rudy Behlmer,
Viking Press, New York, 1972.

Monty and John Huston on the set of Freud.

many things to recommend him for the role—as against which he seems a little lightweight, and perhaps too peculiar in appearance and personality for the part. . . ."

Monty's behavior kept him from consideration for other roles as well. Robert Thom, a writer who knew Monty during this period, suggested Monty for a role in MGM's *The Brother's Karamazov*, which producer Pandro S. Berman was then casting. Berman told Thom, "He's unusable. He should never work again."

*   *   *

In July 1959, there was a fire in Monty's duplex on East 61st Street. Whether it was caused by Monty's smoking in bed, as he claimed, or as the result of carelessness on the part of painters who were working on the entryway, was not determined. In any event, Monty decided to give the place up and bought a brownstone on the same street. He moved into it in January 1960. In the meantime he made *Wild River* and *Suddenly, Last Summer*.

Lyn Tornabene, in a *Cosmopolitan* article on Monty, described the interior of Monty's house as having "a monastery-like bareness . . . texture, no color. All the wooden pieces are sanded down and oil-finished to show the grain. Almost everything in sight is beige—walls, upholstery. There are few paintings or wall hangings, but many exquisite silver *objets* everywhere and jewel-like crystal ash trays." There was also a seven-foot long desk, with a top made from an old fire door, crafted of many layers of wood. Brooks has it now—along with the Vuitton trunk which carried their clothes to Europe when they were children—in his home in Washington.

*   *   *

Although Monty was considered a bad risk, Elizabeth Taylor came to his rescue. She had signed to star as Catherine Holly in *Suddenly, Last Summer* for producer Sam Spiegel and director Joseph L. Mankiewicz, and she wanted Monty to play Dr. Cukrowicz opposite her. The third co-star was Katharine Hepburn (as Mrs. Violet Venable) and Monty was delighted not only with the idea of working with Elizabeth again, but with Hepburn, whom he admired enormously.

From the beginning, the filming of *Suddenly* went badly. In his book* on Mankiewicz's career, Kenneth L. Geist (who was a theater student in London at the time of the filming) observed Monty on the set: "It was a considerable shock to see this sensitive actor's deplorable condition. . . . He was now a mass of tics and spasms." Geist states that Monty passed out on the plane carrying him to London and again in the limousine which carried him and others connected with the film to various social functions.

There are two versions of the way in which Mankiewicz treated Monty. In the first, and most widely reported, account, Mankiewicz was far from sympathetic to Monty's reliance on drugs and booze. As producer Spiegel phrased it: "Mankiewicz is an excellent director but devoid of a great many human considerations when it comes to weaker beings than himself."

The second report of the activities on the set of *Suddenly, Last Summer*—given by Kenneth Geist—is considerably more favorable to Mankiewicz. Geist quotes Mankiewicz as saying that Monty "was on all sorts of tranquilizers" and "in bad shape."

Geist watched Mankiewicz during a scene at the home of Mrs. Venable when a malfunctioning fountain refused to gush water on cue. "Mankiewicz grasped Clift by the shoulders and began to impart his directorial suggestions. While riveting Clift's attention with a piercing gaze, Mankiewicz surreptitiously started to massage Clift's neck and shoulders. Clift's tremors subsided and . . . he maintained his composure through a *series* of repeated takes."

The editorial consultant of *Suddenly*, William Hornbeck, had met Monty when he edited *A Place in the Sun*, and Mankiewicz asked Hornbeck to talk to Monty and find out what he was doing to himself so that he couldn't work. "Joe thought," says Hornbeck, "he was either smoking or taking dope or putting booze into his orange juice."

Monty was often late reporting to work and when he did get there sometimes could not remember his lines. At one point it was discovered that some of Monty's dialogue was unusable because it was overlaid with automobile noises, but he arbitrarily refused to dub new dialogue, stating, "The lines in the picture are better."

Pictures Will Talk, The Life and Films of Joseph L. Mankiewicz, Charles Scribner's Sons, New York, 1978.

Monty and Paramount photographer J. E. Richardson, 1949.

Patricia Bosworth's biography of Montgomery Clift.

According to Hornbeck, Monty then "lay down and rolled around on the floor like a naughty child. He was so infantile and nasty that I grew very irritated at him." Monty finally dubbed the lines, and, as a way of excusing himself, sent Hornbeck a pound of caviar.

* * *

After filming *The Young Lions*, Monty met a young Frenchman, identified as "Giles" in Patricia Bosworth's biography, whom he installed as a lover *cum* servant in his duplex. Marge Stengel had taken over from Arlene Cunningham as Monty's secretary late in 1953 and had traveled with Monty to London for *Suddenly, Last Summer*. Her mission was to keep Monty sober while he was working, and she was supposed to fulfill the same function when Monty made *Wild River*. When Monty felt that Marge was becoming too bossy, he warned her that he might take Giles along as his secretary/assistant. Actually, Donna Carnegie, a beautiful young actress who met Monty through their mutual friend, Ben Piazza, accompanied him to Cleveland, Tennessee, where *Wild River* was filmed. Donna acted as Monty's secretary, but, like Marge, her job was to see that Monty was in condition to perform.

Kazan started working on the script of *Wild River* himself, then Ben Maddow and Calder Willingham tried their hands at it, but Paul Osborn was the only one to get screen credit. Kazan wanted to develop the characters as they went along. He observed the members of the cast reacting to one another and integrated their attitudes with what he felt the thrust of the scene should be. Pictures taken on the set during filming show Monty, his hands in motion, crouched on the ground talking to Kazan. The rapport Kazan and Monty felt toward each other was paralleled by Monty's relationship with Lee Remick; what the audience sees on the screen emerged from their real-life friendship. She also recalled what eventually appeared on film as the fruition of their off-screen companionship: "Insofar as Monty was incapable of being the dominant partner in a male-female relationship [Kazan] went along. . . . The film showed a very different kind of relationship than what one usually sees."

Brooks remembers how much Monty liked the cinematographer, Ellsworth Fredericks: "He loved that guy, off duty as well as on. There's an empathy that Monty had for him—his sense of humor and his ability to communicate."

When *Wild River* was released, it garnered respectful but largely unenthusiastic reviews, and it was a financial disaster. Eleven years after its release, Kazan reflected on his film's fate: "*Wild River* and *America, America* came closest to my theory of the humble and poetic, the unnoticed poetry that's all around us. *Wild River* was never even shown anywhere. All kinds of pictures are being revived, but not *Wild River*."

*Judy Balaban and Monty with announcer Warren Hull
at the premiere of* A Place in the Sun.

When Monty returned to New York, he told his doctor, Arthur
Ludwig, that he sometimes lost his memory and could not maintain
his balance. Dr. Ludwig discovered that Monty had premature
cataracts and a thyroid condition which kept his parathyroid glands
from producing enough calcium. Monty's calcium deficiency gave
him cramps and seemed to be the cause of his other symptoms.
Calcium and Vitamin D improved his condition somewhat, a situation Monty undermined by continuing to drink heavily in spite of
specific orders not to. He wound up in Mt. Sinai Hospital suffering
from alcoholic hepatitis.

*   *   *

In July, 1960, Monty started shooting *The Misfits* in Reno, Nevada. As it had been with *Wild River*, Marge Stengel did not accompany him to the location—she had quit, partly because of
Giles's continued presence in Monty's house. Marge believed
Giles was a bad influence on Monty; moreover, she felt her own
life was being taken over by Monty's demands on her.

Monty told Henderson Cleaves of the *New York World Telegram and Sun* why he had accepted the part of Perce Howland, the
punchy rodeo rider: "I decided to do *The Misfits* because I don't
appear until page 57. In my last two pictures, I am on the screen
constantly. I only read ten pages of the script [where Perce is in the
phone booth] and I called Arthur [Miller] and said I would do it."

Director John Huston assembled a highly volatile cast to star in

*Monty accepts Gary Cooper's Silver Spurs Award,
with Fred Zinnemann.*

the film: Clark Gable, Marilyn Monroe, Eli Wallach, Thelma Ritter, and Monty. Huston, notorious for being tough on actors, apparently decided not to add to the potential difficulties of working with this group, and was on his best behavior. Monty told Bob Thomas of the Associated Press: "I must say that Huston never once gave any evidence of impatience. Whether this was due to his own serenity or whether he reasoned that things might get worse if he did blow up, I don't know."

The set of *The Misfits* was like a circus. Hordes of writers and photographers turned up to chronicle what they thought would be the breakup of the Miller/Monroe marriage. (The *Time* reporter wrote: "Known to be just as explosive as Marilyn, Montgomery Clift was variously happy, snide, exploding with nervous laughter, once fell to the ground and rolled with joy on seeing some old friends. Drinking whisky and Seven-Up with assorted cowboys, making an elaborate do about picking up their speech and mannerisms. . .") Miller had adapted his *Esquire* short story for the screen, changing the plot so that it centered on Rosalyn Taber (Marilyn), rather than on the cowboys. Now, ironically, he was at odds with his wife. Although they pretended to be happy for the benefit of the press, the marriage was over.

In addition (according to James Goode,* who wrote an account of the filming), there were over 200 people connected with the production itself, including a doctor, makeup men for each of the principals, two dogs and their trainer, a whistle blower and a five-man catering service. All of this contributed to making *The Misfits* the most expensive black and white movie ever filmed up until then; it finished forty days over schedule and $500,000 over budget.

Miller was rewriting the script, Monty fought with Libby Holman when she visited him in Reno, Huston took off to go hunting on weekends, Gable tore around the desert in his new Mercedes, and Marilyn was, as expected, chronically late reporting to work.

Marilyn's illness halted filming three times. On August 27, she was flown to Los Angeles and hospitalized for acute exhaustion. Once, Monty flew to San Francisco with the film's press agent, Harry Mines, for some sight seeing; another time he flew back to New York. On another occasion Monty took a chartered flight to Los Angeles to hear Ella Fitzgerald sing. Producer Frank Taylor called it "Monty's little treat." When he arrived in the city, he asked Fred and Jeanne Green to come along, but no one had a very good time.

Monty excused Marilyn, telling Bob Thomas: "When Marilyn was really sick, we had to suspend production. As for her lateness, we adjusted to it. I can sympathize with it. I know how a person feels when facing a big scene. You can get so worked up over it that you become physically sick. I think that was the case with Marilyn."

Monty loved working with her. After Marilyn's death, he spoke about her to several writers. "On *The Misfits* we would be working, and we would be playing to each other, and something would happen. And the scene would escalate! She was much more than a beautiful female, she was a fine actress. I remember the look in her eyes. She was so real. I never met anybody I liked so much to work with."

When filming was over, Monty compared her with himself for journalist W.J. Weatherby.† "I have the same problem as Marylyn. We attract people the way honey does bees, but they're generally the wrong kind of people. People who want something from us, if only our energy. We need a period of being alone to become ourselves. To be an actor, you can't afford defenses, a thick skin. You've got to be open and people can hurt you easily."

Marilyn was fond of Monty, too. She said: "I look at him and see the brother I never had and feel braver and get protective."

*The Story of The Misfits, Bobbs-Merrill, New York, 1963
† Conversations with Marilyn, Mason/Charters Publishers, Inc. New York, 1963

She spoke up against labeling people to Weatherby: "People who aren't't fit to open the door for him sneer at his homosexuality. What do they know about it?" She also commented to Weatherby that Monty was not ambitious enough for his talent.

Publicist John Springer talked about Marilyn and Monty: "Even to Marilyn, the most vulnerable person in the world, he was someone who needed protection. You should have seen them together; they were like two babes in the woods."

Clark Gable, on the other hand, was not so taken with Monty. Lyn Tornabene* wrote in her biography of Gable: "He treated Monty Clift as though he were a mental patient—but he was fascinated by his talent and showed up on the set to watch him work even when he wasn't on call himself." He once greeted Monty's arrival on the set with "If it isn't the little shepherd of kingdom come!" but he was concerned enough about his health to comment to Huston after the mustang-roping sequence that Monty's face was a sickly gray.

Kevin McCarthy had a small scene in *The Misfits*—as the husband Marilyn is in Reno to divorce. Before filming started, he and Monty, along with Huston, the Gables, and others of the cast and crew, met in Frank Taylor's rented house. Kevin and Monty talked about their acting techniques. When Kevin stated that the Method gives an actor things he can use, Monty rejoined: "Yes, Kevin, you and I have hung on to our purity of diction," with some sarcasm. Otherwise, they had nothing to do with each other and after Kevin left, they never saw one another again.

As for the filming itself, it was physically hard on everyone. The temperature stayed at 100° and some of the location work was murderous. On the dry lake bed where the mustang roundup was filmed, the wind whipped alkali dust into the cast's faces.

Toward the end of filming, Arthur Miller commented to Huston: "You know who was a great satisfaction in this picture . . . Monty." And Huston replied: "He always was and always is. Monty couldn't have been better, and he gave a wonderful performance."

The Misfits was Gable's and Marilyn's last film; he died twelve days after shooting was completed, she less than a year later. But before tragedy overcame them, everyone had plans. Gable was looking forward to making *Diamond Head* and to the birth of his first child (his wife, Kay, was pregnant during the filming). Marilyn said: "As far as I'm concerned there's a future and I can't wait to get to it." Her next film was to be *Something's Got to Give*.

Monty, too, was full of the future, telling Joe Hyams: "Two weeks ago I was forty and I feel that my life is just beginning. I want so much to be a director. To be limited by my body is to be

Long Live the King, G.P. Putnam's Sons, New York, 1976

limited professionally. If the part of a sixteen-year-old peasant fascinates you, you might not be able to play it, but you could direct it.''

John Huston also had plans—among them to direct *Freud*.

*   *   *

Producer/director Stanley Kramer originally wanted Monty for a major part in his blockbuster about the German war crimes trials, *Judgment at Nuremberg*, but Monty turned him down in favor of another, less prominent part, which he would do for nothing, just expenses. Monty explained his reasoning to the *Times*: ''There's nothing altruistic about it. I felt the original part they wanted me to play—the American prosecuting-attorney [a role eventually taken by Richard Widmark]—was wrong for me, but I was tremendously intrigued by a smaller role which obviously doesn't deserve my usual salary. Kramer almost fell out of his chair when I offered to do it for nothing, but he wasn't too startled to agree.'' Kramer had offered Monty $50,000 for the part of the mentally deficient witness, Rudolf Petersen, but he preferred doing it for nothing, lest he set a precedent of working for less than his usual salary.

Kramer felt that ''Clift is one of the three or four greatest actors extant,'' and he did everything he could to pull Monty through his role. He told Donald Spoto:* ''. . . by the time of our film [his automobile accident] had affected him emotionally, he was drinking heavily, and he had severe problems. . . . He needed somebody to be terribly kind, somebody who would say, 'You're wonderful and I know that you're having a little trouble and you don't remember the lines, but what difference? Within the scope of the thing, you just do it as you feel it should be done, and we'll manage. But Monty, you're wonderful and I wanted you for the part,' etc., etc. I had to bolster his confidence all the time.''

Kramer told another writer what happened on the set: ''It was [Spencer] Tracy who pulled him through. Monty couldn't remember the lines—he was literally going to pieces. Tracy just grabbed his shoulders and told him he was the greatest young actor of his time and to look deep into his eyes and play to him and the hell with the lines. He did, and Monty . . . got an Academy Award nomination, and he was proud of it.''

Monty commented on the Oscars: ''I'm not in the least annoyed by not having actually won any, but I do feel that the awards pay too much attention to popularity and not enough to merit. You know, neither Chaplin nor Garbo ever got one. The ones that really merit it haven't gotten it.''

*   *   *

*Stanley Kramer, Filmmaker, G.P. Putnam's Sons, New York, 1978

From the first, John Huston had been set on having Monty star as Freud. Universal reported his odd conduct during *Lonelyhearts* and *Suddenly, Last Summer*, but Huston's experience with Monty on *The Misfits* had been nothing but positive. Huston recalled his feelings about Monty on that film: "He was very good in the picture, and all the stories about troubles people had with him in other pictures were refuted by his behavior on *The Misfits*. The reassurance led me to doing *Freud* with Monty."

"I told John that Monty was simply not right for the role," producer Wolfgang Reinhardt stated, "and that he might not get through it. John . . . insisted Monty could do it because of him."

Jean-Paul Sartre had agreed to write the script for *Freud* in 1957. Eventually Sartre turned in a 1600-page screenplay that appalled Huston with its detailing of homosexuality, incest, masturbation, etc. He had had no idea that Freud was so concerned with sexuality and perversion. Reinhardt argued vehemently with the director about Freud's theories: "He'd call in psychiatrists to read this script and prove that I was wrong, but instead they all proved that the script was accurate."

Monty was better prepared than Huston to grapple with Freud. He had read Ernest Jones' biography of Freud and he conferred with Billy Silverberg, cross-questioning him about Freud's attitudes toward his patients. But once filming started, Huston hired two psychiatric consultants to examine Monty: Dr. Steven Black, whose attempts to hypnotize Monty made him uncomfortable, and Dr. David Stafford-Clark, who returned to the set when things began going badly.

The screenplay was finally compressed into 200 pages by Reinhardt and Charles Kaufman (Sartre gets no credit) and shooting began in Munich in the fall of 1961.

Monty felt that his speeches forced him to think aloud in blinding flashes of inspiration. (At one point Monty has to beat his hand in the air and exclaim: "Yes! Yes! Yes! The truth has emerged upside down!" while formulating Freud's theory of reversal.) He complained repeatedly about the script, unaware that Huston had written much of the dialogue he was criticizing. In addition the script was constantly being rewritten. Monty later remarked: "This was surely the hardest part I ever did. For one thing, they kept changing the script on me. I'd go to bed knowing one set of lines and wake up to another whole new scene! I sometimes never saw the next day's script till 10, 11. . . . For five and a half months, I averaged four hours sleep a night. God knows how one stood it." Monty expressed himself very mildly considering how much tension there was on the set.

Monty and Huston disagreed over the way in which a key sequence—one in which Freud lectures his fellow doctors about his concept of the unconscious—should be filmed. Monty argued that

Monty and Edward Dymytrk on the set of The Young Lions.

since Freud always spoke from notes, he did not need to learn his
lines. Huston countered that it would be visually uninteresting if
Monty's head were bowed over his papers. Monty memorized the
lines, but Huston would yell, "Cut!" if Monty's interpretation
varied in the least from the script. Eventually, Huston got what he
wanted, but it seemed to Monty that Huston had deliberately mor-
tified him in front of the crew. They continued to quarrel throughout the rest of the filming over the interpretation of many of the
scenes.

Early on, Huston had declared: "Monty has a photographic
memory. He's one of those rare people whose brain is a sensitized
plate as far as visual impressions are concerned." Huston did not
know that Monty's thyroid condition had gotten worse, that he was
losing his balance and having trouble memorizing his lines.

While Monty was shooting a scene with some extras, his hat
accidentally struck his eye and he protested that something was
wrong with his eyesight. Monty flew from the Vienna location to
London to see a specialist, a delay which outraged Huston. Huston's response to a telegram stating that he had cataracts was a
thoughtless remark about Monty needing a Seeing Eye dog. Monty
returned to the set, but he could not see.

Huston remembered it this way for Gerald Pratley:* "Monty
was very, very hard to work with. He couldn't remember lines.

*The Cinema of John Huston, Barnes/Tantivy, New York and London, 1977

Finally we were writing the lines for him to read, off screen . . . and tricking the scenes. His vision was such that he literally couldn't read. I would see him look at the script very closely and wonder why. I thought he was just nearsighted. Monty was also drinking.''

But during the filming Huston had told columnist Sheilah Graham: "He is never late, always ready to work, and when he works he does nothing else."

By the time Monty got back from London, the *Freud* company was divided into two camps: those who felt that Huston was persecuting Monty for an alleged inability to remember lines, and those who felt Monty was being difficult over the constant script revisions.

But it was more serious than that. Eventually, Universal sued Monty for $686,383 because of the delays purportedly caused by Monty's leaving the set and refusing to learn his lines. "I can memorize lines in one second if they're *valid!*" Monty told Brooks. "I couldn't memorize a line that I don't believe. They [Universal's lawyers] put it that I wouldn't. In other words, I sat back like a naughty child and said 'I won't memorize lines,' but the difference between couldn't and wouldn't is very large." Universal wound up owing Monty $131,000 in overtime which they refused to pay until their suit was cleared up. Monty lodged a countersuit charging that the delays were caused by rewriting the screenplay. It was not until mid-1963 that the suit was settled—in Monty's favor.

In spite of this victory, Monty actually lost: the result of all the adverse publicity was that he was uninsurable.

Huston now has kind memories of Monty: "In the end, I thought he gave quite an extraordinary performance. Freud was a tortured man himself . . . at least I got a tortured actor."

*   *   *

In January 1962, Monty was operated on at Mt. Sinai Hospital for a hernia and varicose veins. Then, early in December, just before *Freud* opened, Monty underwent the first of two operations for cataracts. Monty spoke about his doctors to Brooks: "I'm terribly fortunate because they all care." He was terrified of going blind, telling Brooks: "You know from the picture what my eyes mean to me. Because me listening is like no other actor alive today!

"So you can imagine the traumatic experience of having an operation on one's eyes and now in ten days, I have another. It's hard to describe." But, Monty said: "I have to cope with it and I'm man enough to cope with it."

Sunny came to the hospital, and although at first Monty refused to see her, he finally let her in and they talked.

Monty, Brooks and Nancy Walker attended a special screening

of *Freud*. Afterwards, Monty told Brooks: "This was my opening night, which was pretty meagre in the large sense . . . of what I went through and of what I think I accomplished." Nancy felt that the film was a vindication for Monty and told Brooks: "The fresh, clean air has come in on him."

In March of that year, Monty had cancelled out of *Antonia*, saying: "I have withdrawn my offer to play opposite Sophia Loren in *Antonia* because of my dissatisfaction with the screen treatment. . . . My first consideration is and always will be [the] story. I have not always guessed right in this respect, but I have never made a film of which I am ashamed."

In 1963, Monty wanted to make *The Heart Is a Lonely Hunter*, from the Carson McCullers story, but when his new agent, Robbie Lantz, approached 20th Century-Fox, he was told Monty was unbankable. The company offered him *John Goldfarb, Please Come Home*, but Monty found the script unacceptable.

Unable to get work, Monty began drinking again, and, where he had always been discreet in his private life, he now became more open, soliciting men in public.

Frank Taylor was still Monty's friend, although many others had disappeared, and, during this period, he would often stop by Monty's house for drinks before going home. Taylor remembers the last time he saw Monty, in the summer of 1963. He, Monty, and Giles got drunk together, then they all got in a limousine and headed down to Greenwich Village. Giles and Monty went into a bar, and while Taylor waited in the limo, a squad car stopped and a cop said that if he knew Montgomery Clift, he had better get him out of the bar or there would be trouble. Taylor was frightened, but conquered his fear and entered. He found Monty in the back of the saloon, lying on a table, unconscious and surrounded by people of every sexual persuasion who were fondling his body and kissing him. "It was the most debauched scene I'd ever witnessed," Taylor said. He carried Monty, who at that time weighed about 135 pounds, out to the car and delivered him home.

Giles and Monty tormented each other with one another's weaknesses until their relationship had deteriorated completely. When Giles attempted suicide, Sunny and Bill Clift contrived to separate the two for their own sakes. Dr. Ludwig found a companion for Monty, a black singer and actor named Lorenzo James.

Lorenzo took complete charge of Monty's life, making sure he ate nutritious food, exercised, took the medicine for his calcium deficiency, and cut down on the liquor and pills. During this period when he was not working, Monty had become a recluse; Lorenzo made him go out and asked old friends (and new ones like Roddy McDowall) to come visit him. Some did—Bill Le Massena, Nancy Walker, photographer Blaine Waller, Ned Smith—and some didn't —Kevin McCarthy, Thornton Wilder and others.

May Britt and Monty at the premiere of The Young Lions.

Through Lorenzo, Sunny and Monty attempted a reconciliation. She would come to dinner where Monty would be alternately nice or hostile to her. She was seventy-six at that time and still had not been recognized by the Andersons or Blairs. In February 1964, Bill Clift died. Monty, worried that Sunny would not have enough money to live on, arranged (over her objections) to give her a weekly allowance.

*   *   *

Although it seemed that Elizabeth Taylor was ignoring Monty, she had never forgotten him. Worried about his drinking, she talked about him to Truman Capote for a *Playboy* interview: ''Nobody beats that rap forever. It will kill him.'' When her husband, Richard Burton, starred in *Hamlet* on Broadway, she came` to town with him and, at her invitation, Monty went to the opening night. They began talking about making Carson McCullers' *Reflections in a Golden Eye* into a movie. Elizabeth would play the wife of an Army officer (Monty), a repressed homosexual in love with a young private. The producer, Ray Stark, reminded Elizabeth that

Monty was uninsurable, whereupon Elizabeth—in a gesture of enormous generosity—said that she would put up the bond for Monty's insurance with her own money.

When John Huston was signed as director, Monty seemed resigned. He couldn't wait to get started, but Elizabeth had other commitments to fulfill before she could get to *Reflections*. Monty, dependent on his work for a sense of self, became anxious wondering if he could still act. He narrated a documentary, *William Faulkner's Mississippi*, for WNEW–TV. It was broadcast in April 1965. Alternately soft and firm, he speaks in a slurred old/young voice, but he is touching as he decries Southern racism (the month before Martin Luther King, Jr., led a civil rights march from Selma to Montgomery, Alabama) in Faulkner's words: "We love despite, not toward the virtues, but despite the faults," he says, and it could be Monty describing Prewitt's love of the Army twelve years earlier in *From Here to Eternity*.

Monty recorded Tennessee Williams's *The Glass Menagerie* with Julie Harris, Jessica Tandy, and David Wayne for Caedmon records. He narrates and plays Tom, the brother who escapes the stifling atmosphere of his mother's house. Although his voice is not flexible enough for the part, Monty's breaths and pauses mask the stiffness, and he is immensely moving in the final speech in which Tom breaks down remembering Laura, the sister he left behind to wait for gentlemen callers who never come.

In October 1965, Salka Viertel, whom Monty had met while making *The Heiress*, recommended him for a part in a movie her friend, Raoul Lévy, was planning to produce and direct in Europe. Monty hated the screenplay of *The Defector*, but agreed to do it to prove he could still act. It would be a sort of test for *Reflections*.

* * *

In 1964, Monty, who still suffered constant pain, went to Nancy Walker's doctor, Richard Bachrach. Bachrach found that Monty had bursitis, arthritis, and a slipped disc. He was taking Demerol, which combined with liquor, could make him hallucinate. Bachrach recommended DMSO, which relieved Monty's pain for a while until the FDA, calling it unsafe, removed it from the market.

When Brooks's fourth wife Eleanor was pregnant, Brooks wanted to name the child—if it was a boy—after Monty. Brooks says: "It took a lot of courage for me to ask my brother this because it implies he isn't going to have an heir. When I asked him, he replied, 'How can you *ask* me such a thing? I would be so— honored!' Then, when Eddie was four months old, we went over to Monty's house, and he zoomed upstairs and came zooming down again with a check to Edward M. Clift from E. Montgomery Clift.''

Monty told Brooks: "If you want to cash this, OK, but maybe he'd like to keep it." The check is framed and hangs now in the study of Brooks's home.

*   *   *

Leslie Caron was originally cast opposite Monty in *The Defector* and when he went to London in January 1966, she and Monty tried to rewrite the script before filming began. Caron left the film, saying she could not get along with Lévy, whereupon Monty, frightened that the movie would be cancelled, tried to persuade Simone Signoret to make it with him. Lévy also considered Monica Vitti and Nicole Courcel, finally settling on Macha Méril.

Filming took place in and around Munich from February to April. The weather was miserable, but Monty insisted on doing his own stunts, jumping into the freezing Elbe River for a scene in which the character he plays, James Bower, escapes from East Germany. He pushed himself very hard trying to prove he could still act.

Mira Rostova was there, as Monty's acting coach, and Lorenzo, as his secretary. They worried that Monty was working too hard; the effort of bicycling a few hundred feet exhausted him. Once, on a lunch break, he had to be helped into an inn and up some stairs to lie down.

Macha Méril was amazed at Monty's intensity. "I have never acted with anyone like Monty Clift. He gives so much it is almost painful. His acting is all . . . torn . . . from inside. Almost as though he were acting to destroy himself." Monty's passion was wasted on a confused, contrived, nonsensical movie.

In Munich, Monty talked with Anthony Haden-Guest about his hopes for *Reflections in a Golden Eye*, which finally had a starting date, in August. He was philosophical about working with Huston again: "Yes, this is going to be . . . another film with Huston. . . . He can be very pleasant, and he can be charming. And he can be ruthless." He praised Elizabeth Taylor: "How do you describe the quality of an *actress?* She is an extraordinary girl with an extraordinary sense of humor."

When the picture was finished, Monty flew to London, where Leslie Caron gave him a party. He visited Fred Zinnemann on the set of *A Man for All Seasons*. Several years after they made *The Search* together, Zinnemann had taken Monty to a restaurant in Venice and introduced him to the head waiter, who, according to Zinnemann, "took one look at Monty, said spontaneously, 'You're an artist,' and promptly burst into tears. Thereupon Monty also burst into tears and these two strangers hugged each other, sobbing away. How many artists will inspire that sort of love and devotion?"

Now almost the same thing happened again. Zinnemann reported that the cast all wanted to meet Monty and talk to him. "Monty was still a legend to other actors. He knew that and I think it moved him."

* * *

Monty had never reconciled himself to his appearance after the accident, and when Lorenzo told him he had had plastic surgery years before, Monty wanted to meet the man who had performed it. Lorenzo introduced Monty to Manfred Von Linde, a man with a bizarre past. He had been suspected of murdering his wife and had been sued for malpractice by an actress who claimed he had botched surgery on her breasts. Friends of Monty's who met him called Von Linde "evil" and "sinister," but Monty was enthralled by his strange history and what he considered Von Linde's medical expertise.

After Monty filmed *The Defector* he had Von Linde perform corrective surgery around his eyes.

* * *

Working on *The Defector* had apparently exhausted Monty. He had varicose veins, his thyroid condition was worse, and his hands were gnarled. In addition, the Demerol injections caused violent mood swings, from paranoia to something approaching happiness. In spite of his physical problems, he told Barbara Long of *Vogue* that he was looking forward to *Reflections.* "I feel like a young man just getting started."

When Lorenzo went to wake Monty at 6 A.M., Saturday, July 23, 1966, he found the door to his bedroom locked. There was no answer to his repeated knocking and he couldn't force the door, so he climbed a ladder from the garden and entered the room through a window. He found Monty dead on his king-size bed.

Lorenzo called Dr. Ludwig's office, but the doctor was out of town and an associate, Dr. Howard Kline, came over to examine the body. Lorenzo also notified Monty's lawyer, Jack Clareman.

Monty's body was taken to the city morgue where the associate medical examiner, Dr. Michael M. Baden, performed an autopsy and stated that Monty had died of "occlusive coronary artery disease."

Lorenzo stayed on the phone talking to old friends who called to express their sympathy, and reporters. Monty had said he wanted a simple Quaker funeral like his father's, but Monty's sister, Ethel, who flew from her home in Austin, Texas, insisted on a church ceremony. Sunny agreed with Monty, but Ethel overruled her and

Montgomery Clift's grave in Brooklyn.

arrangements were made to have the service at St. James Episcopal Church on Madison Avenue.

The funeral was private. The family, Sunny, Brooks and Ethel, sat in the front row. Celebrities and friends, Mira Rostova, Lauren Bacall, Nancy Walker, Dore Schary, Ned Smith, Libby Holman, José Quintero, Susan Kohner, Jerome Robbins, and Lorenzo James—sat around them. Two large bouquets of white chrysanthemums from Elizabeth Taylor stood with flowers from Myrna Loy, Roddy McDowall, Richard Burton, Lew Wasserman, and Raoul Lévy near the mahogany coffin in front of the altar. There was a selection of organ music from pieces Monty had liked: Bach's "Sinfonia," the "Cathedral Prelude," and the "Fugue in E Minor." Canon William J. Chase read from the Bible and the congregation recited prayers. A benediction ended the brief service.

Monty's agent Robbie Lantz arranged, through Ethel, to sell Monty's house to some friends of his, a young couple with three children. But there was a condition, to which the couple agreed. Ethel wanted a bronze plaque affixed to the house. It says: "Residence of Montgomery Clift, Actor, 1960–1966."

Monty's estate was valued at $200,000, with most of it going to Ethel and Sunny. Brooks, Mira, Lorenzo, and Marge Stengel received lesser bequests.

* * *

Montgomery Clift's grave stands on a low hill in a small, private cemetery in Brooklyn. He is buried near his father, and running ivy covers both their graves. People who know about the grave visit there, although there are fewer and fewer as the years pass. Recently, a Malaysian student stopped by and placed white carnations next to the simple headstone. It is very peaceful.

THE FILMS

Steve tries to trace Karel.

THE SEARCH

1948

MGM. *Directed by* Fred Zinnemann. *Produced by* Lazar Wechsler. *Original screenplay:* Richard Schweizer. *Collaborator on screenplay:* David Wechsler, *with additional dialogue by* Paul Jarrico, *based on* Therese Bonney's Europe's Children. *Director of photography:* Emil Berna. *Film editor:* Hermann Haller. *Music:* Robert Blum. *Technical adviser and military liaison:* Therese Bonney. *Assistant director:* Mila Mellanova. *Associate producer:* Oscar Düby. *Technical advisers:* Robert D. Mockler and Eva Landsberg. *Made with the cooperation of the* U.S. Army *and* the International Rescue Organization. *Produced for MGM by* Praesens-Film, Zurich. *Locations:* Zurich, Switzerland; U.S. Occupied Zone of Germany; Würzburg, Frankfurt, Munich and Nuremberg. 105 minutes.

CAST

Ralph Stevenson, Montgomery Clift; *Mrs. Deborah R. Murray,* Aline MacMahon; *Mrs. Hannah Malik,* Jarmila Novotna; *Karel Malik,* Ivan Jandl; *Jerry Fisher,* Wendell Corey; *Mrs. Fisher,* Mary Patton; *Mr. Crookes,* Ewart G. Morrison; *Tom Fisher,* William Rogers; *Joel Makowsky,* Leopold Borkowsi; *Raoul Dubois,* Claude Gambier.

Steve (Montgomery Clift) first spots Karel in the ruins.

The frightened boy (Ivan Jandl) struggles as Steve brings him into the house.

Near the completion of *Red River*, director Fred Zinnemann contacted Clift about a film he wanted to make in Europe, a semi-documentary about displaced persons. Unbeknownst to Clift, the role of Steve would be his initial appearance in a part that he would repeat, with variations, over the years: the decent young man who becomes involved in other people's problems.

Clift liked Peter Viertel's script, but it was rewritten by the son of the producer, Lazar Wechsler, so Clift improvised his own dialogue. Wechsler was furious at Clift's tampering and both sides ended by summoning their lawyers to the set. The final irony was that David Wechsler and Richard Schweizer, who had written a previous treatment, won an Academy Award for the script of *The Search*—a script for which Clift was very much responsible.

The disputed screenplay concerns Steve, an Army engineer, who finds ten-year-old Karel Malik, hungry and ragged, wandering in a German ruin. He brings him home and, despite the boy's hostility, makes him feel cared for. A parallel plot concerns the boy's mother, Mrs. Hannah Malik, who roams Europe looking for her lost son, working for a time in an UNRRA camp. There, mother and son are reunited when Steve has to bring the boy to the camp to stay before he can get him to America.

Fred Zinnemann's film is an almost perfect tale

of disillusionment, trust, and unflagging, selfless effort. It is marred, unfortunately, by a sentimental and superfluous narration. The lost expressions on the children's faces are enough; no one has to be told these are silent, hopeless, frightened children. There are no villains, except the vanquished Nazis, so everyone is a hero: Aline McMahon as a tireless, sympathetic UNRRA worker; Jarmila Novotna as Mrs. Malik; and Clift, who strives to win Ivan Jandl's (Karel's) trust, to teach him and, finally, to adopt him.

All the performances are unaffected and unadorned. Clift is rail thin and already, at twenty-seven, stooped but devastatingly handsome. By the time of his next two films, *The Heiress* and *The Big Lift*, he was no longer as raw-looking, nor was he as open. He is relaxed, light, and playful with Jandl, but it is the relaxation of a coiled spring. Underneath he is attentive; as he thinks, his mobile expression reflects his thoughts, his eyes search Jandl's face for a solution to the puzzle he represents. When the film was released, Zinnemann was asked, "Where did you find a soldier who could act?" a tribute to the authenticity of Clift's portrayal.

Clift's best scene takes place when Jandl, believing Clift will not help him look for his mother, runs away from home. Clift finds him in the country and tells him he thinks Jandl's mother is dead. The boy struggles not to cry, gives up, and embraces Clift. Clift rumples his hair and tells him: "Don't say anything, I know." Clift recognizes the uselessness of words in moments of stress and their inability to convey the profound, incoherent emotions the boy is experiencing.

Despite the talk of gassing, homelessness, and hunger, there is a refreshing undercurrent of humor in *The Search*. Clift, trying to teach Jandl to say "No," gives up and says: "Thank you for your patience. I think I'll get drunk." He teaches Jandl the word "tomato" for pretty girl and kids him as he would his own son. Once the initial barriers are overcome, Clift quickly forms a father/son relationship with Jandl, rumpling his hair, telling him to eat, and buttoning his jacket. There is nothing affected about this; Clift slips

Steve and Jerry (Wendell Corey) learn that Karel cannot be traced.

Steve teases Karel with a present.

Steve and Karel's cherished gift—a new pair of shoes.

easily into the role, unthinkingly treating Jandl as if he were his natural son.

The Search was made before the Clift persona had been clearly established on screen. He was not yet the introverted, neurotic young man, driven and alone. His Steve is a relaxed, charming individual, and if he is not *with* anyone, he is not lonely; he is merely alone. He is self-sufficient and competent, realizing instinctively the kind of behavior that is likely to have the best effect on Jandl.

Mira Rostova accompanied Clift—who was getting $75,000 for *The Search*—to Zurich and, although no explanation was given for her presence, it became obvious when she stood behind the camera and indicated either approval or disapproval that she was his acting coach. A few days into the filming, Zinnemann told Clift she was distracting the cast and would have to stay away from the set. Clift agreed, but Mira stayed

Karel's English lesson: a pretty girl is a "tomato."

on, working with him on the script, choreograph-
ing each gesture of every scene.

Although the reviewers generally praised the
film, there were occasional exceptions. *Time*
noted: "Producer Wechsler and director Fred
Zinnemann are not, at best, very vigorous or inventive moviemakers. Their subject . . . is frequently reduced to the scale of gracious
sentimentality."

Arthur Knight, writing for the *National Board
of Review*, said: "Montgomery Clift gives an extraordinary sense of actuality to his Steve, the
A.M.G. engineer. In the truest sense, *The Search*
is an exceptional film."

John Mason Brown of *Saturday Review* found
Clift "honest as the likable American soldier."

The Search made *The New York Times* Ten
Best list, and the paper's critic, Bosley Crowther,
found the film "an absorbing and gratifying emotional drama of the highest sort," and said that
" . . . the young American actor, Montgomery
Clift, gets precisely the right combination of intensity and casualness into [his] role."

Ivan Jandl won an Oscar in the special category
of juvenile actor, and Clift—for this, his second
film—was nominated for his first Academy
Award.

*Steve leaves Karel at the UNRRA camp with Mrs.
Murray (Aline MacMahon).*

Groot (Walter Brennan) argues with Tom Dunson
(John Wayne) that he wants to come along on the cattle
drive, as Matthew Garth (Montgomery Clift) looks on.

RED RIVER

1948

United Artists. *Directed and produced by* Howard Hawks. *Screenplay:* Borden Chase and Charles Schnee, *based on the Saturday Evening Post story* "The Chisholm Trail" *by* Borden Chase. *Music:* Dimitri Tiomkin. *Song:* "Settle Down" *by* Dimitri Tiomkin. *Co-director:* Arthur Rosson. *Director of photography:* Russell Harlan. *Film editor:* Christian Nyby. *Art director:* John Datu Arensma. *Sound:* Richard DeWeese. *Makeup:* Lee Greenway. *Special Effects:* Donald Steward. *Assistant director:* William McGarry. *Special photographic effects:* Allan Thompson. *Music recorder:* Vinton Vernon. *Production manager:* Norman Cook. *Location:* Rain Valley, Arizona. 126 minutes.

CAST

Thomas Dunson, John Wayne; *Matthew Garth*, Montgomery Clift; *Tess Millay*, Joanne Dru; *Groot*, Walter Brennan; *Fen*, Coleen Gray; *Cherry Valance*, John Ireland; *Buster*, Noah Berry, Jr.; *Quo*, Chief Yowlachie; *Melville*, Harry Carey, Sr.; *Dan Latimer*, Harry Carey, Jr.; *Matt (as a boy)*, Mickey Kuhn; *Teeler*, Paul Fix; *Sims*, Hank Worden; *Bunk Kenneally*, Ivan Parry; *Old Leather*, Hal Taliaferro; *Fernandez*, Paul Fiero; *Wounded Wrangler*, Billie Self; *Walt Jergens*, Ray Hyke; *Laredo*, Dan White; *Quitter*, Tom Tyler; *Colonel*, Lane Chandler; *Naylor*, Glenn Strange; *Dance hall girl*, Shelley Winters; *Clift's double*, Richard Farnsworth.

The can-shooting contest between Cherry Valance (John Ireland) and Matt.

Matt and his horse.

Matt wounds one of the rebellious cowboys before Tom can kill him.

Matt tells Tom, as he takes his cattle, "I'll get your herd to Abilene."

Buster (Noah Beery, Jr.), Matt, and Groot try to outguess Tom Dunson.

In 1946, director Howard Hawks, who had seen Clift in *You Touched Me!* offered him the role of Matthew Garth, John Wayne's foster son in *Red River*. Clift was paid $60,000 for his first screen role and since he was $1,300 in debt and collecting unemployment insurance, the proposal looked good to him. Clift faltered briefly before shooting began, wondering if he would be able to stand up to Wayne's imposing cinematic presence. Leland Hayward—his former agent—Hawks, Kay Brown, a friend who was also David O. Selznick's representative in New York, and his parents all encouraged him to make the film.

The script for *Red River*, a disguised rendering of the saga of the King Ranch in Texas, was taken by Borden Chase and Charles Schnee from Chase's *Saturday Evening Post* story, "The Chisholm Trail." A brief prologue sets the stage for the events and rationale behind the movie's main action and introduces the three principals: Tom Dunson, Garth, and Groot, Dunson's friend (played by Wayne, Clift and Walter Brennan). The narrative picks up fourteen years later and begins at the start of the first cattle drive over the Chisholm Trail 1,000 miles from north of the Rio Grande to Abilene, Kansas. Matthew, back from

the Civil War which has bankrupted the South and forced Dunson to take his herd north, helps lead the trek. En route, under pressure to get the herd through, Dunson becomes increasingly ruthless, killing deserters and threatening others with hanging and whipping, until Matthew sides with the mutinous men and takes the steers from Dunson. He leads them to Abilene (where, it is rumored, there is a railway) instead of Sedalia, Missouri (the original terminal point), farther away, and faces Dunson, who has sworn to kill him. The two men square off, but their knock-down, drag-out fight is interrupted by Tess Millay (Joanne Dru), a dance-hall girl whose troupe Matt and the men rescued from an Indian attack. Her anger, the gun she fires to quiet them down, and the logic with which she explains that Dunson could never kill Matt because the two men love each other too much, diffuses the conflict and fosters a reconciliation.

Clift, who had learned to ride at a military academy in Munich, Germany while traveling with his family, expended considerable time and effort mastering a cowboy's skills. He perfected a rolling gait for Matt and trained himself to jump into the stirrup when mounting his horse. Noah

*Matt pulls the Indian arrow from Tess Millay's
(Joanne Dru) shoulder as Cherry watches.*

Beery, Jr., who plays the cowpoke Buster in the
film, became friends with Clift while on location.
He recalled that "the thing he enjoyed most was
becoming a hell of a good cowboy and horseman.
He never asked for help on how to be a better
cowboy, but he was always watching things
closely. You could see him watching the people
who really knew what they were doing." As a
result, whether twirling a lariat to keep the cattle
in line or rolling a cigarette to hand over to
Wayne, Clift looks completely natural, as relaxed
carrying his saddle into camp as he is brandishing
a gun.

Clift's is a quiet, unshowy performance. He
knew he couldn't overwhelm Wayne physically
or dramatically, so he listened to Hawk's advice
and underplayed each scene, watching the byplay
between two men talking—say Wayne and Brennan—with an intensity that demands attention by
virtue of being so still.

Clift is so slight, he seems almost overpowered
by his ten gallon hat, but he is at ease in his chaps
and fringed buckskins. He nearly throws away
some of his lines: hiding his mouth with his hand,
speaking into a cup while drinking coffee, or run-

ning a finger alongside his nose in a gesture imita-
tive of his "father," Wayne.

Clift's love scenes with Joanne Dru, his first on
film, display the tender sensibility and intensity
which would become his hallmark throughout his
career. Dru goes to Clift in the fog, he fondles her
neck and hair, drinking in her welcome femininity
with the night air. As rain envelops them, she
leans against his chest while he explains Wayne's
motivation. She embraces Clift and he flirts with
her, saying: "I've always been kinda slow making up my mind"; he wants her to kiss him again.
This attitude of appearing to consume his leading
lady with his eyes (recapitulated in subsequent
pictures with stars as diverse as Cornell Borchers, Elizabeth Taylor, Jennifer Jones, and Lee
Remick) is one of Clift's most potent instruments
as an actor, and is largely responsible for his reputation as one of the screen's most ardent and
convincing romantic figures.

Red River is as much a film about rites of passage—an older man giving way to a younger one,
the younger one maturing as he performs an impossible task—as it is an epic about a cattle drive.
The movie contrasts Clift's behavior, his assump-

tion of power, and his growth as a humane leader, with that of two younger men: Ivan Parry, as Bunk Kenneally, the sugar thief whose pan-rattling precipitates the stampede; and Harry Carey, Jr. as Dan Latimer, the stammering youngster who wants to bring back a pair of red shoes as a present for his wife.

Wayne is at first presented as tough and autocratic, but also as a man who takes time to listen to his men's opinions and is interested in their welfare. As he grows progressively more callous, sympathy is transferred to the younger man, so that when Clift takes over the journey it seems a natural and necessary act. Wayne is in danger of losing his humanity; Clift is given the opportunity of achieving manhood.

But Clift also repeats Wayne's earlier mistake of leaving his woman behind with a wagon train. The film's opening shows Wayne parting from Colleen Gray (as Fen) despite her pleas, then recovering the snake bracelet he gave her from the

Indian who has killed her. Clift leaves Joanne Dru with *her* caravan and when Wayne shows up, eight days later, Dru has the bracelet, which has been passed on from Wayne to Clift. Wayne takes Dru to Abilene where she confronts Clift, knowing that she can't talk him out of the inevitable fight with Wayne. When they face each other, Wayne tries to make Clift draw by shooting at his feet, his hat, winging him on the cheek and, finally, slugging him almost senseless, before Clift can bring himself to retaliate. Clift gives as good as he gets and as the two fall brawling into the chuck wagon, Dru intercedes, shooting at and missing both men. She tells them that anyone can see they care for each other too much to hurt each other, that the fight is ridiculous, and all they have succeeded in doing is bloodying one another to no purpose. Wayne smiles ruefully at Clift and advises him to marry Dru. Clift retorts: "When are you going to stop telling people what to do?" and Wayne tells him as soon as he has

Matt surprises Buster in the fog.

Tess and Matt fall in love in the rain.

ordered Clift to change the Red River brand to include an "M" for Matthew. "You've earned it," Wayne says, referring to the prologue in which Mickey Kuhn (as the boy Matt) complains that there is only a "D" for Dunson on the brand, and Wayne replies that his initial will be put on when he deserves it.

The story has come full circle. Clift is virtually at the point Wayne was when the film began: mature, responsible, and accompanied by a strong woman like the one Wayne could have had, had he not been too stubborn to take her with him. Wayne has mellowed, and he has achieved the continuity he wanted (symbolized by the snake bracelet) and thought lost when Clift defected, by being able to pass his ranch on to his "son."

Wayne, who did not like Clift any more than Clift liked him—he found Wayne's and Hawk's macho attitudes and dirty stories repellent—was worried that he and Clift might not be able to generate any excitement between them, especially during the fight sequence. Hawks told Richard Schickel for his television series, *The Men Who Made the Movies:* "It took us three days to make Montgomery Clift look good enough to be pitted against Wayne because he didn't know to

punch or move when we rehearsed." As staged by Hawks and enacted by Clift and Wayne, the battle has an utterly convincing fury to it, an electricity matched by their other encounters. The air around the two men fairly crackles with tension, but it is subordinate to their friendship and mutual interests, exploding only when Clift commandeers the herd and in their final conflict.

Red River is one of Howard Hawks's most beautiful and intensely physical movies. The opening shot of the wagons trailing across the plains, the start of the cattle drive with its pan around the waiting herd, followed by the shots of the cowboys yelling exuberantly as they start out, puts the audience right in the middle of the proceedings. Russell Harlan's camera is seldom an objective observer; it is in the thick of things, whether it is the stampede, with the camera *under* the hurtling steers, or the river crossing, filmed amid the herd and from inside the chuck wagon. And the viewer can see the stars in the center of the action. During the stampede there are a few process shots, but while they are fording the Red, it is Clift and Wayne in the water, directing the men and cattle.

Shooting began in Rain Valley, Arizona in June

1946. The location was aptly named; the rain was so heavy it had to be written into the script so that work could progress. The conclusion was altered so that Wayne did not die as had been originally planned. Photography continued on location through November, ending at the studio in December. The release of *Red River*—scheduled for August 1948—was delayed when Howard Hughes alleged that the ending infringed on that of *The Outlaw,* his 1940 film on which Hawks had worked for a time. Hughes stated that *Red River* contained a scene like the one in *The Outlaw* in which Billy the Kid resists Doc's efforts to make him go for his gun even though Doc is shooting at him. Wayne finally interceded and persuaded Hughes to let United Artists leave the disputed sequence in. The movie, originally budgeted at $1,750,000, ultimately cost $3,200,000—an unprecedented figure for that time. Not the least of the expenditures contributing to that rise was one for the rental of 6,000 head of cattle at $10 per day per steer. *Red River* finally opened while Clift was completing work on *The Heiress.*

Clift decided that he didn't like *Red River*—it was ordinary, weakened in his estimation by the changed ending and by Joanne Dru's intervention in the climactic fight, and he hated his own performance. While filming *The Defector,* Clift told interviewer Anthony Haden-Guest:* "Just before it all happened, I was in Hollywood with Kevin McCarthy, and we watched a rough-cut version of *Red River.* I decided I was awful, and that was it—back to Broadway and never go back to Hollywood again. But then, of course, I made it."

Red River made it, too, becoming one of the classic Westerns, an enduring record of masculine determination and camaraderie. It was Wayne's first portrayal of a middle-aged man, and the veteran actor turns in a blistering, gutsy performance, fully the equal of his best work in *The Searchers* and *The Man Who Shot Liberty Valance.*

Otis L. Guernsey, Jr. of the *New York Herald Tribune* disagreed, saying: "Wayne plays what

New York World Journal Tribune, November 20, 1966

Tom creases Matt's cheek at the beginning of the fight. (Frame enlargement)

Tom lands a punch in the climactic fight.

Matt gets even.

can best be described as a typical John Wayne role—tall, wooden and brute stubborn. Clift is much more interesting as a lean, dangerous, capable young man, and he demonstrates that he can saunter into a Western with the best of them . . . an excellent performance as Wayne's foster son, a lanky, straight-shooting youth . . .''

The New York Times's Bosley Crowther praised the film: "Mr. Hawks has filled it with credible substance and detail, with action and understanding, humor and masculine ranginess. He has made it look raw and dusty, made it smell of beef and sweat. . . .

". . . a withering job of acting a boss-wrangler done by Mr. Wayne. This consistently able portrayer of two-fisted, two-gunned outdoor men surpasses himself in this picture. We wouldn't want to tangle with him. Mr. Clift has our admiration as the lean and leathery kid who does undertake that assignment, and he carries it off splendidly."

Time stated: "*Red River* is a high promise for

actor Montgomery Clift, who plays the thorny young man with a fresh blend of toughness and charm."

Pauline Kael reappraised the movie in *Kiss Kiss, Bang Bang:** "In 1948 one of the finest young actors in the country put on cowboy jeans and overnight Montgomery Clift became the hottest thing in Hollywood. Clift—in his most aggressively sexual screen performance—is angular and tense and audacious. . . ."

Under the heading, "The new sensitivity," Richard Schickel discusses Clift in *The Stars*†: ". . . *Red River*, Howard Hawks's bruising, gritty Western; and it might be said that in Clift's epochal brawl with John Wayne the new Hollywood man fought it out with the old. Significantly, it ended in a draw, but Clift was a star from that point on."

*Atlantic-Little Brown and Company, Boston, 1968

†Bonanza Books, New York, 1968

"You musn't be too much bent on a fortune." Dr. Sloper (Ralph Richardson) uses the occasion of a dinner with Mrs. Penniman (Miriam Hopkins) and his

daughter Catherine (Olivia de Havilland) to warn Morris Townsend (Montgomery Clift) subtly that he won't allow Catherine to marry him.

THE HEIRESS

1949

Paramount Pictures. *Directed and produced by* William Wyler. *Associate producers:* Lester Koenig and Robert Wyler. *Screenplay:* Ruth and Augustus Goetz, *based on their play and on* Washington Square *by* Henry James. *Music:* Aaron Copland. *Director of photography:* Leo Tover. *Production designer:* Harry Horner. *Art director:* John Meehan. *Set decoration:* Emil Kuri. *Film editor:* William Hornbeck. *Assistant director:* C. C. Coleman, Jr. *Sound engineers:* Hugo Grenzbach and John Cope. *Sound supervision:* Leon Becker. *Special photographic effects:* Gordon Jennings. *Makeup:* Wally Westmore. *Costumes:* Edith Head. *Men's costumes:* Gile Steele. 115 minutes.

CAST

Catherine Sloper, Olivia de Havilland; *Morris Townsend*, Montgomery Clift; *Dr. Austin Sloper*, Ralph Richardson; *Lavinia Penniman*, Miriam Hopkins; *Maria*, Vanessa Brown; *Marian Almond*, Mona Freeman; *Jefferson Almond*, Ray Collins; *Mrs. Montgomery*, Betty Linley; *Elizabeth Almond*, Selena Royle; *Arthur Townsend*, Paul Lees; *Mr. Abeel*, Harry Antrim; *Quintus*, Russ Conway; *Geier*, David Thursby.

Morris proposes to Catherine.

"Your father thinks you will forget me, Catherine."
Dr. Sloper refuses to permit Catherine to marry Morris.

In 1947, Wendy Hiller and Basil Rathbone
were playing Catherine and Austin Sloper,
daughter and father, respectively, in *The Heiress*
on Broadway. (Peter Cookson was Morris Townsend.) Ruth and Augustus Goetz had adapted
Henry James' *Washington Square* for the stage
and it was a considerable success. Milly (Mrs.
Lewis) Milestone, the wife of the director, told
Olivia de Havilland that Catherine would be a
wonderful part for her; de Havilland rushed to
New York to see the play and persuaded William
Wyler to do likewise. He saw to it that Paramount
bought the screen rights (the Goetzes adapted
their play for the film) and agreed to direct it.
Ralph Richardson (who had depicted Dr. Sloper
on the London stage) was cast; Miriam Hopkins
was Catherine's Aunt Penniman; and Clift was
signed, at $100,000, to portray Morris, the charm-
ing, conniving fortune hunter.

James's and the Goetzes' narrative concerns
Catherine, who is despised by her widowed father as gauche and unmarriageable. In quick succession, she meets Morris Townsend, is courted
by him and consents to marriage, a circumstance
her father disapproves of to the point of disinher-
iting her. On the night they are to elope, Morris
jilts her, returning ten years later, after Dr. Sloper has died and left his daughter rich and alone,
to reopen the courtship. Seeming to accept Morris again, Catherine finally leaves her suitor, who
has called to take her away, pounding at her door
as she now rejects *him*.

The Heiress is Catherine's story, and although
Clift had taken the part of the bounder after two
sympathetic roles to avoid being typecast, he was
not prepared for Wyler's favoring of de Havilland. Though Wyler gives Clift many close-ups
and medium shots, Leo Tover's photography
consistently emphasizes de Havilland, *her* reactions, *her* face, and *her* body, bending from
Clift's blandishments or straining toward Richardson for approval.

Clift complained that Miriam Hopkins up-
staged him in their scenes together and he
groused at Richardson's consummate technique.
He felt that de Havilland was mechanical, the

Morris gives Catherine a hand-warmer as a going-away present.

spaces in her performance being filled in by Wyler's polished directorial style.

De Havilland, for her part, was disconcerted by both Clift *and* Richardson, and years later had this to say about the experience: "The one thing I liked about Monty was that he had a very talented woman on the set, sort of a coach for him, and he would play a scene and then look up to see what she had to say at the back of the set. So that was really rather trying. But what I liked about him was that he cared so much, that he cared enough to have a dialogue coach hidden behind the set, signaling him. He was tremendously interested in caring about his work."

Richardson tried to disconcert de Havilland by walking up and down during their scenes together or by slapping his gloves against his hand. "Willy was afraid to talk to him about them. But he got the cameraman to frame just above the gloves and it worked," de Havilland reported.

Altogether it was quite a nestful and hardly surprising that the cast of *The Heiress* barely spoke to one another when they weren't together on the set.

Wyler changed the conception of Morris Townsend's role when *The Heiress* made the transition from New York to Hollywood. On Broadway the character was unambiguously calculating; his behavior was a surprise to no one. But when the play reached the screen, Wyler recalled that people "had expected a happy ending because he had been charming through most of the picture. Well, of course they didn't expect it. Neither did Catherine Sloper. If she had, she wouldn't have fallen in love with him. [She believed] that he was honest and straightforward."

Although Clift agonized over his part and believed that he was not doing his best work as Morris—he was too modern and facile—he was clearly successful using the interpretation Wyler had worked out. Against the complementary styles de Havilland and Richardson employ, Clift *is*, in fact, too much a man of the twentieth century in nineteenth-century clothes, but his method is not all that jarring.

When de Havilland leaves Clift at the dance where she has just met him, Wyler moves in for a medium close-up as Clift stares after her, his face unreadable. Does he, as he will later say, find her "a delightful girl," or is he simply thinking of her money? Is the audience to believe, as his courtship progresses, that he finds in de Havilland values unknown to anyone but himself, or that, when he admires the Sloper home, he is thinking of it as his future property? Clift flatters her: "That's what I like about you, you're so honest"; woos her by singing *"Plaisir d'Amour"*; calls her "my dearest girl"; and finally, disarms her by bringing attention to his own penury when he proposes.

Richardson, correctly and cold-heartedly, sees through Clift, refusing to consider him as a candidate for son-in-law. Here, Clift is at his most convincing. When de Havilland and he are reunited after the European trip which Richardson had hoped would dissuade her from marrying Clift, they meet in the mews behind her house. Rain pours down, Clift wipes her face dry, cradles her head in his hands, and covers her face with kisses as he talks about "our elopement." But when de Havilland tells him that they must expect nothing from Richardson—neither recognition nor her inheritance—Clift loses his boyish impetuousness. Although Clift tries to smile, he becomes slightly —but clearly—calculating and distant. In his early courtship he was the ardent wooer, bending toward her passionately, worshipping her adoration of himself. Now, briefly, he has separated himself and it is quite clear what will follow.

Clift's ability to devour a woman with his gaze, already evident in *Red River*, serves the character of Morris Townsend well. Clift drinks in de Havilland's admiration with his eyes, consuming her, yet leaving her free to protest, to move away from him, and at last to succumb to his ardor. De Havilland is five-feet-three inches tall and as Clift leans toward her, he is also above her, so that she must look up, increasing the sense of worship her eyes convey so well.

Rarely can the audience discern Clift's cupidity; he dissembles too well. But as he appreciates the Sloper home, helping himself to Richardson's

Morris keeps Mrs. Penniman company while Catherine is in Europe.

brandy and cigars just before de Havilland returns from Europe, viewers can see the deliberation if not any outright scheming.

When the two are reunited and de Havilland has changed into a beautiful, poised woman, it is Clift who is almost gauche. Telling her he had to work as a common seaman to earn the passage back to New York, Clift pleads for her understanding.

Once again, despite his having abandoned her, it is hard to know that Clift is insincere. When he runs his hand across the back of a chair in the old proprietary manner, is he merely glad to be where he feels he belongs or does he believe he has triumphed? Clift's performance keeps the viewer off balance, although de Havilland declares he is greedier than ever. *She* sees through him; previously he wanted her money, now he wants her love, too.

The last scene shows de Havilland, proud and resolved, climbing the stairs away from the door upon which Clift is raining blows. The final image

Morris enjoys the pleasures of a house he hopes will be his.

Catherine presents Morris with the ruby and pearl buttons she would have given him when they were married.

Morris and Catherine's last embrace.

117

is of his face, sweating, desperate, yelling "Catherine! Catherine!" as he realizes he has lost everything.

The Heiress opened at Radio City Music Hall in October 1949 to respectable, but not exhilarating, business. *The New York Times* critic, Bosley Crowther, said: "As the mercenary suitor Montgomery Clift seems a little young and a wee bit too glibly modern in his verbal inflections and attitudes. But he brings a vast deal of vitality and romantic charm to the role."

Howard Barnes of the *New York Herald Tribune* remarked: "Here is a stern and uncompromising motion picture which is worthy of Henry James's original.

"Clift plays the self-seeking suitor with immense conviction. . . . Wyler has undertaken a perilous assignment, but he has handled it magnificently."

The following year *The Heiress* was nominated for six Academy Awards; only Wyler, as Best Director, and Richardson, as Best Supporting Actor, did not win. Olivia de Havilland won her second Best Actress award; Aaron Copland garnered one for scoring of a dramatic picture; it won an art direction and set decoration award; and Edith Head won for her period costumes.

In August, Clift appeared at the command performance of *The Heiress* in London. He was presented to the Queen wearing an uncharacteristic outfit, except—perhaps—for Morris Townsend: a top hat, cane, white tie, and tails.

118

Danny MacCullough (Montgomery Clift) and Hank (Paul Douglas) watch American supply planes fly into Tempelhof Airbase.

THE BIG LIFT

1950

20th Century-Fox. *Directed by* George Seaton. *Produced by* William Perlberg. *Screenplay:* George Seaton. *Music:* Alfred Newman. *Director of photography:* Charles G. Clarke. *Film editors:* Robert Simpson and William Reynolds. *Costumes:* Bobbie Brox. *Art directors:* Lyle R. Wheeler and Russell Spencer. *Orchestrations:* Edward Powell. *Special photographic effects:* Fred Sersen. *Sound engineers:* Charles Hisserich and Roger Heman. *Locations:* Frankfurt; Tempelhof Airbase, West Berlin, Germany. 120 minutes.

CAST

Danny MacCullough, Montgomery Clift; *Hank,* Paul Douglas; *Frederica,* Cornell Borchers; *Gerda,* Brunie Löbel; *Stieber,* O.E. Hasse; *Private,* Danny Davenport; *Gunther,* Fritz Nichlisch; *Himself,* Capt. Dante V. Morel; *Himself,* Capt. John Mason; *Himself,* Capt. Gail Plush; *Himself,* Capt. Mack Blevins; *Himself,* Maj. R.L. Hetzl; *Himself,* Capt. William A. Stewart; *Himself,* 1st Lt. Alfred L. Freidburger; *Himself,* 1st Lt. Gerald Arons; *Himself,* 1st Lt. James Wilson; *Himself,* 1st Lt. Richard A. Kellogg; *Himself,* 1st Lt. Roy R. Steele; *Himself,* S/Sgt. James H. Blankenship; *Himself,* S/Sgt. Harold E. Bamford; *Himself,* S/Sgt. D. R. Simmons; *Himself,* S/Sgt. O. B. Schultz; *Himself,* Sgt. Andrew Shamless; *Himself,* Sgt. Elbert Garrett; *Himself,* Sgt. Billy Pierson; *Himself,* Cpl. Donald R. Neild; *Himself,* Pfc. William L. Davenport; *Himself,* Pfc. William J. Hardiman; *Himself,* Sgt. Herman Dornbusch; *AP Correspondent,* Richard O'Malley; *ABC Correspondent,* Lyford Moore.

In a screen career that numbered only seventeen films, five placed Clift in the service and/or in Germany. *The Search*, the first of his films to be released, cast him as an Army engineer stationed in Germany; in *The Big Lift* he is an Air Force engineer assigned to Berlin's Tempelhof air base. He was a buck private in *From Here to Eternity* and a soldier fighting in Germany in *The Young Lions*. Although *Judgment at Nuremberg* is set in Germany Clift's scenes were not shot on location like those of his previous films, but in Hollywood. Additionally, *Freud* is set in Austria and *The Defector* takes place in East Germany. The period in which Clift made these films—the post-war and Cold War eras—are as responsible as any other factor for the preoccupation with war-related subject matter.

The plot of *The Big Lift* follows two Air Force men, ground controller Hank and engineer Danny MacCullough, who join a unit ferrying supplies to Tempelhof in blockaded Berlin. Hank has a girl, Gerda, whom he belittles as dumb when she tries to understand democracy—as taught by Hank—and the mistakes of her forefathers. Danny falls in love with Frederica, whom he arranges to take to the States with him. Just before their wedding he learns that she plans to leave him for her German lover, now settled in America, as soon as she has made it to the United States. Danny confronts her with this information and they part. Hank announces that he plans to stay on in Germany and marry Gerda. The film ends with the news that the Russians are about to lift the blockade.

Like Clift's earlier role in *The Search*, which he described as a "plot business," Danny's story is intended (with Hank's) to make certain points about the American way of life, and to contrast them with the Germans' historical tendency to obey a stronger "father"—be it Bismarck or Hitler.

The Big Lift is saturated with bald propaganda, most of it delivered by Paul Douglas in response to Brunie Löbel's bottomless curiosity and endless questions. Löbel is very sweet and were she not such an effective counter to Douglas's rude, blustery didacticism, these "lessons" would be

Danny on the job as a flight engineer.

Danny surveys the ruins of Berlin as he waits for Frederica to finish work.

Paint covers Danny and the precious loaf of bread Frederica (Cornell Borchers) has just bought.

much harder to take. Douglas plays the grump with a heart of gold. From the beginning, as he surveys Berlin, saying, "This is where they shoudda used the A-bomb," through the sequences wherein he instructs Löbel in "democracy," to the end in which he realizes that Germans and Americans belong to one big, fallible family of man and sees himself as a "salesman" for American principles, Douglas is an ambulatory mouthpiece for these values. It is laid on too thick to take at times, but when one realizes that the film was made in 1949 (only four years after the end of World War II and during the height of the Cold War), one can see it as an effective teaching mechanism. Löbel's indoctrination is an anti-Russian weapon as much as it is anti-German, and mirrors the ambivalence many Americans felt about going to the rescue of their recent enemy.

Even Clift's romance with Borchers is a form of propaganda. She is the "bad" Kraut, conniving and selfish, contrasted with Löbel's open, concerned innocence.

Propaganda aside, *The Big Lift* is fairly slim stuff: boy meets girl, boy overcomes obstacles (posed by an indifferent bureaucracy) to woo girl, boy gets girl (who turns out not to be the girl of his dreams), boy gives girl up. Without the doctrinal embellishments, there would be almost no story at all. The narrative of the airlift itself, with the drudgery involved in moving tons of food and coal past harassing Russian planes and barrage balloons, is certainly not enough to sustain a two-hour film.

Caviling aside, there are some very nice moments in *The Big Lift*. The first occurs when Clift meets Borchers at a presentation ceremony in which the Germans express their gratitude for the efforts of the servicemen. Borchers, as a representative of the German people, gives Clift a briefcase on the occasion of the 100,000th flight into the city. Clift, who has not had a leave in months, moves in on Borchers, intent on dating her. And Borchers, with her fresh face and rumpled hair, is the image of the girl men leave home for. In Clift's performance here, there is none of that androgynous sexuality critics would later remark on. He is an average horny young man determined to make time with the pretty Fräulein.

Another effective scene involves O. E. Hasse

Danny watches Stieber (O.E. Hasse) spying for the Russians.

(who would shortly appear with Clift in *I Confess*) as a plane spotter working for the Russians and sharing Borchers' building. With self-deprecating humor, Hasse mocks the Russians who only believe other Russians and thus make his efforts worthless. Hasse is dry and sardonic, a man with no illusions about his position as a parasite who can function only as long as the blockade continues.

Because his uniform has gotten stained, Clift has to borrow Hasse's clothes. He, Borchers, Douglas and Löbel go to a jazz joint where they sing and dance. The blockade has created a situation in which all human relationships are speeded up, Clift explains, including courtship, and—as if to demonstrate this thesis—Clift proceeds to fall in love. Borchers croons the English lyrics to a German song in Clift's ear—"Perhaps, maybe"—and one can see Clift falling for her. He consumes her with his eyes. It's been so long since he has been with a woman and, despite her drab clothes, Borchers is very feminine. Through Clift's rapt expression one understands that he is investing her with all the longing he has had to suppress over the past months.

The M.P.s enter the bar and Clift suddenly becomes the fourth member of a German trio, enthusiastically massacring "Chattanooga Choo Choo." When the others switch to German, Clift fakes it by going "Choo choo!" and turning in circles when the soldiers get too close. It is one of the lightest moments in any Clift film and hints at a totally untapped gift for comedy, which Clift had shown on stage but never had a chance to exhibit on screen.

Clift is charming in *The Big Lift*, displaying none of the neurotic tension that marked many of his portrayals. He is like a male *Daisy Miller*, the naive American abroad whose innocence is his undoing. With his crooked smile and burning gaze, Clift is the personification of the unsophisticated serviceman, eager to absorb new experiences. So moving was Clift during the scene in which he reads Borchers' letter and discovers she has deceived him that the crew applauded his performance.

Douglas has his own rough fascination; he is

Danny and Frederica in the jazz bar.

like a bad-tempered teddy bear. All he needs to regain his good humor is to realize what it is like to be on the receiving end of his black moods. Cornell Borchers is lovely, yet her apparent accessibility disguises a complexity and duplicity for which Clift's Danny is no match. It is too bad her American film career was so brief, comprising only this and a few other films. Brunie Löbel is the feminine version of the part Clift plays: the gullible but shrewdly questioning woman who is quick to spot the holes in Douglas's arguments and only a little slower to develop her own set of values.

Like *The Search, The Big Lift* was shot entirely on location. Clift stopped off in London on his way to Berlin and discovered that after only two films (*The Heiress* had not been released yet) he was an even bigger star in England than in the United States. Director George Seaton had found a house in West Berlin for Clift and Mira Rostova to share, taking great pains to see that it was comfortably furnished, and was chagrined when Clift

insisted on a house with a garden. Seaton accommodated his star by asking the commander of the American forces, General Lucius Clay, to help out. Clay came through; a colonel gave Clift the loan of his house while Clift was filming. Seaton was under additional pressure: Clift was due to begin shooting *A Place in the Sun* as soon as *The Big Lift* was finished and Seaton had to keep the production on schedule.

Trouble developed immediately between Clift and Paul Douglas. Clift tried to upstage Douglas by leaning into their two-shots and Douglas complained to Seaton. The next time Clift attempted this trick, Douglas stepped on his foot so hard Clift yelled in pain. Clift learned his lesson.

Seaton wasn't happy to have Mira around either. She was always on the set, nodding approval or shaking her head when she thought a take went badly. But Clift insisted he needed her and on the set she stayed.

Clift and Seaton had begun by getting along well, feeling that they understood each other and

Hank gives Danny his orders to go home.

Frederica and Stieber worry about Danny's plight.

wanted the same things for the film. By the end of shooting this harmony had disappeared. Seaton remembers unhappily that Clift used to sell cigarettes he had bought at the PX on the black market.

The critics were largely indifferent to *The Big Lift. Time*'s reviewer said: "In attempting so much, *The Big Lift* becomes overlong and somewhat unwieldy. But where the picture really goes wrong, and badly, is in having Douglas spout repeated primer-level sales talks for democracy at his girl friend; the result is clumsy propaganda in a movie that would be excellent propaganda without it.

"Clift and Douglas give unaffected performances that blend nicely with the acting of director Seaton's remarkable non-professionals."

Bosley Crowther, writing in *The New York Times*, noted: "Not to belittle the straight performance which is given by Montgomery Clift as the sergeant, it must be acknowledged that the most interesting performances are given by Cornell Borchers as the fraulein and by Paul Douglas as the hater of the 'Krauts.'"

Otis L. Guernsey, Jr. of the *New York Herald Tribune* summed up the critical reaction: "The performances of Douglas and Clift have the color to support themselves on the screen, but these and other roles stay too close to the convention of the slangy, indifferent, wise-cracking G.I. Joe. . . . [Seaton's] planes fly gallantly to their moral victory, but his human relations are not so constructed as to become airborne."

George Eastman (Montgomery Clift) applies for a job at his uncle's factory.

A PLACE IN THE SUN

1951

Paramount Pictures. *Directed and produced by* George Stevens. *Associate producer:* Ivan Moffat. *Screenplay:* Michael Wilson and Harry Brown, *based on* An American Tragedy *by* Theodore Dreiser *and the* Patrick Kearney *play adapted from the novel. Music:* Franz Waxman. *Director of photography:* William C. Mellor. *Film editor:* William Hornbeck. *Set decoration:* Emile Kuri. *Sound engineers:* Gene Merritt and Gene Garvin. *Art directors:* Hans Dreier and Walter Tyler. *Assistant director:* C.C. Coleman, Jr. *Associate director:* Fred Guiol. *Assistant to the producer:* Howie Horwitz. *Special photographic effects:* Gordon Jennings. *Process photography:* Farciot Edouart and Loyal Griggs. *Costumes:* Edith Head. *Makeup:* Wally Westmore. *Locations:* Cascade Lake and Lake Tahoe, Nevada. 122 minutes.

CAST

George Eastman, Montgomery Clift; *Angela Vickers,* Elizabeth Taylor; *Alice Tripp,* Shelley Winters; *Hannah Eastman,* Anne Revere; *Earl Eastman,* Keefe Brasselle; *Bellows,* Fred Clark; *R. Frank Marlowe, District Attorney,* Raymond Burr; *Charles Eastman,* Herbert Heyes; *Anthony Vickers,* Shepperd Strudwick; *Mrs. Ann Vickers,* Frieda Inescourt; *Mrs. Louis Eastman,* Kathryn Givney; *Jansen,* Walter Sande; *Judge R. S. Oldendorff,* Ted de Corsia; *Coroner,* John Ridgely; *Marsha,* Lois Chartrand; *Mr. Whiting,* William R. Murphy; *Boatkeeper,* Douglas Spencer; *Kelly,* Charles Dayton; *Morrison,* Paul Frees; *Dr. Williams,* Ian Wolfe; *Martha,* Kathleen Freeman; *Joe Parker,* John Reed; *Frances Brand,* Marilyn Dialon; *Sec'y to Charles Eastman,* Josephine Whittell; *Truck Driver,* Frank Yaconelli; *Police-*

George takes Alice Tripp (Shelley Winters), a girl from the factory, out on a date.

George tries to get ahead by working at home.

man, Ralph A. Dunn; *Eagle Scout,* Bob Anderson; *Maid,* Lisa Golm; *Mrs. Roberts, landlady,* Mary Kent; *Warden,* Ken Christy; *Eastman butler,* Hans Moebus; *Butler,* Eric Wilton; *Motorcycle officer,* Mike Mahoney; *Bailiff,* Al Ferguson; *Tom Tipton,* James W. Horne; *Miss Harper,* Laura Elliot; *Miss Newton,* Pearl Miller; *Jailer,* Major Philip Kieffer; *Man,* Major Sam Harris; *Executive,* Jay Morley; *Receptionist,* Ezelle Poule; *Factory guard,* Wallace E. Scott; *Guard,* Robert Malcolm; *Guard,* Len Hendry; *Guard,* Frank Hyers; *Joe Parker,* John Reed; *Deputy,* Ed O'Neill; *Maid,* Frances Driver; *Bus Driver,* Lee Miller; *Court Clerk,* Bill Sheehan; *Jury Foreman,* Harold McNulty; *Prisoners,* Mike Pat Donovan, Joe Recht, Martin Mason; *Bit players:* Louise Lane, Lula Mae Bohrman, Cliff Storey, Gertrude Astor, Harold Miller, Pat Combs, Marion Gray, Ann Fredericks, Carmencita Johnson, La Verne "Sonny" Howe, Dolores Hall.

Theodore Dreiser was so appalled at Hollywood's 1931 version of his novel, *An American Tragedy,* that he sued, unsuccessfully, to prevent its release. He felt that Paramount had watered the story—which starred Sylvia Sidney, Phillips Holmes, and Frances Dee as the ill-fated trio—down to a simple murder melodrama. The Josef Von Sternberg film, in which Holmes had played Dreiser's Clyde Griffiths as a scoundrel unworthy of audience sympathy, had gotten reviews calling it everything from mediocre to "a shrewd and effective courtroom drama."

George Stevens's two-and-a-half million dollar budget had presumably convinced the director that he had better stress romance at the expense of social comment, and bit by bit he reneged on his original conception. He had intended to film the Dreiser story more or less straight, retaining Dreiser's plot, which was based on a 1906 murder and trial in Herkimer, New York. But Paramount was afraid of commercial failure and of anything that smacked of being un-American (the blacklist was still in effect).

But even with a changed title *A Place in the Sun,* with its emphasis on personal and career ambitions, is still *An American Tragedy,* the ac-

Angela Vickers (Elizabeth Taylor) eavesdrops on George's conversation with his mother.

count of an Everyman who, dislocated in changing social strata, falters and fails. Although Stevens does not specifically indict the perversion of American enterprise and misdirected aspirations with the vigor of Dreiser's anti-Horatio Alger ethic, the message is present as background, the force which drives George Eastman and whose influence he is unable to escape. Stevens narrative is a romance and its attention is on two contrasting loves: one born of loneliness and need, the other of ambition and the fascination of glamour.

George Eastman, a young man without education or social standing, hitches a ride to "the city" (any mid-Western city; Stevens deliberately leaves the locus vague) where his uncle finds him a job in the family bathing-suit factory. There, despite a ban on fraternization, he befriends Alice Tripp, an ordinary assembly line worker. Eventually she becomes pregnant by George. At the same time he is introduced to the world of his wealthy relations, and particularly to a beautiful young socialite, Angela Vickers. Angela and George fall in love, but Alice nags and chases George until he agrees to marry her. He

has a half-formulated plan to kill her, but hesitates. Finding that they can't get married over the Labor Day weekend, George takes Alice rowing. Although he cannot bring himself to murder her, fate intervenes, the boat overturns, and Alice is drowned. George is charged with murder and found guilty. Although he believes he is guilty in thought but not in deed, George faces death with equanimity.

From the opening shot on the highway George is drawn to the dual images representing luxury. First, Angela speeds by in her convertible—a symbol of all that is unattainable and desirable—but he settles for a ride in a junk wagon. Second, a billboard bathing beauty is shown reclining in her Eastman swimsuit. Clearly Stevens is determined to demonstrate the opposing forces which have formed and will influence George's behaviour throughout the film.

George is basically a decent young man who, coming from a background of poverty and piety (his mother runs a religious mission) is naturally attracted to wealth and position. He knows, however, that such a life is beyond his grasp so, realistically and ambitiously, he applies himself to

"Are they watching us?" Angela is afraid people can see her falling in love with George.

"It scares me." Angela and George fall in love.

getting ahead on his own. George dates Alice Tripp and genuinely seems to find her companionship all he needs until his uncle takes him in hand, promotes him, and gives him a glimpse of the milieu he had thought forever beyond his reach. As Angela claims more of his time and they realize they are in love, George abandons his scruples. He lies to Alice and ignores her to vacation with Angela. At heart George is an honest person; he is torn and unwilling to desert Alice, especially since she has threatened to make a scene and spoil his new-found social status. But he is reluctant to give up Angela for the humdrum existence to which he will surely be sentenced with Alice.

Stevens continually counterposes the drives at work within George. He observes Angela arriving at a party as he looks through the gates of the Eastman mansion; then he reconciles himself to a night at the movies where coincidentally, he meets Alice. In a later scene he leaves Angela, with whom he has fallen in love, and goes to the meager birthday party Alice has laid out in her furnished room, where she will wreck his ambitions by announcing that she is expecting his child. Stevens places George in T-shirt and work

pants next to Alice on the assembly line and later in a new dark suit dancing with Angela. Even the names convey status: drab Alice Tripp with her stultifying motto: "It's the little things in life that count"; glamourous Angela Vickers with her seductive invitation: "I'll take you dancing on your birthday!"

Walking with Alice, George passes a boy singing with a sidewalk mission group as he had done when he was young. When he calls home, his mother tells him she has kept his bed for him in the mission. Meanwhile, Angela is at his side, flirting, luring him away. The audience is always made aware of the past George is struggling to escape and the future he is trying to make for himself. On the desk, where George labors on a "production report" he hopes will impress his uncle, sits a copy of "High School—Self Taught." That future includes Angela Vickers, but after George realizes what is within his grasp, it can no longer encompass Alice Tripp.

George's is a world dominated by women and their demands on him. It is no wonder he has a hard time making a place for himself. He is given little opportunity to discover an identity that is not defined by the conflicting urgencies of the

Angela and George get away from the party.

"You'll be my pickup." Angela and George plan an idyllic summer.

females who constrain his life: his mother who wants him to be good, Angela who yearns for him, and Alice who needs his name.

Shooting began in October 1949 and continued through January 1950 with location work at Lake Tahoe, Nevada. Stevens worked hard to create an ambience conducive to obtaining the most thoughtful, expressive work from his performers. One tactic was to play mood music, usually Franz Waxman's haunting score for the film; another was to have Clift and Taylor, or Clift and Winters, rehearse a scene without dialogue, communicating their performances only through looks and gestures.

Taylor, who was impressed with Clift's "seriousness"—he had read *An American Tragedy*—and with his reputation as a "method" actor, relied on him to coach her portrayal of Angela. They ran scenes together, with Clift showing Taylor the intentions and subtle implications of her role. Clift, who had enormous presence even when he took a woman's part, would play Angela for Taylor with an utterly convincing feminine persona. While he was working with Mira Rostova, Clift taught Taylor to dig beneath the surface sophistication of this girl to the tender

woman beneath. There is no doubt that the womanly creature she depicted on screen, far surpassing in quality any work Taylor had accomplished previously (even her affecting performances as a child in *National Velvet* and *Jane Eyre*), is as much the creation of Clift as it is of Stevens. Subsequently Taylor wrote: "It was my first real chance to probe myself and Monty helped me. . . ."

Stevens later recalled his reasons for casting Taylor: "Liz was a teen-ager, but she had all the emotional capabilities. She had the intelligence, sharp as a tack. She was seventeen and she had been an actress all her life. So there was no problem there. The only thing was to prod her a bit into realizing her dramatic potential." Taylor was somewhat lazy; no director before Stevens had ever demanded so much from her. He cajoled and bullied her, ordering retake after retake until he got what he wanted.

When Clift confessed his love for Taylor, Stevens gave her the lines he wanted her to use to coax him. As Stevens remembered for an American Film Institute Seminar:* "Elizabeth Taylor

*Dialogue on Film, May/June 1975

129

Alice tells George she is pregnant.

almost dissolved when she had to say them. She said, 'Tell Mama,' and she thought it was outrageous that she had to say that. Jumping into a sophistication that is beyond her sophistication at the time. . . . it was spasmodic.'' In their first love scene they are both overwhelmed by the surge of emotion they feel for each other. '' . . . she took him out where they could be alone. That let something loose. That let him loose and he was impassioned. . . . He felt so moved by this girl that it touched her loose. She was just revelatory. She wanted to tell him that he was so exciting, interesting, lovable, whatever it was to her that it had to be kind of staccato and vibratory.''

They had to throw the lines at one another, conveying both desire and reticence. In the memorable moment to which Stevens refers, Taylor, frightened by her own passion, looks up, startled, and asks, ''Are they watching us?'' She's so stirred by their response to one another, she has

The picture of Ophelia gives George the idea of drowning Alice.

to hide. She drags Clift out onto the terrace where, in a series of immense close-ups shot with a six-inch lens, Stevens records their yearning. Taylor is at once maternal and sensuous; Clift is reserved but overwhelmed with ardor. As Stevens said: "Monty had that kind of emotion that he got steamed up in it."

Stevens went on to explain how he worked with Clift and Taylor: "I went from one side of the face to the other and then created a tempo with the thing in which as fast as it could be said, it was said. I explained that I'd like to get [the lines] into their heads and then get them in there and throw them at one another and move twice as fast, compulsively, one talk on top of another. . . . It's an instinctive thing that they want to join. So just throw these words at one another."

When it came time to edit this sequence, Stevens used two projectors placed side by side and viewed Clift's and Taylor's closeups simultaneously. He then cut the scene so that the shots dissolve into each other. He created the impression of two people consumed in their heat, getting lost in one another, becoming one.

Clift surpassed himself in *A Place in the Sun.* The quality he possessed of appearing removed from others around him—as though he is both a participant in the action and an outsider looking on—helps him convey equally George Eastman's torment and his consuming infatuation. He is both private and exploding out of himself, the ex-mission boy who wants so much he can contemplate murder to achieve it. "I guess maybe I loved you before I saw you," Clift tells Taylor in a confession of abstract longing made concrete in the person of this adorable creature.

Clift's much-heralded "vulnerability" serves him well in *A Place in the Sun.* He aches with unvoiced longings; his introversion and ambivalence is as appealing as other actors' expressiveness. The hint of neurosis and sexual ambiguity Clift brings to his role are qualities he would employ in differing measure throughout his career.

Although Winters has the showier and, in some respects, more sympathetic part, Taylor is more than able to hold her own as the superficial social-

On the assembly line. Alice wants George to marry her.

131

George excuses himself to Mrs. Vickers (Frieda Inescourt)
when Alice calls him away, as Angela looks on in alarm.

ite transformed by love into a responsive woman. But Winters is extraordinary as Alice Tripp. She makes the dowdy, wistful factory girl aggravating and appealing, a shrew of understandable human dimensions. As she sits in the rowboat, unconsciously torturing Clift with her view of their mundane future together, Winters is both pathetic and a self-made victim, a natural candidate for murder.

The critics were almost unanimous in their praise for *A Place in the Sun*, with A. H. Weiler of *The New York Times* finding it "a work of beauty, tenderness, power and insight . . . scenarists Michael Wilson and Harry Brown have distilled the essence of tragedy and romance that is both moving and memorable. Retained too . . . are characterizations which cleave to the Dreiser originals. And it is a tribute to deft dramatization that the young principals are projected as fully as the maelstrom of life in which they are trapped and with which they are unable to cope.

"There may be some belief that Montgomery Clift, as the tortured George Eastman, is not nearly the designing and grasping youth conceived by Dreiser. But his portrayal, often terse and hesitating, is full, rich, restrained and, above all, generally credible and poignant. He is, in effect, a believable mama's boy gone wrong.

" . . . Miss Winters, in our opinion, has never been seen to better advantage than as the colorless factory hand. . . . Elizabeth Taylor's delineation . . . also is the top effort of her career. It is a shaded, tender performance. . . ."

The *New York Herald Tribune* reviewer found that "the success of *A Place in the Sun* is probably attributable to George Stevens, who produced and directed it with workmanlike restraint and without tricks or sociological harangue. He has drawn excellent performances from Montgomery Clift, who is thoroughly believable as the young man; Elizabeth Taylor, who is remarkably well cast as the daughter of a wealthy social clan, and Shelley Winters, who is particularly moving in the role of the unwanted sweetheart.''

Time's critic stated: ''Thanks to director Stevens, all three of the picture's stars do the best acting of their careers. In the pivotal role, actor Clift's sensitive, natural performance gives the film a solid core of conviction. Actress Taylor plays with a tenderness and intensity that may surprise even her warmest fans. In a film of less uniform excellence, Shelley Winters' mousy factory girl would completely steal the show. Shy, petulant, or shrilly nagging by turns, she makes the most of her unconventional role. . . .

''Stevens's unerring timing, and his skill at filling any situation with the last shade of emotion and meaning, enable him to direct the picture at a deliberately slow pace that still weaves a spell without dragging for a moment.

''He makes imaginative use of his sound track; the cry of a loon, the distant whine of sirens, the barking of dogs become recurring motifs bound up with the action. His camera is effectively restrained; it peeks through doorways or stands patiently in the corner like a hidden witness; and when it moves suddenly into closeups, the effect of intimacy is breathtaking.''

Pauline Kael, in reappraising the film, found: ''George Steven's most highly respected work is an almost incredibly painstaking movie. . . . Perhaps because Stevens's methods here are studied, slow, and accumulative, the work was acclaimed as ''realistic''—which it most certainly is not. It is . . . designed to affect you emotionally without your conscious awareness [and] mannered enough for a very fancy Gothic murder mystery. . . .

''Having expressed rather major reservations, I should point out that this is definitely not the

George tries to explain his actions to Jansen (Walter Sande) during his murder trial.

George struggles to be as honest as possible with District Attorney Marlowe (Raymond Burr).

accepted view, and that the movie is almost universally honored as an example of adult cinema. . . . Whatever one thinks about it, it is a famous and impressive film. The performances by Montgomery Clift, Shelley Winters, and Elizabeth Taylor are good enough (and Clift is almost too good, too sensitive), though they appear to be over-directed pawns.''*

A Place in the Sun won six Academy Awards: George Stevens for best director; Michael Wilson and Harry Brown for best screenplay; William C. Mellor for best black-and-white cinematography; Franz Waxman for best scoring of a dramatic picture; William Hornbeck for best editing; and Edith Head for best black-and-white costuming. Only Montgomery Clift, nominated as best actor, failed to win an Oscar.

The impact of *A Place in the Sun* relies on a moral climate that has ceased to exist. Pre-marital sex is no longer frowned upon and abortions are easier to obtain. But the film's power resides in its convincing depiction of the problems created by these situations. Stevens accurately and sympathetically conveys the urgency of young people trapped in insoluble moral and emotional dilemmas. Because of the skill with which it is written, directed and acted, *A Place in the Sun* is transported beyond its time and has become an enduring and universal drama. As Charlie Chaplin stated upon seeing the movie: ''This is the best film ever to come out of Hollywood.''

Kiss Kiss, Bang Bang, Atlantic-Little Brown and Co., Boston, 1968

Otto Keller (O.E. Hasse) confesses his crime to Father Michael Logan (Montgomery Clift).

I CONFESS

1953

Warner Bros. *Directed and produced by* Alfred Hitchcock. *Associate Producer:* Barbara Keon. *Supervisory Producer:* Sherry Shourdes. *Screenplay:* George Tabori *and* William Archibald, *based on the play* Our Two Consciences *by* Paul Anthelme. *Music:* Dimitri Tiomkin, *conducted by* Ray Heindorf. *Director of Photography:* Robert Burks. *Film Editor:* Rudi Fehr. *Costumes:* Orry-Kelly. *Sets:* Edward S. Haworth *and* George James Hopkins. *Sound Engineer:* Oliver S. Garretson. *Technical Consultant:* Father Paul la Couline. *Police Consultant:* Inspector Oliver Tangvay. *Location:* Quebec. 92 minutes.

CAST

Father Michael William Logan, Montgomery Clift; *Ruth Grandfort,* Anne Baxter; *Inspector Larrue,* Karl Malden; *Willy Robertson, attorney,* Brian Aherne; *Otto Keller,* O. E. Hasse; *Alma Keller,* Dolly Haas; *Pierre Grandfort,* Roger Dann; *Father Millais,* Charles Andre; *Murphy, a policeman,* Judson Pratt; *Vilette, the lawyer,* Ovila Legare; *Father Benoit,* Gilles Pelletier; *Maid,* Nan Boardman; *Farouche,* Henry Corden; *1st French girl,* Carmen Gingras; *2nd French girl,* Renée Hudson; *Nightwatchman,* Albert Godderis.

*Michael says goodbye to his girl, Ruth (Anne Baxter),
as he leaves for the war.*

*After the war: Michael and Ruth enjoy
a day in the country.*

Alfred Hitchcock's *I Confess* contains a central
coincidence which unfortunately strains one's
credulity at the same time it provides the motivation on which the plot hinges.

A German refugee, Keller (O.E. Hasse), murders a lawyer named Vilette (Ovila Legare) when
he is caught stealing. Keller thereupon confesses
his crime to Father Michael Logan (Montgomery
Clift), a priest at the Quebec church where he is a
sexton. Vilette was blackmailing Ruth Grandfort
(Anne Baxter), who was in love with Logan before he was ordained and who continues to love
him in spite of his religious vows and her subsequent marriage to Pierre Grandfort (Roger Dann).
Keller wore a cassock when he committed the
crime and Logan is unable to supply an alibi for
the time of the murder—a series of coincidences
which eventually find Logan on trial for murder.

In spite of the extremity of his predicament,
Logan is bound by his holy orders not to reveal
the secrets of the confessional and is unable to
say anything in his own defense. The jury reluc-
tantly acquits him on the grounds of reasonable
doubt, but an unruly crowd harangues him as he
leaves the courtroom. Keller's wife, Alma (Dolly
Haas), turns against him and, defending Father
Logan, accuses her husband. Keller shoots her

Willy Robertson (Brian Aherne) accuses Father Michael of murder.

and is himself wounded by the police as he attempts to escape. Logan gives Keller extreme unction as he dies in his arms.

The pivotal dilemma of *I Confess* relates to Catholic church law which specifically forbids the clergy from disclosing those sins exposed in the privacy of the confessional. Thus forced into complicity with the murderer, Father Logan behaves as though he is guilty despite his innocence, in much the same way Guy Haines takes on some of Bruno's guilt in the same director's *Strangers on a Train.* The film's tension derives from the audience's knowledge of the cleric's ethical problem and its desire to see him break his vows to save his own life.

Despite the romantic angle, *I Confess* has a semi-documentary feeling about it, very much like Elia Kazan's 1947 film, *Boomerang,* which benefited, as Hitchcock's does, from being shot on location. Robert Burks's striking low-key lighting also contributes to the documentary flavor, each scene being lit with a penumbral gloom which pervades the mood of the film.

I Confess is marred, however, by a strident and over-emphatic score by Dimitri Tiomkin which intrudes jarringly on one's consciousness. Tiomkin redeems himself by providing a lushly ro-

Inspector Larrue (Karl Malden) receives an important piece of information as Father Michael looks on.

Father Michael on trial.

Alma Keller (Dolly Haas) accuses her husband.

mantic song for the extended flashback in which Ruth describes her early romantic relationship with Logan. Over scenes of Ruth waiting tremulously for her boyfriend, meeting him after the war and enjoying a pastoral tryst with him, Hitchcock has superimposed Tiomkin's intentionally sappy aria. The words are unimportant; Hitchcock means it as a commentary on Ruth's blind love for a man who is about to renounce her for the priesthood. Ruth sacrifices fulfillment in the present with her husband by clinging to a romantic fantasy of the past. In a sense, it is as much her guilt which circumstantially dooms Father Logan as it is the murder confessed to by Keller.

In spite of his former affection for Ruth, Logan obviously has a profound inner life which precludes his violating his oath. This faith sustains him and yet, surprisingly, Hitchcock makes little use of Catholicism as the bedrock upon which the priest's life is grounded, the one thing which supports him when everything else fails. The director's method of showing Clift's turmoil and indecisiveness when faced with arrest is to depict him walking the streets of Quebec deep in thought. It is a measure of Clift's skill as an actor that the audience understands his extreme tension and the insolubility of his problem without recourse to dialogue. Clift makes the clergyman's inner torment apparent simply by the anguished expression in his eyes, and creates sympathy for a man who could be an object of derision by maintaining his dignity. Even when Inspector Larrue (Karl Malden) humiliates him by prying into his alliance

The chase through the Chateau Frontenac. Inspector Larrue cautions Father Michael.

with Ruth, Clift's solemnity prevents him from yielding to the temptation to retaliate. Compassionate, grave, and restrained, Clift delineates the priest's conflicting emotions with the subtlest nuances of expression. His face, vulnerable but enlivened by discerning yet kind eyes, reveals his suffering with eloquent intensity.

The critics were divided about the movie, with Otis L. Guernsey, Jr. of the *New York Herald Tribune* declaring: ''Montgomery Clift's usual underplaying is perfect for his role of a man forced to keep his own counsel lest he betray his highest ideals.'' Guernsey was not favorably disposed, however, to the film in general, finding that ''the whetted knife of Hitchcock's direction blunts itself on a ponderous, equivocal situation.''

Bosley Crowther of *The New York Times* also decided against the film: ''Even though moments in the picture do have some tension and power, and the whole thing is scrupulously acted by a tightly professional cast, the consequence is an entertainment that tends to drag, sag and generally grow dull.''

"What's the treatment?" Lorene asks about the trouble Prew is in.

FROM HERE TO ETERNITY

1953

Columbia Pictures. *Directed by* Fred Zinnemann. *Produced by* Buddy Adler. *Screenplay:* Daniel Taradash, *based on the novel by* James Jones. *Music:* George Duning. *Musical director:* Morris Stoloff. *"Re-enlistment Blues"* by James Jones, Fred Karger and Robert Wells. *Orchestrations:* Arthur Morton. *Director of photography:* Burnett Guffey. *Film editor:* William Lyon. *Costumes:* Jean Louis. *Set decoration:* Frank Tuttle. *Sound:* Lodge Cunningham. *Art director:* Gary Odell. *Assistant director:* Earl Bellamy. *Hair styles:* Helen Hunt. *Makeup:* Clay Campbell. *Technical adviser:* Brig. Gen. Kendall J. Fiedler, Ret. *Location:* Schofield Barracks, Hawaii. 118 minutes.

CAST

Sgt. Milton Warden, Burt Lancaster; *Karen Holmes,* Deborah Kerr; *Robert E. Lee Prewitt,* Montgomery Clift; *Angelo Maggio,* Frank Sinatra; *Alma/Lorene,* Donna Reed; *Sgt. "Fatso" Judson,* Ernest Borgnine; *Capt. Dana Holmes,* Philip Ober; *Corp. Buckley,* Jack Warden; *Sgt. Leva,* Mickey Shaughnessy; *Mazzioli,* Harry Bellaver; *Sgt. Maylon Stark,* George Reeves; *Sgt. Ike Galovitch,* John Dennis; *Sgt. Pete Karelsen,* Tim Ryan; *Mrs. Kipfer,* Barbara Morrison; *Georgette,* Kristine Miller; *Annette,* Jean Willes; *Sal Anderson,* Merle Travis; *Treadwell,* Arthur Keegan; *Sgt. Baldy Thom,* Claude Akins; *Sgt. Turp Thornhill,* Robert Karnes; *Sgt. Henderson,* Robert Wilke; *Cpl. Champ Wilson,* Douglas Henderson; *Friday Clark,* Don Dubbins; *Cpl. Paluso,* John Cason; *Capt. Ross,* John Bryant; *Sandra,* Joan Shawlee; *Jean,* Angela Stevens; *Nancy,* Mary Carver; *Suzanne,* Vicki Bakken; *Roxanne,* Margaret Barstow; *Billie,* Delia Salvi; *Lt. Colonel,* Willis Bouchey; *Nair,* Al Sargent; *Bartender,* Weaver Levy; *Major Stern,* Tyler McVey; *Bill,* William Lundmark; *Soldier,* Robert Healy; *Military guard,* Brick Sullivan; *Rose, waitress,* Moana Gleason; *Col. Wood,* Freeman Lusk; *Maj. Bonds,* Robert Pike; *Col. Ayres,* Carleton Young; *Gen. Slater,* Fay Roope; *Bit players:* Louise Saraydar, Joe Roach, Patrick Miller, Nor-

The morning roll call.

Angelo Maggio (Frank Sinatra) and Robert E. Lee Prewitt (Montgomery Clift) return from extra duty as

Sgt. Warden (Burt Lancaster) and Sgt. Leva (Mickey Shaughnessy) look on.

man Wayne, Joe Sargent, Mack Chandler, Edward Laguna, John D. Veitch, John Davis, Carey Leverette, Alan Pinson, Guy Way, James Jones. Manny Klein and his trumpet.

James Jones's *From Here to Eternity* was one of the most important novels to emerge from the postwar period and, along with Norman Mailer's *The Naked and the Dead,* one of the most influential. Harry Cohn, the tyrannical head of Columbia Pictures, had bought it for $82,000 and had been dissatisfied with the many screen adaptations various writers, including Jones, had come up with. Cohn didn't want to tamper with the volatile mix of sex and sadism or the audacity—dependent, in large measure, on the four–letter words which had so shocked the reading public—which had made the book sell so well. But he had to have a script that could get past the production code. Daniel Taradash finally derived a screenplay Cohn was willing to shoot, one which nevertheless is much toned down from Jones's savage indictment of army morality.

In the book, Capt. Dana Holmes is promoted to major; in the film he is made into an isolated case and cashiered out of the service. The brutal stockade sequences are deleted and a scene is substituted in which a soldier describes to Prewitt the cruel treatment Maggio is undergoing. Columbia also had to have the Pentagon's cooperation. Someone who followed the negotiations between the army and the studio reported: "The army would never have allowed us to shoot the picture at Schofield Barracks if we hadn't [made those changes] and it would have been awfully expensive to build a set like Schofield Barracks." The army saw each draft of the script before shooting began, and the producer, Buddy Adler, went more than once to Washington to bargain with the army about the script.

Fred Zinnemann, already set as director, was aghast at Cohn's suggestion that either Aldo Ray or John Derek—two Columbia contract players—should portray Robert E. Lee Prewitt. "I'd like to have Montgomery Clift," Zinnemann announced, pointing out the first paragraph of the

Maggio offers Prew and Lorene (Donna Reed) a drink.

novel which describes Prewitt as "a very neat
and deceptively slim young man." Cohn hit the
ceiling, whereupon Zinnemann handed him back
the script and prepared to walk out. Cohn eventually agreed to cast Clift.

"This is the way we started and this is the way
it went all through the picture," Zinnemann related. "He got me so mad that out of sheer fury I
worked better than normally. I think he did it on
purpose."

But there were more casting problems. Joan
Crawford was signed as Karen Holmes, but
bowed out in an argument over her wardrobe.
Buddy Ehrenberg, Deborah Kerr's agent, looking
for a role that would revive her stalled career,

suggested to Zinnemann that Karen's sluttishness
would be more interesting if played against
Kerr's cool gentility. Kerr was then cast in place
of Crawford. Frank Sinatra, whose career was
also waning, campaigned vigorously for the part
of Angelo Maggio, the feisty Italian. His wife at
the time, Ava Gardner, pleaded personally with
Cohn. The two flew to Africa where Gardner was
starting *Mogambo;* Sinatra returned to test for
the role that did, in fact, give him a whole new
career as a dramatic actor.

In the movie that Taradash culled from Jones's
860 pages, many characters are excised while the
focus remains on five major individuals. The narrative follows Prewitt as he interacts with the oth-

Sgt. Warden teases Prew about getting the treatment.

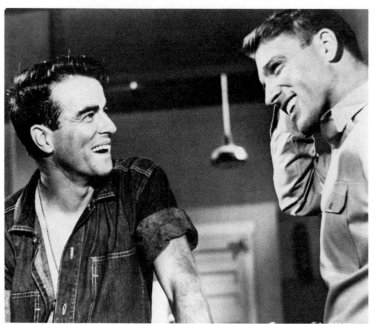

Prew kids Sgt. Warden about the possibility of finding a pearl while on KP duty.

ers—with the exception of Karen Holmes, who is told about him by Sgt. Milt Warden—beginning with his first day at Schofield Barracks. He is transferred there on a matter of honor—his honor. Another bugler was promoted over him and he believes he is the better man. Capt. Dana Holmes runs the regimental boxing team and wants Prewitt to fight for him. Prew once blinded a friend in the ring and now refuses to box. Because of his intransigence, Prew is given "the treatment": hard duty designed to soften him up and persuade him to box. On leave he meets Lorene (who, in the book is a whore at the New Congress Hotel, a bordello), a "hostess" at a club, and falls in love. Prew's story is interwoven with those of Karen, the Captain's wife, who has a passionate, unsuccessful affair with Warden, and Maggio, the rebellious private whose defiance of Fatso Judson eventually costs him his life. As revenge for Judson's killing Maggio in the stockade, where he was sent for being AWOL, Prew murders Judson and is himself seriously wounded. While recuperating at Lorene's, he hears that the Japanese have invaded Pearl Harbor. He tries to rejoin his unit, and, refusing to answer a guard's challenge, is shot as the enemy.

From Here to Eternity is the story of three men with Prewitt as the pivotal figure. Each man—Prew, Maggio and Warden—has his code of honor. Prew's involves not submitting to pressure and not accepting the promotion of an inferior bugler over him, even if it means being broken in rank. Warden's principles revolve around his love of the army and not becoming that most hated of men: an officer. As the film depicts him Maggio is a pig-headed runt who hates injustice and will not shut up. His mouth is his best weapon and his worst enemy. As Prew defines it for all of them, "A man don't go his own way, he's nothin'!"

The movie involves each of the men as they try to live up to that code. It is significant that the only one of the three alive at the end is Warden, the man who knows how to bend his rule without breaking it, and the most politically astute of them all. Together they embody a military version of the Westerner's credo: "A man's gotta do

"Why don't you learn to play the bugle?" Prew astounds the company bugler and Maggio with his prowess.

what a man's gotta do." As Prew says, explaining his limitations, "A man should be what he can do."

Prew and Warden are good at what they do. Prew is justifiably proud of his ability as a bugler ("I play the bugle well," he tells Lorene); he's a middle-weight whose reputation has preceeded him to the company, and he is a skillful pool player. Warden is an efficient, fair, and—in his way—compassionate aide to the Captain, and when the barracks are under assault, he proves himself an inspiriting leader of men. Maggio is good with his mouth; he is funny, hip, and a worthy friend. He is almost like a mascot, ready with a quip or a bottle and all too anxious to fight.

All three are stubborn: Maggio to the extreme that he dies in defense of his honor; Warden to the point that he gives up the woman he loves in order to be true to his principles; and Prew also to the extent of dying as he attempts to return to his company when it's attacked, despite his wounds and in defiance of his loved one's wishes. As Warden says when he sees Prew dead in the sand

trap where he has fallen: "He was always a hard-head."

Like Maggio, Prew is obstinate to the point of stupidity. When his unit pours on the treatment, Prew tells the men, "I can take anything you can dish out." He won't complain and he won't back down. When he is finally goaded into fighting Galovitch, he refuses to go for his head because he once injured a friend. Only when he is losing, crumpling under Galovitch's blows, does he disobey his resolve and punch his opponent in the face.

Eternity is also about loneliness, that of men minus the camaraderie that war often instills in fighting units. It is the kind of solitude that will drive a man like Warden to risk a prison term in order to have an affair with his captain's wife. It impels Prew to seek a relationship with Lorene, who describes herself as being about "two steps up from the pavement." When Lorene and Prew discuss marriage, Lorene refuses because she doesn't want to marry a soldier, but she admits she is lonely. Prew says, looking at her regret-

Prew squares off against Sgt. Ike Galovitch (John Dennis) as the company looks on.

"Prewitt stays right here till the bitter end." Prew and Warden drunk in the middle of the road.

fully, "Nobody ever lies about being lonely." He left home when he was seventeen, and the army is the only real family he has ever had. "I'm a 30-year man," he tells Lorene, "I'm in for the whole ride." The army will provide the refuge he has been looking for.

Once Schofield is under attack, Prew believes he can return safely to his company. He confirms this view to Lorene: "I'll be all right once I get back." The army is like a big mother who gathers all the strays and misfits into her arms. But Prew is wrong: the army also has room for sadists like Fatso and incompetents like Holmes. It has killed Maggio and Prew has been virtually ostracized. At last, although it is his own fault, the army kills him. Prew is loyal to the army, but the army does not repay him in kind. Prew recognizes the reality of this situation by stating: "I love the army. Man loves a thing, that don't mean it's gotta love him back." He clings stubbornly to his faith despite the evidence of his own experience.

Prew insists on his individuality, even though the army tries to mold all men into an amorphous mass that acts only for the good of the unit. When

Lorene tells him she has to treat all the men at the club alike—it's her job—Prew rejoins: "We may look all alike. We ain't all alike." But his exigence wins through and she does treat him differently. "You're a funny one," she muses in an effort to comprehend him.

There are only two ways Prew can stand out, however. One is to box and the other is to bugle. He denies himself the first avenue and is refused the second. But the audience does get an opportunity to see what bugling means to him. At the local beer joint, Prew grabs the horn of a young soldier who is blowing ineffectively on it. "Why don't you learn to play the bugle?" he snarls and proceeds to demonstrate how it is done. He loses himself in the effort of playing; lifted from his chair by the force of his music, he seems at one with the instrument. The blues come rushing out, expelled from his body by the power of his emotions. Even drunk, Prew has a unique ability to communicate his feeling for music. He noodles away on the mouthpiece he always carries with him (telling Lorene proudly that he played "Taps" at Arlington before the President on Armistice Day), and spews the sensuous notes of "Re-enlistment Blues" into the night air. When Maggio dies, Prew plays "Taps" as a tribute to his friend, the tears running down his face, once more pouring his inexpressible sentiments into the horn. When he removes his mouthpiece and gives the instrument back to the bugler, the man looks at it as though it is a foreign object; he has never heard "Taps" played so eloquently before, never knew music could convey such intensity.

Clift insisted on learning how to box and bugle as well as Prew would be able to. He studied bugling with Manny Klein; even though a professional would be heard on the sound track, he wanted the motions of his mouth and throat to be exactly right. An ex-fighter named Mushy Calahan coached Clift for the fight scene and, although he looks good enough in the close-ups, Zinnemann used a double in the long shots where the movements of Clift's not very graceful body would have been more pronounced.

Eternity provides Clift with the second of the many brutal beatings he received on screen. The first came in *Red River* at the hands of John Wayne, and there were others in *The Young Lions* and *Wild River*. Clift is subdued by broncs and bulls in *The Misfits* instead of human hands, but his body absorbs savage punishment nevertheless. If Clift was physically whipped on screen, his animus remained unconquered. His spiritual courage transcended the assault on his flesh and he emerged somehow purified and stronger.

As he had when working in Zinnemann's *The Search*, Clift pared his dialogue down to the minimum. He perceived Prew as inarticulate, uneducated, his speech full of grammatical lapses. Mira Rostova flew to California to work on *Eternity* and they labored over Clift's lines as they had on previous films.

Clift developed other friendships and other sounding boards for his ideas on his performance. Deborah Kerr remembered Clift: "His concentration was positively violent." Donna Reed had never performed with anyone who had Clift's intensity about his work; his efforts lifted the level of her acting higher than she had ever

Maggio dies in Prew's arms.

147

"This is a real attack." The radio warns of the Japanese invasion as Prew, Lorene, and Georgette (Kristine Miller) listen.

been able to go before. Reed recalled the almost physical shock she would get when Clift began performing with her: "No actor ever affected me that way. After our scenes, I'd go home and our work would push me into myself."

But his closest relationship was with Frank Sinatra. Clift admired the fact that Sinatra had worked hard all his life to establish himself as a singer, and now he had had the guts to break that mold and fight for the non-singing role of Maggio. Sinatra respected Clift as a serious actor, so Clift guided him in his performance as well. Ironically, Reed and Sinatra both won Academy Awards for roles Clift helped them with, while Clift himself was ignored in his third bid for an Oscar.

Clift and Sinatra became drinking buddies. Sinatra, however, was able to hold his liquor while Clift could not. Clift even began drinking during working hours. He was drunk when he and Lancaster (acting drunk for the scene and sitting in the middle of a road) had to shoot Maggio's death

scene. Sinatra has to stumble out of the bushes, collapse in Clift's arms and die. There was a tag to the sequence in which Clift watches the soldiers put Sinatra on the back of a truck and says, "See his head don't bump." But Clift could not get the line out correctly. Hours after they should have been done, Zinnemann called a halt to the filming and cut the scene short.

None of these problems is visible on the screen and Maggio's death is an extraordinarily moving scene. Sinatra lies cradled in Clift's arms, clutching at his shirt and brokenly whispering a warning to Clift. It is his way of expressing his love for his buddy and Sinatra plays it in a very understated manner. His sweating face and frail body speak more eloquently than any words. Clift doesn't cheat the shot; he makes no attempt to upstage Sinatra by turning his face toward the camera, but looks directly at his fellow actor.

Clift's endless probing of the nuances and significance of Prew's behavior paid off. His per-

Prew gets ready to return to his company after being AWOL.

formance is an exercise in economy of gesture and expression, the struggle of a non-verbal man to reveal himself with movement and thought. His restless eyes examine Reed's face in their scenes together, searching for a response to his need. Under pressure Clift's teeth clench and his jaw works as he pushes himself to discipline his temper. Against Lancaster's more expansive performance and Sinatra's cocky, humorous one, Clift comes across as almost rigidly controlled, expressing himself exclusively through his bugle: an inanimate object which affords him the release he finds otherwise only with his buddy, Sinatra, and in his love for Reed. His is an extreme sensitivity tinged with neurosis, an almost monomaniacal insistence on being true to himself. Fred Zinnemann described what Clift added to the film: ". . . of ten suggestions he makes, eight or nine are good; he makes marvelous contributions to a film. I will go so far as to say he was the basic reason for what excellence *Eternity* had. The other actors, excited by his attitude, drew a tre-

mendous amount from him. He'd have made a wonderful director. Monty Clift was an inspired actor."

From Here to Eternity was made at the time of the Korean War when Americans were becoming ambivalent about their commitment to "holy wars," and the film mirrors that uneasiness. It admires the hard-driving, leather-lunged "top" sergeant, but questions the appropriateness of the power his superiors wield and misuse. The movie esteems the spirit of the gutsy G.I. "dog face," yet challenges the rectitude of the arena in which he must operate: the politics, the obsequiousness, and the general misery of his position. If the film is not the hard-driving denunciation Jones's novel was, it nevertheless raised some important questions about the men we ask to do our fighting and dying for us and about those who direct their actions.

Pauline Kael* summed up the movie this way: "*From Here to Eternity* did not convert its hero into a socially accepted leader, did not reduce issues to black and white, and it was a huge popular success. But a curious displacement occurred in the course of the film: Prewitt's fate as hero got buried in the commotion of the attack on Pearl Harbor, and it was easy to get the impression that it didn't really matter what happened to him as he would probably have gotten killed anyway. And, as a related phenomenon, Montgomery Clift's fine performance as Prewitt was buried in the public praise for Frank Sinatra and Burt Lancaster. It was almost as if Prewitt wasn't there at all, as if the public wanted to forget his troublesome presence. Or perhaps Prewitt wasn't troublesome enough: there was no mystery or confusion about why he behaved as he did. He had his own value system, and perhaps his clarity prevented him from stirring the audience. *Formulated* alienation seems already part of the past; Prewitt is the last Hollywood representative of depression-style alienation."

The critics coined new superlatives to express their admiration for *From Here to Eternity*. A.H. Weiler of *The New York Times* said, "Mont-

*I Lost It at the Movies, Atlantic-Little Brown, Boston, 1965

"I'm a soldier." Prew says goodbye to Lorene.

gomery Clift adds another sensitive portrait to an already imposing gallery with his portrayal of Prewitt."

Time's reviewer reported: "The three male leads in the film turn in the finest performances of their careers. Montgomery Clift displays a marvelous, snail-like capacity to contract his feeling and intelligence into the close little shell of Prew's personality, and yet he also manages to convey that within this very limited man blazes a large spirit.

"The performers have that curious and captivating air which director Zinnemann calls 'be-having rather than acting,' an artless-seeming form of art. . . . [The film] tries to tell a truth about life, about the inviolability of the human spirit, and in some measure it fails. Yet the picture does succeed, perhaps without quite intending to, in saying something important about America. It says that many Americans, in a way that is often confused and sometimes forgotten, care deeply, care to the quick about a man's right 'to go his own way,' though all the world and the times be contrary."

Otis L. Guernsey, Jr., writing in the *New York Herald Tribune*, noted: "Played by Montgomery Clift with slim, muscular efficiency and deep-set, brooding eyes, Prewitt commits himself to perfection—that is his tragedy. Clift's version of Prewitt is both taut and sensitive. . . ."

In yet another consideration of the film, Guernsey wrote: "Montgomery Clift plays Prewitt as a tense but capable fellow, an excellent soldier but flaring at small irritations if they happen to touch a certain nerve of his personality. His performance is as economical as it is effective, in a curious role which is almost the male counterpart of the melodrama heroine. . . ."

The critic for *Saturday Review* said: "Montgomery Clift, as Prewitt, reveals again his uncanny ability to lend eloquence to an incoherent personality. His eye, his gesture, unfailingly suggest the nuances of feeling that the script writer dare not let him speak.

From Here to Eternity walked off with eight Oscars, including one for Zinnemann (who told the reporters at the ceremony, "I couldn't have gotten this without Monty"), one for best picture, and a third for Daniel Taradash's script. Clift was distraught that he did not win, and as a kind of consolation prize, Renée Zinnemann, the director's wife, bought him a miniature gold trumpet mounted like an Oscar. Clift kept it with him for the rest of his life.

Coffee in the station: Giovanni Doria (Montgomery Clift) tries to talk his beloved out of leaving Rome.

INDISCRETION OF AN AMERICAN WIFE

1953

Columbia Pictures. *Directed and produced by* Vittorio de Sica. *Associate producers:* Marcello Girosi and Wolfgang Reinhardt. *Screenplay:* Cesare Zavattini, Luigi Chiarini and Giorgio Prosperi, *with dialogue by* Truman Capote. *From the story* "Terminal Station" *by* Cesare Zavattini. *Director of photography:* G.R. Aldo. *Music:* Alessandro Cicognini. *Conducted by* Franco Ferrara. *Film editor:* Eraldo da Roma and Jean Barker. *Art director:* Virgillio Marchi. *Post-production audio:* James G. Stewart. *Production manager:* Nino Misiano. *Music editor:* Audray Granville. *Sound engineers:* Bruno Brunacci and Alberto Bartolomé. *Jennifer Jones's costumes designed by* Christian Dior. *Costumes:* Alessandro Antonelli. *Technical associate:* Richard van Hessen. *Cameraman:* Sergio Bergamini. *Location:* Stazione di Roma. 75 minutes.

CAST

Mary Forbes, Jennifer Jones; *Giovanni Doria*, Montgomery Clift; *Commissariat*, Gino Cervi; *Mary's nephew, Paul*, Richard Beymer; *Baggage clerk*, Paolo Stoppa; *Employee*, Mando Bruno; Clelia Matania, Enrico Viarisio, Giuseppe Forelli, Enrico Olorio, Maria Pia Casillo-Ciro.

151

Giovanni looks for Mary.

As soon as *I Confess* was completed, Clift went to Rome to star in *Indiscretion of an American Wife*. (The film was released after *From Here to Eternity*.) The movie was in difficulty even before shooting started. Although David O. Selznick was not the producer, or even officially connected with the film, he had raised the money and supplied the stars (including his wife, Jennifer Jones) and the script. The screenplay had been worked on by Carson McCullers, Alberto Moravia, Paul Gallico and Truman Capote, who gets credit for the dialogue. By the time it reached the screen it was a hodge-podge of director Vittorio de Sica's visual asides on the activities in the Rome railroad station where it was filmed—many of which Selznick cut for the American version— and the variable quality of the script itself.

Furthermore, it was de Sica's first film in English and the director suggested, only half facetiously, that since he couldn't speak English he would hire an Italian actor to stand in for Clift before the camera. De Sica would tell this actor— in Italian—how to move and speak, and Clift would imitate him. Understandably, Clift refused angrily to have anything to do with the idea.

Jones, who did not know of Clift's predilection for men, developed a crush on him. When she discovered the truth of the situation she reportedly became so overwrought that she stuffed a mink jacket down the toilet of a portable dressing room.

De Sica rented the newest railroad station in Rome and filmed there every night from ten P.M. to five A.M. In addition to contending with the extras and trains, de Sica had to cope with Selznick's legendary memos, most of which concerned Jones. Selznick actively directed Jones's career, since his own was virtually ended, and he was interested in everything that involved her. Clift was furious at Selznick's interference. Selznick wanted the movie to look like a glossy Hollywood romance—he was responsible for changing the title from *Terminal Station* to *Indiscretion of an American Wife*, which he deemed more commercial—while Clift agreed with de Sica that it should be the story of a doomed love affair.

The plot, as pared down by Selznick, is sim-

Mary Forbes (Jennifer Jones) and Giovanni are
escorted to the police station.

plicity itself. Mary, determined to end her relationship with Giovanni (whose embodiment as
Montgomery Clift is carefully explained by giving
him an American mother), arranges to leave
Rome by train. Giovanni follows her to the terminal and importunes her not to desert him. They
seek the privacy of an empty railway car for
some last-minute passion. (In the original version
their love-making was considerably more ex-
plicit.) There they are discovered by a worker
and haled before a railroad official for improper
behavior. The commissariat decides not to charge
them formally and dismisses the unhappy couple.
At last Mary departs, leaving Giovanni alone on
the platform.

Clift looks properly European in his baggy
overcoat, wearing a sweater under his jacket. He
is appropriately macho, telling Jones: "In this
country, it's the men that count. You American
women are too emancipated." But Clift is hardly
the picture of a dashing, romantic Italian. He is a
rather drab university professor, undistinguished
looking and—as the script expresses it—with his
calf-eyed yearning, quite banal.

Jones is a rather ordinary Philadelphia house-
wife, although the screenplay makes a great point
of explaining, both through Clift's words and her
behavior, how special she is. Clift worships her;
he can't take his hands or his eyes off her. She is

Giovanni flares up at a comment by the arresting officer, as the Commissariat looks on.

Mary removes lipstick from Giovanni's mouth in the police station.

Giovanni pleads with the Commissariat to let Mary go.

*Giovanni argues with an officer as the Commissariat
(Gino Cervi) disposes of the case.*

dignified, soft spoken and thoughtful; she buys
chocolate for the three sons of a distressed pregnant lady whom she tries to help, and she talks to
them, trying to allay their fears.

De Sica's forte is the small vignettes like this
one which he has scattered throughout the film.
The faces of the three boys are heartbreaking and
de Sica lingers on them just long enough to mov-
ingly communicate their concern for their
mother. Another sequence shows a little man
climbing on the door of the commissariat's office,
trying to get a look at the scandalous couple. In
the office Jones tells Clift to wipe her lipstick off
his face, then does it for him, screwing her face
up in concentration. There were many more of
these stories—virtually subplots—most of which
Selznick removed when he trimmed the film from
over two hours (its length in Europe, where Selz-

After saying goodbye to Mary, Giovanni falls to the platform, jumping from the train.

nick controlled neither the editing nor distribution) to 75 minutes.

Clift and Jones are both effective as the disconsolate lovers. Clift is desirous, ardent, voluptuously surrendering his dignity for a few minutes of passion with his inamorata. Flirting even as they say goodbye, he fantasizes about the life they could have shared. "If you didn't behave yourself, I'd beat you," he tells her mock-seriously. Jones is vulnerable yet determined. Her acting has a wistful quality that is right for the part, but at times she's so Philadelphia-proper it is hard to imagine her in the throes of rapture with Clift, or even to see what he finds so fascinating in her.

De Sica's film could have been another neo-Realistic documentary, but as distributed in the United States, it is neither a bittersweet romance nor a visual essay on the lives of the people who move through a great metropolitan terminus. He has cast it scrupulously with character actors whose faces say more with one look than Capote's heartfelt speeches express in pages of dialogue. (Capote, by the way, claims he wrote only two scenes.)

The critics, without exception, loathed the film. Otis L. Guernsey, Jr. of the *New York Herald Tribune* said: "The film is short—but it soon exhausts the resources of its stars. Once Miss Jones has established that she is tense with emotion; once Mr. Clift has broken up his dialogue in his impetuous style of speech and launched his eagle-eyed look of desire, they find nothing to do except more of the same. The words change, but not the pitch of performance or its overtones."

The New York Times's Bosley Crowther found: "Miss Jones performs the troubled lady with dignity and sentiment. In the course of an hour, she makes a woman of little sympathy look much better. Less can be said in favor of her lover, played by Montgomery Clift. He droops in dreary fashion and appears a pretty futile sort of man."

Garwood Jones (Rod Taylor) makes fun of Johnny's idealism as Nell defends him.

RAINTREE COUNTY

1957

MGM. *Directed by* Edward Dmytryk. *Produced by* David Lewis. *Screenplay:* Millard Kaufman, *based on the novel by* Ross Lockridge, Jr. *Associate producer:* Millard Kaufman. *Music:* Johnny Green. *"The Song of Raintree County" sung by* Nat "King" Cole. *Lyric by* Paul Francis Webster. *Director of photography:* Robert Surtees. *Film editor:* John Dunning. *Costumes:* Walter Plunkett. *Set decoration:* Edwin B. Willis and Hugh Hunt. *Recording supervision:* Dr. Wesley C. Miller. *Art directors:* William A. Horning and Urie McCleary. *Assistant director:* Ridgeway

Callow. *Special effects:* Warren Newcombe. *Makeup:* William Tuttle. *Hair styles:* Sydney Guilaroff. *Unit production manager:* Eddie Woehler. *Dialect coach:* Marguerite Lamkin. *Technicolor consultant:* Charles H. Hagedon. *Locations:* Danville, Kentucky; Natchez, Missisippi and Reelfoot Lake, Tennessee. Technicolor, Camera 65 and Panavision. 165 minutes.

CAST

John Wickliff Shawnessy, Montgomery Clift, *Susanna Drake*, Elizabeth Taylor; *Nell Gaither*, Eva Marie Saint; *Prof. Jerusalem Webster Stiles*, Ni-

157

Nell Gaither (Eva Marie Saint) gives John Shawnessy (Montgomery Clift) his graduation present.

Nell and Johnny first hear of the golden raintree.

gel Patrick; *Orville "Flash" Perkins*, Lee Marvin; *Garwood B. Jones*, Rod Taylor; *Ellen Shawnessy*, Agnes Moorehead; *T. D. Shawnessy*, Walter Abel; *Barbara Drake*, Jarma Lewis; *Bobby Drake*, Tom Drake; *Ezra Gray*, Rhys Williams; *Niles Foster*, Russell Collins; *Southern Officer*, DeForest Kelley; *Lydia Gray*, Myrna Hansen; *Jake, the bartender*, Oliver Blake; *Cousin Sam*, John Eldredge; *Soona*, Isabelle Cooley; *Parthenia*, Ruth Attaway; *Miss Roman*, Eileene Stevens; *Bessie*, Rosalind Hayes; *Tom Conway*, Don Burnett; *Nat Franklin*, Michael Dugan; *Jesse Gardner*, Ralph Vitti (Michael Dante); *Starter*, Phil Chambers; *Man with gun*, James Griffith; *Granpa Peters*, Burt Mustin; *Madame Gaubert*, Dorothy Granger; *Blind Man*, Owen McGiveney; *Party guest*, Charles Watts; *Union Lieutenant*, Stacy Harris; *Jim Shawnessy (age 2½ years)*, Donald Losby; *Jim Shawnessy (age 4 years)*, Mickey Maga; *Pantomimist in blackface*, Robert Foulk; *Photographer*, Jack Daly; *Old Negro man*, Bill Walker; *Bearded soldier*, Gardner McKay; *1st spectator*, William Challee; *2nd spectator*, Frank Kreig; *Spectator*, Joe Brown; *1st girl*, Janet Lake; *2nd girl*, Luana Lee; *3rd girl*, Judi Jordan; *4th girl*, Phyllis Douglas; *5th girl*, Sue George; *Spectator*, Nesdon Booth; *Spectator*, Robert Forrest; *Woman*, Josephine Cummins; *Bit player*, Mil Patrick.

Ross Lockridge, Jr.'s *Raintree County* was a best seller when it appeared in 1948. Metro-Goldwyn-Mayer snapped up the movie rights, but no one at the studio was able to come up with a satisfactory screen treatment. Dore Schary, then vice-president in charge of production, decided it would be too expensive to film and abandoned the project. Seven years later Millard Kaufman was assigned to transform Lockridge's 1,066-page blockbuster into a screenplay and Schary agreed to put *Raintree County* on the production schedule.

Raintree County is a novel that reads like a film: full of flashbacks, historical events, and colorful characters whose dialogue enlivens the scenario. The film is constructed like a novel:

Johnny and his father (Walter Abel) talk over the young man's future.

with a beginning, middle, and an end—in that order. It starts in 1859 with John Wickliff Shawnessy's and Nell Gaither's graduation from secondary school in Fairhaven, Indiana. Their teacher, "Perfesser" Jerusalem Webster Stiles, tells them of a golden raintree, representing truth and fulfillment, hidden somewhere in the county, whereupon Johnny immediately sets out in quest of it. Although Nell and Johnny are sweethearts, he marries visiting Southern belle Susanna Drake when she informs him she is carrying his child. Susanna has lied to make Johnny marry her, but after a trip to the South where Johnny becomes aware of her confused mental state—involving fears of miscegenation and a mystery surrounding her parents' death in a fire—Susanna does become pregnant. The Civil War erupts but Johnny stays home, teaches school, and cares for his son Jimmy and his increasingly distraught wife. Susanna runs off with Jimmy and Johnny enlists in the Union Army to try to track them down. Eventually he finds his son sheltered by Susanna's former slaves and carries him back to the Union lines. After the war, Johnny locates

Susanna in an insane asylum and returns with her to Indiana. Apparently recovered, but believing that her behavior has impeded Johnny's pursuit of the mythical raintree, Susanna takes off one night in search of it, followed by Jimmy. The next day, Susanna is found dead in the swamp. Johnny and Nell, reunited at last, find Jimmy nearby at the foot of a golden tree.

Raintree County was MGM's attempt to recapture on film those elements that had made *Gone With the Wind* great: passionate, vital characters swept up in epic historical events. Although it cost $6 million and the money is evident on the screen—in battles, a ball, and the re-creation of towns, farms and elegant houses—the movie is a turgid soap opera bereft of spectacle or any convincing feeling (on the part of director Edward Dmytryk or scenarist Kaufman) for the period or the individuals.

Raintree County pits a dark-haired seductress —warm, insane and destructive—against a cool, blonde virgin—rational and loyal—for the love of an idealistic schoolteacher. But these dramatis personae, cardboard clichés all, never come to

Professor Stiles (Nigel Patrick) plans to bet on Johnny in the big Fourth of July race.

Johnny helps the philandering Professor escape from an irate husband.

life. The film has no values of its own, only people who posture while talking about their values. They embody attitudes toward the issues of their day—slavery, war and secession—without actually coming to grips with these problems on a personal level. The most interesting individuals, by default, are Nigel Patrick as the "Perfesser" who introduces Clift to the concept of the raintree, and Lee Marvin as Flash Perkins, the colorful local cut-up whom Clift beats in the Fourth of July footrace. Patrick gives an outrageous performance—all hyperbole, foppish curls and lechery—as he tries to fix the race or lusts after one of his nubile students. Marvin starts out as a gaudy rakehell, but grows in stature during the war. He and Clift go scouting for the Union through the South and when they are on the run with Mickey Maga (as Clift's son, Jimmy), Marvin stops a rebel bullet. He keeps the Confederate soldier talking long enough for Clift and Maga to get away. At first blustery and ornate, Marvin's portrayal is toned down as the character matures while the war progresses, becoming generous and considerate as his friendship with Clift develops.

Eva Marie Saint (as saintly as her name implies throughout a career comprised of virtuous roles) is sweet as the girl who never stops loving her worthy swain, but she has little to do except stand around and reaffirm her faith in Clift. At graduation she gives Clift a history of Raintree County and the notables who originated there, telling him that one day he will be in the book; he will be a "great writer." Later, when he has survived the war and his wife's illness, Saint informs him: "Your great book is your own life."

Elizabeth Taylor depicts Susanna as a florid, superficial yet deeply troubled belle, a precursor of the Southerners she would play in *Cat on a Hot Tin Roof* (the vixen) and *Suddenly Last Summer* (the neurotic, again opposite Clift as the patient protector). She has some moments of flirtatious charm, and her long speech toward the end when Clift finds her in the asylum is quite moving. Here Taylor is subdued, longing for the peace of sanity and blaming herself because Clift never found the raintree. "There is no raintree," Clift intones, acknowledging that it is mythical and symbolic (echoing the sound track theme song which says that "the raintree's a state of mind or a dream . . ."), and absolving Taylor of wasting his life. For this performance, Taylor received her first Academy Award nomination. Seven years after she played the young Angela Vickers to Clift's George Eastman in *A Place in the Sun*, Elizabeth Taylor's looks have changed. She is womanly and voluptuous, no longer the sweet teenager, but a siren more than capable of luring the gullible lad Clift portrays.

At thirty-six, Clift is too old to be convincing as the twenty-year-old Johnny Shawnessy and too urban to be believable as a country boy, striding across the fields with a scythe over his shoulder, or tearing off his shoes to race with Marvin. (No matter how often his father and mother call him "son" or Rod Taylor refers to him as "sprout," Clift no longer looks like a young man.) It is not a question of looking out of place in period clothes —Clift is completely right in Western garb for *Red River*, but less at home in the nineteenth-century costumes he wore in *The Heiress*—but one of attitude. Clift's sensibility is that of the city: sensitive, modern, although not necessarily hip, and more at home on the pavements of *Lonelyhearts* or in the New Congress Club of *From Here to Eternity*. Clift's physical stance is that of

Johnny argues that Susanna (Elizabeth Taylor) cannot continue to keep slaves in the North.

the twentieth century, his vocal inflections have a modern rhythm, and his overall mien bespeaks the present rather than the past.

Clift's problems are not simply those of having the wrong demeanor in the right clothes. The script is fundamentally silly and his character's idealism as expressed in pretentious aphorisms (like "To see the raintree is not nearly as important as what you find looking for it") is undiscerning. Hopeless optimist that he is, he persists in trying to help the obviously mad Taylor when it is apparent she is a lost cause. If the script were clearer about the principles Clift is supposed to be abandoning while engaged in this lifelong rescue attempt, the audience might feel a greater sense of loss at his so-called failure.

The entire dramatis personae seem to feel that Clift is precious, but this is communicated through dialogue, not through any overt intention on the part of scenarist Kaufman. Clift's parents (played by Agnes Moorehead and Walter Abel) cluck over him; Eva Marie Saint informs him that he is fated for greatness; Marvin calls him "the fastest man in Raintree County" and Taylor exclaims, "You're too good for me!" But Clift's John Shawnessy is an ordinary young man with an ordinary destiny. The events in his life (the Civil War; the death of Abraham Lincoln; his quest through the South for his son) may have an aura of grandeur, but no touch of greatness is conferred on the man himself.

Clift, like Taylor, has intervals in which his presence is effective: he is gentle and understanding with Taylor, tender with his son, and has some nice moments with Saint, talking about his future. A fellow actor, observing Clift on the set, noted: "He comes over strong and quiet and furthermore with a mysterious sensual quality that isn't there in real life. . . ."

Unlike some scenes in *Red River*, *A Place in the Sun*, and *From Here to Eternity*, which remain in the mind long after the rest of the film has faded from one's memory, there are no sublimely felt sequences in *Raintree County*. Audiences in 1957 (when the film was released) and now are curious to discover, with an understandable ghoulishness, the difference in Clift's looks between the scenes photographed before and after his accident. As Janet Maslin, writing in *The New York Times* on the occasion of the film's revival in June, 1978, observed: "In *Raintree County*, which alternates scenes of a young, vital Clift with a stiffly sad-faced, deeper-voiced man, there are moments when the actor attempts his old coquettishness with his new face, with agonizing results."

Johnny and Susanna just after their son's birth.

Johnny and Jim (Donald Losby) at bedtime.

Another major defect in the movie is its complete lack of humor. With the exception of Marvin's country bumpkin hijinks and Patrick's oratorical flourishes, *Raintree County* takes itself all too seriously, as though aware that it is supposed to be making a serious *statement.*

Filming began at MGM in April 1956. The studio was worried about Clift's drinking; Dore Schary insured the film—something that had never been done before—for $500,000 to cover any problems that might occur during production. *Raintree County* was about half completed when Clift's car accident halted photography for nine weeks. His mouth was twisted; a nerve had been cut in his left cheek so that side of his face was stiff; his nose had been broken; and his jaw was wired so that he now spoke as though through clenched teeth. In addition, Clift had lost two teeth and suffered a concussion. Although he was in constant pain and dosing himself regularly with codeine and an assortment of pills from his bottomless satchel, Clift felt he owed it to the film's company to return to *Raintree County*. It was too soon; his face was still swollen. His right profile was the least damaged so he was filmed from that angle as often as possible.

Clift had previously kept his drinking and his

work separate. Now he sometimes drank while filming and Dmytryk would tell him to quit for the day and sober up. What sustenance he did not derive from liquor and drugs, he got from a concoction of his own devising: "one quart of orange juice and one quart of skim milk for breakfast," was his description, "and for lunch more skim milk and three raw eggs broken into a glass. It keeps me from starving but [keeps me] concentrating, at the peak of tension, for the necessary eight hours."

Millard Kaufman, watching Clift on location in Danville, said: "He is under such tension as I've seen only in service during the war." The Kentucky State Guard stationed a couple of men at his house to keep the fans away. Twice, when Clift—in the throes of a nightmare—ran naked into the street in the middle of the night, they accompanied him home. Clift stumbled on a rock once and broke his toe in four places. As Kaufman observed: "Monty is the worst-coordinated man I've ever seen." Boyd Martin, a journalist for the *Boyle County Courier-Journal*, reported from the Danville location on August 19th: "Clift's recent automobile accident has done things to him. He hardly looks himself in repose. It is only when he plays a scene that you see he is

"Flash" Perkins (Lee Marvin), Johnny, and the Professor watch the war from a hilltop.

the same sensitive young actor who last appeared here with the Lunts in *There Shall Be No Night.*'' Clift was found at 1 A.M. in his Natchez, Mississippi hotel room in a semicoma with a cigarette stub between his fingers. A member of the company stated: "It had burned two of his fingers. He could have burned himself up."

Whatever the cost in mental anguish and pain, Clift kept himself going until filming was completed in October. MGM released the film in December 1957 with a great hoopla, roadshowing *Raintree County* at hard ticket prices for two performances a day. The promotion booklet for the New York invitational premiere effusively enumerated details about the cast, locations, the fact that it was the first movie shot in 65 millimeter (the negative is 65mm, but the prints were reduced to the standard 35mm), and the cost, naturally without mentioning Clift's accident.

The reviews were uniformly bad. William K. Zinsser of the *New York Herald Tribune* declared: "Director Edward Dmytryk could not have made a more sluggish drama if he projected magic lantern slides on the screen. His inability to cut, to frame a scene with any impact or beauty, to put a breath of life into his actors, is shocking.

"Elizabeth Taylor, as the frightened and pathetic wife, is the best of the actors. The other roles have less variety, as the players well realize. Clift is obliged mainly to comfort his wife, which he does with tenderness and insight. . . ."

Bosley Crowther, *The New York Times* critic, found that "the people here are vaporous creatures, without clear personalities or drives, pasted together out of patches of literary clichés and poetic sentiments. What is more, the natures of their problems are too sketchily presented to bring them out.

"Mr. Clift's idealist, for instance, is just a tag-along sort of good guy who falls into traps (such as marriage) and never shows a really positive attitude. . . . We might also mention the strange appearance and the aging, husky voice of Mr. Clift as other minor disturbances in this long picture."

Time's reviewer stated: "Montgomery Clift, talking through his nose and expressing sensitivity by seldom looking other cast members in the eye, jitters through the role of John Shawnessy. . . . Represented to be a kind of rustic 20-year-old Candide of pre–Civil War Indiana, 37-year-old Clift goes lurching through a swamp. . . ."

The *New York Post*'s Archer Winsten wrote: "The performances are of a piece, lusty, lively, and historically human. But Montgomery Clift disturbs because he doesn't look quite as he did before his accident. His performance seems to lack the extra something it used always to have. This slack is not completely taken up by Miss Taylor's unusually strenuous efforts, nor by the fine contribution of Lee Marvin. It is not that Clift lets the picture down. It is simply that he fails to lift and carry it on his own shoulders alone. And someone does need to carry it."

Although Clift later denounced *Raintree County* as a bore, a friend remembers seeing the film with him: "We were watching some *Raintree* rushes in the projection room one day, when all of a sudden a terrible, racking, death-rattle of a sob broke out of him. Even though it was his own performance he was watching, he was so moved he had to rush out of the room."

While making his next movie, *The Young Lions* (again with Dmytryk), Clift told a reporter: "What happened on *Raintree County*, my previous picture, was that the actors and the director, Edward Dmytryk, tried to lift its lousy script from soap-opera level. But we couldn't raise it more than a couple of inches—far from putting it into the realm of merit."

Today, twenty-two years later, the only elements which distinguish *Raintree County* are: the luscious score by Johnny Green (which, until its reissue on the Entr'acte label in 1976, was bringing up to $200); the fact that the detail in the Technicolor prints is still vibrant unlike many other MGM films made in Eastmancolor, which have all deteriorated; and the fact that Montgomery Clift sustained an accident during the filming which significantly changed his looks, the direction his career would take, and his life.

THE PICTURE YOU'VE HEARD SO MUCH ABOUT!
IT'S TREMENDOUS!

In the great tradition of Civil War Romance!

The picture that's the talk of the nation brings you memorable scenes of conflict and love!

M-G-M presents in MGM CAMERA 65

MONTGOMERY CLIFT • ELIZABETH TAYLOR • EVA MARIE SAINT

RAINTREE COUNTY

co-starring NIGEL PATRICK • LEE MARVIN

with ROD TAYLOR • AGNES MOOREHEAD • WALTER ABEL • JARMA LEWIS • TOM DRAKE
Screen Play by MILLARD KAUFMAN Associate Producer • Based on the Novel by Ross Lockridge, Jr.
Print by TECHNICOLOR® Directed by EDWARD DMYTRYK • Produced by DAVID LEWIS

GET MORE OUT OF LIFE ...GO OUT TO A MOVIE!

T H E A T R E

Mr. Plowman (Vaughn Taylor) tells his daughter Hope (Hope Lange) that it's all right to marry Noah *Akerman (Montgomery Clift) even though Noah is a Jew.*

Hope and Noah look at the neighborhood he must leave to go to war.

THE YOUNG LIONS

1958

20th Century-Fox. *Directed by* Edward Dmytryk. *Produced by* Al Lichtman. *Screenplay:* Edward Anhalt, *based on the novel by* Irwin Shaw. *Music:* Hugo Friedhofer. *Conductor:* Lionel Newman. *Director of photography:* Joe MacDonald. *Costumes:* Adele Balkan. *Set decoration:* Walter M. Scott and Stuart A. Reiss. *Sound engineers:* Alfred Bruzlin and Warren B. Delaplain. *Art directors:* Lyle R. Wheeler and Addison Hehr. *Assistant director:* Ad Schaumer. *Special photographic effects:* L. B. Abbott. *Makeup:* Ben Nye. *Hairstyles:* Helen Turpin. *Technical consultant:* Lt. Col. Allison. A. Conrad, USA. *Orchestration:* Edward B. Powell. *Executive wardrobe designer:* Charles LeMaire. *Locations:* Paris *and* Alsace-Lorraine. CinemaScope. 167 minutes.

CAST

Christian Diestl, Marlon Brando; *Noah Ackerman*, Montgomery Clift; *Michael Whiteacre*, Dean Martin; *Hope Plowman*, Hope Lange; *Margaret Freemantle*, Barbara Rush; *Gretchen Hardenberg*, May Britt; *Hardenberg*, Maximilian Schell; *Simone*, Dora Doll; *Sgt. Rickett*, Lee Van Cleef; *Françoise*, Liliane Montevecchi; *Brant*, Parley Baer; *Lt. Green*, Arthur Franz; *Private Burnecker*, Hal Baylor; *Private Cowley*, Richard Gardner; *Capt. Colclough*, Herbert Rudley; *Cpl. Kraus*, John Alderson; *Private Faber*, Sam Gilman; *Private Donnelly*, L. Q. Jones; *Private Brailsford*, Julian Burton; *John Plowman*, Vaughn Taylor; *Cafe manager*, Gene Roth; *German Major*, Stephen Bekassy; *German Colonel*, Ivan Triesault; *British Colonel*, Clive Morgan; *Maier*, Ashley Cowan; *Private Abbott*, Paul Comi; *Private Hagstrom*, Michael Pataki; *Burn*, John Gabriel; *Emerson*, Kendall Scott; *Acaro*, Stan Kamber; *Rabbi*, Robert Ellenstein; *Drunk*, Jeffrey Sayre; *Camp Commandant*, Kurt Katch; *Physician*, Milton Frome; *Bavarian*, Otto Reichow; *Colonel Mead*, Robert Burton; *General Rockland*, Harvey Stephens; *Brunette*, Anne Stebbins; *Young French girl*, Mary Pierce; *French woman*, Ann Codee; *French boy*, Christian Pasques; *Nurse*, Doris Wiss; *German waiter*, Alfred Tonkel; *Burgermeister*, John Banner; *Civilian*, Norbert Schiller; *Sergeant*, Henry Rowland; *Soldiers:* Art Reichle, David Dabov; *Lt. Emerson*, Wade Cagle; *P.F.C.*, Lee Winter; *Medic*, Nicholas King; *Draft board chairman*, Harry Ellerbe; *Draft board secretary*, Craig Karr; *Draft board member*, Michael Smith; *Druggist*, Voltaire Perkins; *Hatcheck girl*, Ann Daniels; *Bartender*, Alberto Morin; *Milkman*, George Meader; *Maid*, Joan Douglas; *Mailman*, Ed Rickard; *Bit players:* Joe Brooks, Hubert Kerns, Ann Paige.

Noah and Hope say goodbye at the front door as he leaves for the war.

In May 1957 Clift was due to start filming *The Young Lions* in Paris, but he never made it to the location. Instead he disappeared and was discovered in a cheap bordello in southern Italy. When he did report to the set, he was all right, but he complained to director Edward Dmytryk that the film had no similarity to Irwin Shaw's novel. (Surprisingly, Clift was working again with the man who had guided him through *Raintree County,* which he despised.) Clift and his co-star, Hope Lange, labored prodigiously on their scenes together, with Clift reinserting much of Shaw's dialogue into his role, at least. Shaw remembers that Clift was angry about the alterations that had taken place when the novel was undergoing its transformation, at the hands of Edward Anhalt, from book to movie. Shaw liked Clift's depiction of Noah and felt that ". . . he was superb—the best and the truest to the character I'd written."

There were other changes, not unlike the temporizing that had taken place when *From Here to Eternity* became a film. The screenplay was changed so that the issue of anti-Semitism in the Army was diluted. The Jewish soldier was still treated unfairly because of his religion, but the officer responsible was punished by the Army for his actions. The script was re-written three times before the Pentagon would agree to cooperate.

Years before, Clift had torn a picture of Franz Kafka from a magazine. He studied it almost daily and now, with its narrow, skeletal face and prominent ears, he based his portrait of Noah Ackerman on that picture. Clift starved himself down from 150 to 139 pounds, he distended his ears with putty, and slightly altered the shape of his nose.

More than a passing resemblance exists between Clift's Noah and the Robert E. Lee Prewitt of *From Here to Eternity.* They are both "hard heads," determined to be faithful to their own principles. There is a self-destructive resolve to go against the prevailing system, in both cases the Army. The chief difference is that Noah is not alone. Throughout the film, he is accompanied by his friend, Michael Whiteacre, who acts as a kind

Noah explains to Michael Whiteacre (Dean Martin) why he has to fight.

of mentor and sounding board. Also Noah gets the girl of his dreams; he even marries her.

The plot of *The Young Lions* follows three soldiers, the German Christian Diestl and the two Americans, the Jewish nobody Noah Ackerman and the Broadway showman, Michael Whiteacre. Michael and Noah meet at their induction into the Army and Michael asks Noah to a party. There Noah encounters Hope Plowman whom he marries shortly thereafter. The film then takes the two through basic training, where Noah is beaten by a quartet of his fellow G.I.s who are vicious anti-Semites. Eventually he earns their respect and they become buddies. The end of the war finds all three at a concentration camp where Michael and Noah are sickened at what the Nazi persecution has wrought. Christian, equally revolted, tries to escape the advancing Americans. The change from Shaw's novel is particularly evident in the character of Christian, who (in the guise of Marlon Brando) has become a kind of super-Aryan saint, the only man in Germany who did not know about the concentration camps. Diestl is followed from his triumphant entry into Paris with the German troops through the Nazis' defeat in North Africa to his death at Michael's hands—the only time he meets the other two.

The Young Lions is concerned with the difference in attitude toward war that the three men represent: Christian, who fights gallantly for the fatherland; Noah, who allows himself to be drafted; and Michael, who pulls strings to avoid induction. Each behaves out of conviction and each is diametrically opposed to the others. As a group they represent a cross section of the kind of men who fought in World War II.

The film is heavy-handed in its exposition, presenting Marlon Brando as a paragon of Aryan virtues who believes that Hitler brings hope to the Germans after years of economic chaos. Martin is the opposite side of the coin; he is the crass opportunist who would grab any chance to duck the Army. Eventually he sees the light and soldiers along with the rest of the men. Clift, the man in the middle, is the third side of this narrative triangle. At one point he tells Hope Lange, "I don't think I have a single opinion in the whole world," but he soon finds himself standing up for his rights and for principles he did not even know he had.

Director Dmytryk never misses an opportunity to underline the obvious. When Brando encounters May Britt (as the wife of his superior officer, Maximilian Schell), she is like a walking cata-

*Noah fights with one of his fellow recruits who hates
him because he is Jewish. One of the many brutal fights
Clift had on screen.*

*On the river bank. Noah helps one of his fellow soldiers
cross a river under fire.*

logue of Nazi vices: corrupt, hedonistic, and, of
course, doomed along with the rest of the deca-
dent Germans. Her suave voluptuary is played as
counterpoint to Brando's idealistic soldier: she
represents all that is base and destructive in the
German people while he is everything noble and
pure.

Dmytryk is less clumsy depicting the relationship between Clift and Lange. Their romance has
a natural feeling about it; they *belong* together.
Like Robert E. Lee Prewitt, Clift's Noah is ill-at-
ease socially. When he meets Lange, he babbles a
lot of half-baked nonsense to make an impression
on her, because, as he tells her later, ''I was
afraid that if I was myself you wouldn't look at
me twice.'' But she sees through his awkward
behavior to what is appealing and genuine in him.
When they become engaged, she takes him to see
her father (played by Vaughn Taylor) who has
never met a Jew before. They walk the streets of
her home town and Taylor gives Clift a lesson in
the importance of having roots, a tradition that
supports one. Taylor confesses that meeting Clift
is a jolt; he has made Taylor examine his principles, but he ends by accepting him. This lovely
brief sequence is so straight-forward and to the
point that it is at odds with the convoluted, extended construction of the rest of the film.

The Young Lions is virtually an inventory of
the Clift acting mannerisms, which, because of
the thought and care underlying his performance,
seems remarkably unmannered. He has a habit of
putting a cigarette in his mouth by folding his
hand over it and placing it on his lower lip. Here
he makes it part of Noah's demeanor, something
indigenously his. Clift bounces on his toes when
he walks; his eyes search Lange's face in the familiar expression of yearning. We have seen the
subtle changes in his features as he thinks, and
his method of grabbing a girl's face with both
hands to kiss her, but he makes them intrinsically
this character's. Lange visits Clift in prison
(where he has been sent for going AWOL), and
he presses his hand against the glass when they
say goodbye, in a gesture he will use in his last
film, *The Defector*. But one is never aware of
these as the artifices of a lazy actor; they are

Michael Whiteacre, Noah's wartime friend, brings him some clothes after Noah has lost his while crossing the river.

fresh and original, a sort of visual compensation for all the dialogue Clift cut out of his role. Typically, he pared his lines to the minimum needed to convey the essence of Noah Ackerman. The prison sequence is almost wordless; the emotional urgency of the young couple is communicated through looks and small gestures.

Clift was happy with his performance, justifiably so, as it is one of the few bright spots in an otherwise turbid and philosophically confused movie. When the film was released he was quoted as saying, ''I always expect the worst when I go to see any performance of mine. But I'm genuinely proud of Noah. . . . I've done some really good things in the picture—or, I should say, I think I've erred less than I have on any of the nine other pictures I made. I feel a great affinity for the character—a shy, introspective man of the people. I'm thirty-seven and Noah is twenty-five, but our characters met in this movie. Strange, isn't it? It's impossible to explain, but I couldn't have played Noah ten years ago.''

During the shooting Clift became friendly with Dean Martin who was, like Frank Sinatra in *From Here to Eternity*, making the switch from singing star to dramatic actor. He helped him with his lines and would crack Martin up when he saw him getting tense. Martin called Clift ''Spider'' because his gestures were so extreme, and persuaded the crew to make up a director's chair with a spider on the back instead of Clift's name.

Clift also ''adopted'' Hope Lange and leaned on her as he had on Liz Taylor and later on Lee Remick when they made *Wild River.* As with his other leading ladies, they probed their parts together and ran lines, with Clift converting Lange into a mother-figure and confidante.

Although they had no scenes together, a sense of strain developed between Clift and Brando. Brando would sneak onto the set to observe Clift filming and hide behind a camera. Clift got a glimpse of Brando once and told Dmytryk, ''Tell Marlon he doesn't have to hide his face when he watches me act.'' For his part, he watched Brando at work only twice.

Brando's part had been softened, idealized, so that he would agree to star in the film. Clift was furious at Brando's alterations in the character of Christian: ''Look at Marlon! He can't stand not being sympathetic, he's turning that bastard Nazi into a martyr.'' Brando wanted a very dramatic death scene, falling across a pile of barbed wire

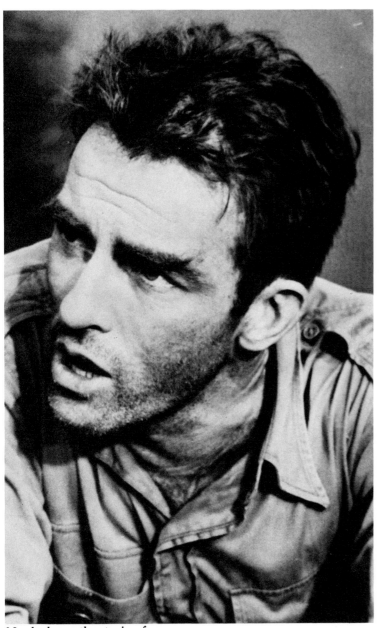

Noah shows the strain of war.

with his arms outstretched, a German Jesus. Clift threatened to walk off the picture if this ending was used and a compromise was effected: Martin shot Brando in the head. As a friend observed: "When Monty was around, there was room for only one Jesus Christ."

The reviewers liked *The Young Lions* when it was released, but over the years a critical reassessment has deemed it less than satisfying. The *Newsweek* commentator found it ". . . excellent film fare for [this reason]: Clift's, Brando's, and Schell's performances are virtually flawless, chiefly because they have insinuated into their roles all the character subtleties at the command of their imagination[s]."

Bosley Crowther of *The New York Times* found Brando a "corn silk blond [with a] German accent reminiscent of Weber and Fields. . . . As it happens, Mr. Brando makes the German much more vital and interesting than Montgomery Clift and Dean Martin make the Americans. Mr. Clift is strangely hollow and lackluster as the sensitive Jew. He acts throughout the picture as if he were in a glassy-eyed daze."

The *Time* critic said, "Clift does a wonderfully funny, touching job of suggesting the sort of man, simple and clear as a bell, who rings true when he takes a beating; but at times he overdoes the job and rambles off in a fugue of mannerisms."

Paul V. Beckley of the *New York Herald Tribune* noted: "Clift . . . is superb in his inarticulate anguish as he walks with his girl's father who has never met a Jew. He is no less so in the trying and brutal scenes in the training camp."

Editor Shrike (Robert Ryan) torments his employee Adam White (Montgomery Clift) by assigning him to write the lonelyhearts column.

LONELYHEARTS

1959

United Artists. *Directed by* Vincent J. Donehue. *Associate producer:* Walter Reilly. *Written for the screen and produced by* Dore Schary. *Based on the novella* Miss Lonelyhearts *by* Nathaniel West, *and the play by* Howard Teichmann. *Music:* Conrad Salinger. *Conductor:* Adolph Deutsch. *Director of photography:* John Alton. *Film editors:* Aaron Steele and John Faure. *Costumes:* Chuck Arrico and Angela Alexander. *Art director:* Serge Krizman. *Set decorator:* Darrell Silvera. *Production supervisor:* Joel Freeman. *Sound mixer:* John Kean. *Property master:* Max Frankel. *Makeup:* Abe Haberman and Frank Laure. *Assistant director:* Clarence Eurist. *Titles:* Pacific Titles *and* Art Studio. Schary Productions, Inc. 102 minutes.

CAST

Adam White, Montgomery Clift; *William Shrike,* Robert Ryan; *Florence Shrike,* Myrna Loy; *Justy Sargent,* Dolores Hart; *Fay Doyle,* Maureen Stapleton; *Pat Doyle,* Frank Maxwell; *Ned Gates,* Jackie Coogan; *Frank Goldsmith,* Mike Kellin; *Mr. Sargent,* Frank Overton; *Don Sargent,* Don Washbrook; *Johnny Sargent,* John Washbrook; *Mr. Lassiter,* Onslow Stevens; *Edna,* Mary Alan Hokanson; *Bartender,* John Gallaudet; *Jerry,* Jack Black; *Charlie,* J. B. Welch; *Smitty,* Charles Fawcett; *Bartender,* Charles Wagenheim; *Taxi driver,* Frank Richards; *Mrs. Cannon,* Dorothy Neumann.

Adam ponders the best way to comfort his readers.

Lonelyhearts was Dore Schary's first film as an independent producer after five years as head of production for MGM. United Artists put up the money with the proviso that Schary keep the budget under $1,000,000. The cast—Clift, Robert Ryan, Myrna Loy, Jackie Coogan and Dolores Hart—were all working for less than their usual salaries. Clift, who was now getting $200,000 per film, appeared in *Lonelyhearts* for something less than $100,000.

Lonelyhearts had been filmed once before, in 1933—just after Nathaniel West's novella was published—as *Advice to the Lovelorn,* a comedy-drama about murder with Lee Tracy as the columnist. The script Schary extracted from *Miss Lonelyhearts* has about as little to do with the cynical, desperate individuals West created as the earlier film. West's characters are represented as beyond redemption and, indeed, they are not saved. One of Schary's changes is to leave Lonelyhearts (called Adam White in the film) alive at the end. In the book, the gun carried by Doyle (the husband of the woman who has seduced Lonelyhearts) goes off, killing the writer. The film's Adam is an all-American boy, filled with compassion and understanding, who goes to work as an advice-giving newspaper columnist. His editor, Shrike, goads him into meeting one of his correspondents, a teary, self-pitying woman who makes a play for him. He leaves the paper and the town with his girl Justy, while Shrike prepares to make up with his longsuffering wife, Florence.

Schary had his own ideas about his film. He believed that the Lonelyhearts character should not be so obviously a Christ figure, suffering for the woes of mankind. In Schary's script there are no lines like these from the book: "I've got a Christ complex. I'm a humanity lover. All the broken bastards. . . ."

Shrike, who sarcastically calls Adam "Pilgrim," is evidently West's idea of a symbolic joke, as a shrike is a bird which impales its prey on thorns. Shrike browbeats his wife for her past adultery, and his employees by assigning them to journalistic jobs for which they have little aptitude or interest. But in Lonelyhearts' case, he is

*Adam asks Shrike for another assignment as Shrike's
sympathetic wife Florence (Myrna Loy) looks on.*

too well-suited to the job, a self-made martyr to
the pain of his readers. Schary played a game
with names too, calling his protagonist Adam
White: Adam, the first man and White as in pure,
instead of retaining West's Lonelyhearts as the
character's only identifier.

Clift's Adam is an ambitious, yet reticent, neo-
phyte. He wants a job on Ryan's paper and accepts the position as Lonelyhearts. It is a job he
is too well qualified for; he is too sympathetic,
too open to the suffering in people's lives. His
idealism, which manifests itself in statements
like, "If someone is in trouble, how can you not
take them seriously?" is contrasted with Ryan's
cynicism. Ryan is an all-purpose monster, hound-
ing his employee with remarks like, "I enjoy
seeing youth betray their promises," and torturing his wife for her infidelity.

Clift is earnest at the paper and charming with
Hart, who plays his girlfriend. He tells her, "I
love you because you love me and because
you're warm and soft." He is relaxed and natural
with her in comparison to his wound-spring attitude at the *Chronicle.* He is both nervous and
spirited with Ryan, fighting for his dignity while

Adam makes a date with one of his readers.

175

Lonelyhearts meets the reader, Fay Doyle (Maureen Stapleton).

*Adam tells his girl Justy (Dolores Hart) that his father
is in jail because he killed his mother.*

Adam tells Justy about his past.

doing the job to which Ryan has assigned him in order to humiliate him.

Mike Kellin, who played Clift's fellow reporter, said of Clift's acting, "There was a solidness about his work—a rocklike quality. . . . he revealed himself as powerfully as a scream."

Ryan, who only has to enter a scene to dominate it, is allowed to overact shamelessly, and all on one ornately voluble note. The part of Shrike is larger than life anyway—with its heavy-handed sarcasm—and, although Ryan creates interest in the role, he overpowers everyone he shares the screen with, especially Clift and Loy, whose methods of underplaying complement one another. In Loy's performance one sees her pain and her love, but also the strong streak of masochism that must prevail in a woman who takes so much abuse from her husband. Dolores Hart is sweet, unaffected, and strong; she is the perfect girl-next-door to Clift's open-souled innocent. Maureen Stapleton's performance is full of Meth-

ody tics, but she is affecting as the bitter, lonely Fay Doyle.

Visually, Vincent J. Donehue's direction is not particularly arresting. The newspaper has an authentically grubby look, but the cinematography is flat and one has the feeling that Donehue (directing his first movie) let the actors guide their own performances. The professionalism of the actors—the leads, Kellin, Stapleton, and Jackie Coogan—provides the impetus for the picture, not any dominating momentum on the part of Donehue.

As Myrna Loy said, "*Lonelyhearts* was a film which Monty always thought should never have been released as a commercial movie. . . . We all had great affection for that movie, which Monty thought would have done well concentrated in art houses." Such was not its fate; *Lonelyhearts* opened to medium reviews and a disappointing box office. It was quickly forgotten. Bosley Crowther of *The New York Times* liked the film,

"That's why I'm drinking—to release the iron grip" of conscience. Adam tells Shrike about his experiences with the fakes and frauds who write to Miss Lonelyhearts.

calling it "a clearly sincere endeavor to say something moving and profound about the danger of too-quick moral judgments and the virtue of loving thy fellow man," but felt that "there is no redemption for the sad sacks in *Lonelyhearts*, and the basic weakness of this picture is the attempt to pretend that there is." Crowther noted: "Mr. Clift is remarkably affecting as the troubled young lovelorn-columnist whose internal battles and soul-searchings get him into some terrible sweats." In his Sunday consideration of the film, Crowther said: "Mr. Clift runs a coruscating gamut of twitching agonies."

The *New York Herald Tribune*'s Paul V. Beckley said: "Although I confess Clift's young newspaper man banging out a 1,000-word lovelorn column daily with a humorless, listless, hurt devotion makes me a bit queasy, still the picture is a respectable, honest and coherent study of some emotional oddballs."

Adam explains to Justy why he's leaving town.

"Whatever's true, we'll find." Dr. Cukrowicz (Montgomery Clift) comforts the distraught Catherine Holly (Elizabeth Taylor).

SUDDENLY, LAST SUMMER

1959

Columbia Pictures. A Horizon (G.B.) Pictures Limited Production. *Directed by* Joseph L. Mankiewicz. *Produced by* Sam Spiegel. *Screenplay:* Gore Vidal and Tennessee Williams, *from the play by* Tennessee Williams. *Music:* Buxton Orr and Malcolm Arnold, *conducted by* Buxton Orr. *Director of photography:* Jack Hildyard. *Camera operator:* Gerry Fisher. *Photographic effects:* Tom Howard. *Editorial consultant:* William Hornbeck. *Film editor:* Thomas G. Stanford. *Assembly editor:* John Jympson. *Production designer:* Oliver Messel. *Art director:* William Kellner. *Set decorator:* Scott Slimon. *Sound:* A. G. Ambler and John Cox. *Sound editor:* Peter Thornton. *Continuity:* Elaine Schreyeck. *Assistant director:* Bluey Hill. *Construction manager:* Peter Dukelow. *Production supervisor:* Bill Kirby. *Makeup:* David Aylott. *Hairdresser:* Joan White. *Associate costume designer:* Joan Ellacott. Shepperton Studios, London. 114 minutes.

CAST

Catherine Holly, Elizabeth Taylor; *Dr. John Cukrowicz,* Montgomery Clift; *Mrs. Violet Venable,* Katharine Hepburn; *Dr. Hockstader,* Albert Dekker; *Mrs. Holly,* Mercedes McCambridge; *George Holly,* Gary Raymond; *Mrs. Foxhill,* Mavis Villiers; *Nurse Benson,* Patricia Marmont; *Sister Felicity,* Joan Young; *Lucy,* Maria Britneva; *Dr. Hockstader's secretary,* Sheila Robbins; *Young blond intern,* David Cameron; *Patient,* Roberta Woolley.

Catherine gives her opinion of Mrs. Venable and her dead son as Dr. Cukrowicz looks on.

A tense confrontation between victim and victimizer.

When Clift applied for insurance in New York to make *Suddenly, Last Summer* he was so tense and incoherent the doctors would not grant it. He tried again in London where the film was shot but he was obviously affected by the drugs he was taking and again the physicians would not pass him. Production on the film started without insurance for Clift.

Mercedes McCambridge, who played Elizabeth Taylor's mother in the picture, recalled: "Everyone connected with the film was going through some kind of personal anguish and it showed. Monty was in torment. I can see him now, with his shoulder blades hunched and pinched in that way of his. . . . there was always that terrible tension."

The unhappy ambiance of the movie itself had its counterpart in the lives of its performers. Katharine Hepburn was worried about Spencer Tracy; Elizabeth Taylor, recently married to Eddie Fisher, was still mourning Mike Todd; Albert Dekker died shortly after the film was completed; and the director, Joseph L. Mankiewicz, wore gloves to hide a skin disease.

The film these actors were involved in was a steamy blend of venality and insanity, derived by Gore Vidal from Tennessee Williams's one-act play. Mrs. Violet Venable will endow a new wing for a crumbling Southern insane asylum if its leading light, Dr. Cukrowicz, will perform a lobotomy on her niece, Catherine Holly. Catherine, who accompanied Mrs. Venable's son Sebastian to Spain last summer, came back with an unspeakable story detailing the circumstances of Sebastian's death. As it develops in Catherine's long climactic monologue, both she and Mrs. Venable before her were used as bait to attract boys to satisfy Sebastian's homosexual appetites. The boys avenged themselves on Sebastian for his cruelty by literally eating him alive.

The film belongs to the women; even McCambridge, in her relatively small role, has a showier part than Clift's. For extended sections of the picture he listens, occasionally asking a question or making a prescient observation. Clift is thoughtful, considering, and considerate. He refuses to be railroaded into performing a lobotomy on someone who needs to be rescued not from her own insanity, as it turns out, but from her aunt's madness. Clift's performance is virtually a catalogue of postures: crossed arms, bowed shoulders, and a furrowed brow.

Clift's best scenes are two with Taylor: when he first meets her there is so much compassion in his expression it is as though the real Montgomery Clift identifies with the pain and confusion of the screen Elizabeth Taylor. Later, just before her final cathartic speech he again reaches out to comfort and calm her, telling Taylor, "Give me all your resistance," and kissing her in a gesture that combines both eros and reassurance.

Considering the impassioned lines she has to utter, Hepburn's performance is quite restrained. Feeding insects to a carnivorous plant in a gesture that is a metaphor for the incestuous nature of the relationship with her son, or declaiming "Sebastian saw the face of God," Hepburn is all cool rationality and sweet reason. Violet Venable is an expert at getting her own way and Hepburn

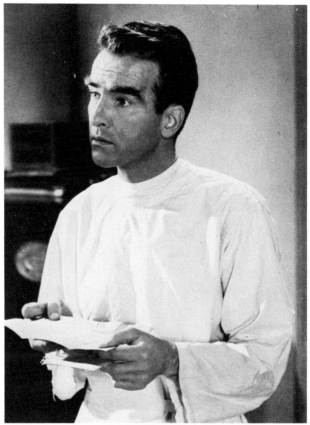

Dr. Cukrowicz and Mrs. Venable's letter offering to build a wing for the hospital if the doctor will lobotomize her niece.

Dr. Cukrowicz, Mrs. Venable, and Catherine's mother, Mrs. Holly (Mercedes McCambridge) talk over Catherine's problem.

Dr. Hockstader tries to convince Dr. Cukrowicz to operate.

Dr. Hockstader (Albert Dekker) tells Dr. Cukrowicz that an operation on Catherine means a new wing for the hospital.

"Give me all your resistance." Dr. Cukrowicz prepares Catherine for her cathartic remembrance.

makes her most outrageous actions seem those of a moderate and kind-hearted woman.

Taylor's performance is like an aria, rising toward the end to an emotional crescendo of desperation and release. And Taylor handles it expertly; she is ironical, self-deprecating, and self-aware. (Catherine Holly is also too obviously sane and healthy to convince the audience that she needs help. As written, Catherine is tormented because she is incarcerated in an asylum, surrounded by real madmen on the inside and an unsympathetic and grasping family on the outside.) For all that Catherine starts out as a neurotic babe-in-the-woods, she ends the film as a creature of startlingly mature perceptions, set free by her confession. Taylor makes the most of Williams's extravagant dialogue, attacking her part head-on, screaming the tortured declaration as though driven by inner demons.

Williams's play is constructed so that the women carry the dramatic weight, making Clift's role that of a receptacle for their neuroses. Calming Taylor, questioning Hepburn, or listening to McCambridge babble about her "poor baby," Clift's part is almost nothing more than a series of reaction shots. Presumably it was truncated not only because of the original material but because Mankiewicz was forced to shoot around Clift when he was unable to remember his lines or to concentrate on what was happening on the set. Clift reportedly was exhausted by the way Vidal had adapted Williams's material, breaking it into extended scenes with long monologues delivered by one or another of the actors. Clift could not manage the lengthy speeches and Mankiewicz had to cut his scenes into shorter takes. Both Mankiewicz and producer Sam Spiegel wanted to dump Clift but Taylor rushed to his defense. The pressures Clift experienced are evident in his performance. He has a slight lisp, he is somewhat glassy-eyed, and his face is almost immobile. When he made his next film, *Wild River*, with the more understanding director Elia Kazan, Clift was more relaxed and his facial problems were less evident.

Hepburn virtually adopted Clift and asked him to spend weekends with her at her country house near London. She tried to persuade Clift to give up drugs and liquor, to no avail. When *Suddenly* was done, Hepburn made a great point of assuring herself that it was, in fact, completely finished. "There's nothing more you're going to need me for?" she asked Mankiewicz. "No looping, no pick-up shots, no retakes?"

"I've got it all, Kate," Mankiewicz replied. "And it's great. *You're* great. What *is* all this?"

"I just want to leave you with this," Hepburn retorted. And with that, she spat in Mankiewicz's face.

She spat again on the floor of Spiegel's office. Later she emphasized, "I didn't spit just for Monty Clift! I spit at them for the way they treated *me*."

The critics respected *Suddenly, Last Summer*, but did not like it. Bosley Crowther of *The New York Times* said: "Montgomery Clift seems racked with pain and indifference as the brain surgeon." Paul V. Beckley of the *New York Herald Tribune* said: "Despite his soft, sympathetic eye, Clift does not strike me as a chap I'd want fiddling with my tonsils, let alone cutting a fantail entrance into my skull."

Taylor and Clift were set to star in *Reflections in a Golden Eye*, but Clift died before work could start on the film. Thus, *Suddenly, Last Summer* stands as their last film together.

Catherine tells what happened last summer. Dr. Cukrowicz, Mrs. Venable (Katherine Hepburn), Dr. Hockstader, George Holly (Gary Raymond), Mrs. Foxhill (Mavis Villiers), Nurse Benson (Patricia Marmont), and Mrs. Holly watch Catherine.

Chuck explains that when his job is done, he will leave and Carol shouldn't count too much on him.

WILD RIVER

1960

Twentieth Century-Fox. *Directed and produced by* Elia Kazan. *Screenplay:* Paul Osborne, *based on* Mud on the Stars *by* William Bradford Huie *and* Dunbar's Cove *by* Borden Deal. *Music:* Kenyon Hopkins. *Director of photography:* Ellsworth Fredricks. *Film editor:* William Reynolds. *Costumes:* Anna Hill Johnstone. *Set decoration:* Walter M. Scott *and* Joseph Kish. *Color consultant:* Leonard Doss. *Sound engineers:* Eugene Grossman and Richard Vorisek. *Art direction:* Lyle R. Wheeler and Herman A. Blumenthal. *Makeup:* Ben Nye. *Hair styles:* Helen Turpin. *Assistant director:* Charles Maguire. *Locations:* Charleston, Hiwassee River, Lake Chickamauga and Cleveland, Tennessee. CinemaScope and Eastmancolor. 115 minutes.

CAST

Chuck Glover, Montgomery Clift; *Carol Baldwin*, Lee Remick; *Ella Garth*, Jo Van Fleet; *F.J. Bailey*, Albert Salmi; *Hamilton Garth*, Jay C. Flippen; *Cal Garth*, James Westerfield; *Joe John Garth*, Big Jeff Bess; *Ben*, Robert Earl Jones; *Walter Clark*, Frank Overton; *Betty Jackson*, Barbara Loden; *Sy Moore*, Malcolm Atterbury; *Jack Roper*, Bruce Dern; *Barbara Baldwin*, Judy Harris; *Jim Baldwin, Jr.*, Jim Menard; *Mayor Tom Maynard*, Jim Steakley; *Mattie*, Patricia Perry; *Todd*, John Dudley; *Thompson*, Alfred E. Smith; *Winters*, Mark Menson.

*Chuck Glover (Montgomery Clift) talks to Cal Garth
(James Westerfield) about the easy life on his mother's island.*

Elia Kazan had visited Chattanooga, Tennessee in 1934–35 and had seen the Tennessee Valley Authority when it was just beginning. As he says: "I got an idea about a film twenty-five years before I actually made it.

"*Wild River* shouldn't be overcrowded, it shouldn't be full of effects, it should just be telling my own love affair with the New Deal; my love affair with the people in the back parts of this country—how much I love and admire them," the director-producer continues. "*Wild River* . . . was shot exactly where it should be, in Tennessee. And the river was there, and the trees were there, the fruit was there, and the people were there. Everything stimulated me and . . . each day we extracted some material from all that was there."

The movie that scenarist Paul Osborn abstracted from the novels of William Bradford Huie and Borden Deal and from Kazan's remembrances is basically a romance. Even at the start when Kazan uses newsreel footage to demonstrate the nature of the problem, he emphasizes the human dimensions rather than the physical hardships engendered by the annual floods. From

the moment Chuck Glover, the TVA administrator, steps off the bus to try to persuade Ella Garth to sell her property so that it can be inundated as part of the TVA's dam network, the film focuses on the personal dilemmas of the people affected, not the technological facilities which make the vast project possible. Ella Garth, a matriarch who rules her family and the blacks who work for her with an iron hand, is the lone holdout who insists on her right not to sell. Her widowed granddaughter, Carol, gradually becomes attracted to Glover. Glover and Carol are married, Ella Garth eventually succumbs, the land is flooded, and she dies shortly after moving into her new house.

Kazan stresses the impact of Glover's socially advanced notions—paying blacks the same wages as whites for the work they do for the TVA—on the town, and the townspeople's resistance which culminates in their beating Glover in an attempt to make him see the light. The director shows Ella Garth as proud and respected, the sort of pioneer woman who cleared the land from which she is being forced. Kazan admires her, but shows that she is an anachronism; she must be swept aside, literally and figuratively, if the project is to advance. But there is a certain amount of regret in her passing.

Kazan accentuates the purely romantic aspects of his story such as the attraction of opposites: city-bred Chuck Glover (Clift), the fine-spirited country girl, Carol (Lee Remick), and the fulfillment they find in one another. *Wild River* is one of Kazan's most sensuous films; one can feel Clift and Remick connect on screen. In one scene Remick returns to the house she lived in with her now-dead husband. Clift watches her closely for a reaction and grabs her shoulders when she seems overwhelmed by her memories. One can *see* him relate to his acting partner; one can see him *know* what the other is thinking. There is an incandescent glow even when his face is in shadow. Remick is equally impressive. She plays a strong-willed woman who makes up her mind to marry Clift and, when he vacillates, there is an urgency and a sensual heat she emits that fuses with Clift's yearning.

Still another sequence stands as one of the most sensuous scenes Clift ever enacted on screen. He and Remick sit in his car in front of her house, the leafless autumn trees contrasting with their warmth as she taunts him: "You can't get enough of me, right now, can you?" and he rejoins, spellbound, "I can't get enough of you." Clift's hand moves involuntarily, momentarily covering his eyes, so powerful is his longing. "Shut up, come here," he commands Remick; there is a craving, a need he has never recognized before. He knows he is losing control, but he is beginning to like the idea. They slip into what seem like relaxed patterns of behavior as their relationship deepens. "Yes, dear," Clift replies to a question from Remick; there is an easy, loving familiarity that makes their union inevitable and right.

Remick is so strong as an actress that she pulls Clift along with her. Not that he needs help as an actor, but the character he plays is not conceived of as a decisive individual. He needs help making up his mind, and Remick's forthright womanliness provides that impetus.

There is one scene that encapsulates and de-

Chuck tries to convince Ella Garth (Jo Van Fleet) to move out of her house so the TVA can flood the island.

Chuck, a townsman, and Ella Garth's sons outside the TVA office. (Unidentified player, James Westerfield and Jay C. Flippen.)

fines their alliance. A band of townsmen beat Clift up for his willingness to pay blacks and whites equally. Remick wades headlong into the battle, jumping on the ringleader's back, striking out at anyone who comes within reach. When it is over, Clift and Remick lying beaten on the damp ground, Clift looks at her admiringly and says, "You were wonderful up there." He continues, in a speech that seems to hearken back to all the beatings he received throughout his screen career; "You know, I wish someday I could win maybe one fight." Remick answers: "I don't care if you ever win a fight." It is Remick's combative, feisty nature that wins Clift over, as well as her femininity, for he proposes on the spot. But not without misgivings: "Marry me. I know I'll probably regret it and I'm sure you'll regret it." Remick gives him a small smile of triumph. She has won this difficult, aloof man at last.

Kazan remembers that Clift liked Remick a lot and that she was as strong off-screen as she was on; she supported him and he leaned on her. Remick recalls this quality in him: "He was very thin and all bones. And he was so sensitive. He was like a wounded bird—so vulnerable. He made me feel needed."

During the location shooting in Cleveland, Tennessee, Remick received news that her husband, producer-director William Colleran, had been seriously injured in a car accident. Remick hurried to California, but before she left Clift rushed to her side. "He was wonderful," Remick recalls, "because he had been through all that himself. . . . he was just like a rock."

But toward the end of the filming Clift was something less than reliable. Kazan had extracted a pledge from Clift that he would stay on the wagon for the duration of shooting. Kazan re-

Chuck and Carol (Lee Remick) fall in love.

members that he was "grateful for his effort to stay off the sauce." Nevertheless, "For the film I found him in terrible shape. I resisted getting Monty Clift because I didn't think he had the strength to do it. I wouldn't have taken him if I could've had Brando. Before the film he was drunk, all the time. I said to him: 'Monty, you must give me your word of honor that you won't take one drink during this production.' I can't work with a drunk. Well, by God, during the production he got better, stronger, more confident. And then, about three days before it was over, he came on the set one day, walked up to me to say hello, and fell flat on his face: he had been drinking again. His hair was getting thin and the make-up man had to put black in it. And he was terribly uncertain with girls—like a homosexual is. Lee Remick helped; it's why she comes out so strong in that film, like an aggressive woman who's made up her mind: 'He's going to marry me and . . . be the father of my children. I'm going to get him.' " Kazan recalls Clift with affection; he felt that he was "ideal to work with and stayed in the part always. He was always earnest, devoted, and terrible sensitive."

The chemistry generated by Clift and Remick was ably complemented by Kenyon Hopkins' sensuous score. From the first searing notes of the opening horn solo, the music comments on and enriches the visual detail with which Kazan has filled the movie. Kazan has made the town emblematic of the entire dramatic situation, a microcosm of the TVA's struggle to harness the flood water's potential to enrich the countryside rather than impoverish it. He has peopled the town with a cross section of back-woods types and good ole boys, with thoughtful men who can see the way the future must take them, and impetuous bigots who know only that their cherished way of life is changing. The film is impeccably cast, from Albert Salmi's down-home racist, to Frank Overton's well-meaning suitor to Lee Remick, and to Jay C. Flippen's practical, wry islander. But Jo Van Fleet's flinty curmudgeon strikes a slightly wrong note. She was forty at the time and playing a woman twice her age. The audience is aware that this is a *performance;* she

Walter Clark (Frank Overton) warns Chuck that the townspeople are out to beat him up for paying blacks the same wages as whites.

is almost too slow, too dignified, and too all-wise. She comes very close to being a caricature; the rest do not, but rather are types. *Wild River* is Elia Kazan's tribute to a time when many things seemed possible and some changed for the better.

The film was not well received when it was released (Kazan described it as a "catastrophe"), but over the years a critical reassessment has brought a more favorable view and renewed interest.

A.H. Weiler of *The New York Times* found *Wild River* a "strangely disturbing drama rather than a smashing study of a historic aspect of the changing American scene.

"Montgomery Clift is reserved but a mite more animated than he has been in recent films."

The *New York Herald Tribune* critic, Paul V.

Beckley, said: "The romantic interludes between Clift and Miss Remick tend to be a little stretched: here the shots grow somewhat redundant, the dialogue a bit torpid. Clift always seems to me a bit pained, even under circumstances that would leave most people happy. Moments of triumph do wrest a wry smile out of him, but his eyes remain fastened on some inner depression. If this unchanging mood fits remarkably well into some dramatic situations, there are times . . . his mopy inarticulateness makes me a trifle impatient, even nervous."

"Kazan's direction produces here some of the more exciting performances of the year. In addition to Miss Van Fleet's portrait of the old lady, which is nothing less than magnificent, there are Miss Remick's distraught young widow . . . Albert Salmi's bluff filling-station operator . . . and Jay C. Flippen and James Westerfield as two of Miss Van Fleet's sons."

Carol welcomes Chuck to her house.

190

Perce Howland (Montgomery Clift) meets Roslyn Taber (Marilyn Monroe) and Gay Langland (Clark Gable) on the way to the rodeo.

THE MISFITS

1961

United Artists. *Directed by* John Huston. *Produced by* Frank E. Taylor. *Assistant producer:* Edward Parone. *Screenplay:* Arthur Miller. *Music:* Alex North. *Director of photography:* Russell Metty. *Film editor:* George Tomasini. *Wardrobe:* Shirley Strahm. *Set decorator:* Frank McKelvy. *Sound:* Philip Mitchell and Charles Grenzbach. *Second unit photography:* Rex Wimpy. *Second unit director:* Tom Shaw. *Art directors:* Stephen Grimes and William Newberry. *Assistant directors:* Carl Beringer, John Gaudioso and Thomas P. Shaw. *Production manager:* C.O. Erickson. *Script supervision:* Angela Allen. *Special effects:* Cline Jones. *Makeup:* Frank La Rue, Frank Prehoda and Allan Snyder. *Hairstyles:* Agnes Flanagan and Sydney Guilaroff. *Wrangler:* Billy Jones. *Masseur:* Ralph Roberts. *Titles:* George Nelson and Co., Inc. United Artists/Seven Arts. 124 minutes.

CAST

Gay Langland, Clark Gable; *Roslyn Taber*, Marilyn Monroe; *Perce Howland*, Montgomery Clift; *Isabelle Steers*, Thelma Ritter; *Guido*, Eli Wallach; *Old Man in Bar*, James Barton; *Church Lady*, Estelle Winwood; *Raymond Taber*, Kevin McCarthy; *Lester, young boy in bar*, Dennis Shaw; *Charles Steers*, Philip Mitchell; *Old Groom*, Walter Ramage; *Young Bride*, Peggy Barton; *Fresh Cowboy at Bar*, J. Lewis Smith; *Susan, at train station*, Marietta Tree; *Bartender*, Bobby LaSalle; *Man in bar*, Ryall Bowker; *Ambulance Attendant*, Ralph Roberts.

Perce surveys the livestock.

"Coming out!" Perce begins his ride.

Although *The Misfits* gives Montgomery Clift billing equal to that of Marilyn Monroe and Clark Gable, it is predominantly their picture. When Gable died twelve days after completing the film *The Misfits* was—naturally enough—publicized as "Gable's last film!" and it proved to be Monroe's as well. In fact, of the five principals—who include Eli Wallach and Thelma Ritter—only Wallach was alive eight years later. John Huston's direction, efficient and illuminating as it was, matters less than the chemistry generated by the stars.

Arthur Miller's threefold message—that men had better learn to adapt to changing times and mores; that each person is alone; and that the innocent are blessed by their sensitivity and openness—is a rather fragile one to support all the heavy philosophical and symbolic weight he attaches to it.

The story concerns three modern cowboys (Gable, Clift, and Wallach as Gay Langland, Perce Howland, and Guido) who prefer eking out a chancy living at rodeos and odd jobs to working steadily. They meet up with a sad-eyed, newly divorced "interpretive dancer" (Monroe as Roslyn Taber) and her landlady (Thelma Ritter as

Isabelle Steers). The five pal around for a while; then the men—each of whom has immediately fallen in love with Monroe—and the girl take to the hills to go mustanging, selling the wild horses to contractors for dog food. The girl, aghast at the fate of the horses, pleads with the men to free them. After a conflict that is both physical and moral, they agree that the five horses they have captured are not worth the trouble and let them go. Monroe and Gable leave the desert together; the implied resolution is that they will try to make some kind of life with one another.

In a sense *The Misfits* is a violation of the Western myth, demonstrating as it does that men are not free, that they are bound to their society despite their claims to the contrary. In spite of the three men's oft-repeated statement that ''Anything's better than wages,'' selling the mustangs is a way of working for a salary and Gable's inability to see this is as hypocritical as Monroe's refusal to consider where the meat she eats comes from.

Gable, unexpectedly virile (in view of his subsequent demise), is the film's most interesting character. As a man who has difficulty fitting himself into the changed and increasingly complex twentieth century, he gives a carefully nuanced performance, full of regret and defeat but also alive with bravado and tenderness. He is confused, discomfited; he has lost the only way of life that had any meaning for him. Gable grasps at Monroe as a kind of corporeal last straw. Through her innocence, he is able to celebrate again the unfettered life.

Marilyn Monroe is half enchanting, half exasperating. She is very much the focal point of Miller's screenplay, but one can get very tired of hearing the men worshiping her: ''When you smile, it's like the sun coming up.'' ''I bless you, girl.'' ''You have the gift of life.''

Monroe is best in her quiet moments. Although her face has a way of lapsing into a series of tics, she is radiant with love for Gable or delighting in nature, charming as a befuddled naïf, sometimes remarkably observant, and often weepy and over-sentimental.

Clift runs into the other four as they are on

Perce, bandaged because of his fall in the rodeo, flirts with Roslyn.

''How did you get such trust in your eyes?'' Perce and Roslyn get better acquainted outside the bar.

193

Roslyn comforts Perce after a fall.

their way to look for a third cowboy to help catch the mustangs. He is sitting by a phone booth, waiting for his long distance call home to come through. They exchange greetings, the phone rings, and Clift encloses himself in the booth. Opening and shutting the door, shifting position, explaining to his mother that he was going to buy her a present but needed a new pair of boots himself, Clift chews his lip and ends by saying into a dead receiver, "I love you too, Mom."

Against such formidable star wattage as that generated by Gable and Monroe, Clift's quiet inward-looking performance, coupled with the fact that he does not appear until the film is one-third over, makes less impact. But he is riveting in this painful introductory scene. One feels the lines of family attachment extended hopefully for contact and withdrawn when the other person fails to respond.

Clift's Perce Howland prides himself on giving rodeo patrons their money's worth. "I don't fake nothin'!" he exclaims. But he is punch drunk; he

Perce and Gay during the mustang roundup. Roslyn and Guido (Eli Wallach) in the cab.

has used himself up the way the overenthusiastic cowboys have demolished the mustang herds. Now there is nothing left but a few more prizes to win—Clift has failed completely at the rodeo— and a few more bones to break.

Clift carefully and, some who saw the shooting say, self-consciously, mastered the wrangler's habits of working with their ropes, rubbing grease into their chaps and the other skills of the professional rodeo circuit rider. He accompanied his stunt double, Dick Pascoe, to a Pocatello, Idaho rodeo so that he could absorb the atmosphere and ''business'' which would add authenticity to his performance.

Clift was rope-burned, kicked, and slashed during his action scenes. Hundreds of feet of film were exposed before anyone noticed that he was not wearing gloves for his roping scenes. Clift's hands looked like raw meat, but he had to continue without gloves so his shots would match. Clift was cut on the bridge of his nose by a bull's horn while helping a cowboy climb onto a brahma bull during the rodeo. Coincidentally, the script called for Perce to cut himself in the same place falling from a bucking horse.

Gable was furious at Clift because he felt Clift had stolen a scene from him by lighting a cigarette in back of him while he was speaking. But when Gable saw the rushes he acknowledged he was wrong, saying: ''That faggot is a hell of an actor!'' Gable was fascinated by Clift's talent and, when he wasn't on call himself, would come to the set to watch Clift work.

All three men are busted gallants who try to connect with their blonde waif. From Clift's ''How do, ma'am'' to his besotted ''Are you lookin' for a fight?'' when a cowpoke pats Monroe's derriere during the famous paddle-ball sequence, he is trying to make an impression.

Clift's most powerful scene is a quiet one with Monroe outside a bar. He lies with his head in her lap and grieves for his lost past: his mother's defection, the insult when his stepfather offered him wages on the ranch *he* was supposed to inherit (with more than a hint of an Oedipal motif here), and the girl he lost to his pals when he was out cold after the last rodeo. Clift is reaching out

Perce lassos a mustang.

Perce looks over the mustangs.

to Monroe, hopeful that she'll respond, but knowing she is already involved with Gable. "How did you get such trust in your eyes?" he asks her from his position on the bottle-strewn ground, the bandage around his head beginning to come loose. He is flattering her with truth.

Clift's last significant act follows his earlier remark: "Fifteen horses—kinda hits me sideways." There *are* too few mustangs to be profitable and the men, despite their scorn of working for wages, know it. Clift jumps into the cab of the truck and drives off to cut the ropes holding the horses to their used-tire anchors. Monroe bumps

along in the cab beside Clift. Sick over what has happened and what she has had to face, not only about these men and their actions, but about herself, she stays in the truck.

Clift's real-life accident, interestingly, works to his advantage in *The Misfits*. His mouth is strained, as though with the ache of too many broken bones and thoughts that are growing hazy. He is thin to the point of illness, and here the familiar stooped posture has him bent into a C–shape. When he dances, he is stiff, graceless; his body cannot respond to the music's demands.

Clift told W.J. Weatherby* that after his accident, "I had to try to master myself, find the real me outside my looks which people were hung up on and so was I." In *The Misfits* Clift does go beyond his looks to tenderness, naivete, and to giving a fully rounded performance full of remembered, unassimilated pain and guileless hope for the future. The reviews of *The Misfits* were mixed. Paul V. Beckley of the *New York Herald Tribune* said: "*The Misfits* is so distinctly American nobody but an American could have made it. The whole picture rouses that sense of contact that can only come when you know everybody that had a hand in it means just what he says, is dealing out an ordered, passionate response to the shock of life.

"And can anyone deny that in this film these performers are at their best. You forget they are performing and feel that they *are*."

But Bosley Crowther of *The New York Times* thought: "Characters and themes do not congeal. There is a lot of absorbing detail in it, but it doesn't add up to a point. Mr. Huston's direction is dynamic, inventive, and colorful. But the picture just doesn't come off."

Roger Angell, writing in the *New Yorker*, said that *The Misfits* was "almost continuously absorbing," yet "a dramatic failure of considerable dimensions." The screenplay was "obtrusively symbolic and so sentimental as to be unintelligent."

*Conversations with Marilyn, Mason/Charters Publishers, Inc., New York, 1976.

The horror of remembering what the Nazis did to him.

JUDGMENT AT NUREMBERG

1961

United Artists. *Directed and produced by* Stanley Kramer. *Associate producer:* Philip Langner. *Screenplay:* Abby Mann, *from his original story.* *Director of photography:* Ernest Laszlo. *Camera Operator:* Charles Wheeler. *Music:* Ernest Gold. *Song:* "Lili Marlene", *music by* Norbert Schultze, *lyrics by* Hans Leip *and* Thomas Connor. *Song:* "Liebeslied", *music by* Ernest Gold, *lyrics by* Alfred Parry. *Film editor:* Frederic Knudtson. *Marlene Dietrich's costumes:* Jean Louis. *Costumes:* Joe King. *Sound engineer:* James Speak. *Sound editor:* Walter Elliott. *Music director:* Art Dunham. *Assistant to the director:* Ivan Volkman. *Script supervisor:* Marshall Schlom. *Makeup:* Robert J. Schiffer. *Set decorator:* George Milo. *Production manager:* Clem Beauchamp. *Production designer:* Rudolph Ster-

nad. *Opticals:* Pacific Title. *Company grip:* Morris Rosen. *Assistant company grip:* Martin Koshuk. *Propery master:* Art Cole. *Chief gaffer:* Don L. Carstensen. *Casting:* Stalmaster-Lister Co. *Cost accountant:* Joe King. *German crew:* Richard Richtsfeld, L. Ostermeier, Lyn Hannes, Pia Arnold, Albrecht Hennings, Laci von Ronay, Hubert Karl, Egon Haedler, Frank Winterstein, Richard Eglseder and Hannelore Winterfeld. *Location:* Nuremberg, Germany. 190 minutes.

CAST

Judge Dan Haywood, Spencer Tracy; *Ernst Janning*, Burt Lancaster; *Col. Tad Lawson*, Richard Widmark; *Mme. Bertholt*, Marlene Dietrich; *Hans Rolfe*, Maximilian Schell; *Irene Hoffman*, Judy Garland; *Rudolf Petersen*, Montgomery

*Before the trial. Col. Tad Lawson (Richard Widmark)
offers Rudolf Petersen (Montgomery Clift) a cigarette
as Major Abe Radnitz (Joseph Bernard) looks on in a
scene cut from the film.*

Clift; *Capt. Harrison Byers*, William Shatner;
Senator Burkette, Edward Binns; *Judge Kenneth
Norris*, Kenneth MacKenna; *Emil Hahn*, Werner
Klemperer; *General Merrin*, Alan Baxter; *Werner
Lammpe*, Torben Meyer; *Judge Curtiss Ives*, Ray
Teal; *Friedrich Hofstetter*, Martin Brandt; *Mrs.
Halbestadt*, Virginia Christine; *Halbestadt*, Ben
Wright; *Maj. Abe Radnitz*, Joseph Bernard; *Dr.
Wieck*, John Wengraf; *Wallner*, Howard Caine;
Schmidt, Paul Busch; *Perkins*, Bernard Kates;
Pohl, Otto Waldis; *Dr. Geuter*, Karl Swenson;
Mrs. Lindnow, Olga Fabian; *Mrs. Ives*, Sheila
Bromley; *Elsa Scheffler*, Jana Taylor; *Spectator*,
Joseph Crahan.

Judgment at Nuremberg, which the *New
Yorker* critic called a "judicial Grand Hotel" be-
cause it was so loaded with stars, boasts Spencer
Tracy, Richard Widmark, Maximilian Schell,

Marlene Dietrich, Judy Garland and Burt Lancaster in its cast. The film is an almost minute-by-
minute detailing of the charges against four German judges who abandoned their principles and
passed pro-Nazi laws in the 1930s. The witnesses
parade to the stand; Widmark, as the American
prosecutor, and Schell, as the German defense
attorney, spar; the American judges ask questions; the accused judges look uncomfortable;
and the process is repeated. There are a few
breaks in this routine as the chief judge, Tracy,
attempts to "understand" the German people by
strolling around the city or talking to Dietrich, the
widow of a German general. But the action is
predominantly confined to the courtroom. To
break up the static quality of the testimony, director Stanley Kramer employs a constantly
moving camera which revolves in 360° pans
around the witnesses.

Kramer offered Clift $50,000 for the seven-
minute part of Rudolf Petersen, the sterilized
mental incompetent, but MCA advised him not to
take it for fear of setting a precedent (Clift had
just gotten $200,000 for *The Misfits*). Kramer
avoided Clift's agents and bargained directly with
the star; Clift signed for the minimum plus
expenses.

Clift had been drinking and was jittery when he
reported for filming in Hollywood, but he did not
want to dry out just to play a scene that would
last five days. (It took ten because Tracy became
ill.) He appeared on the set with a particularly
awful haircut; he believed Petersen would have
his hair cut before such an important occasion.

Clift's testimony is agonizing. From the moment he takes the stand—diffident, awkward, shy
—he is Rudolf Petersen, the man from whom one
of the essential functions of mankind has been
cruelly taken. Clift's shaking hands and his no-
longer-beautiful face are painful to watch and
perfect for the role. As he gets deeper into his
statement, he begins visibly to lose control. To
demonstrate that he is mentally incompetent,
Schell asks him to take a test which he failed
when he was judged defective: composing a sen-
tence from the words, "hare, hunter, field." Clift
falters, his hand flies to his face in a familiar ges-

Clift and Maximilian Schell go over the script.

ture, his eyes wander, and he shifts in his seat. It is original and terrifying, but it comes close to being a performance that Clift pieced together out of *schtik* he has done before.

One can hear Clift's breathing as he struggles to deal with the question; he frowns, scratches his eyebrow, drops, then raises his voice. He makes a fist, then splays his fingers on the side of the witness box, as though motion will help him think. But Rudolf Petersen *is* mentally incompetent, a situation Clift's carefully nuanced performance makes all too credible and poignant.

At the beginning, Clift speaks slowly and softly; later he yells his anguish: ''Since that day I've been half I've ever been!'' His lower lip trembles as he tries to keep himself from crying. Clift's face is contorted and he buries his chin in the lapel of his jacket, his body twisted in his chair. But the most deeply affecting moment occurs when Clift denies that his mother was feeble-minded. He takes her picture from his pocket

In the witness box: Clift and Schell confer before shooting.

Rudolf Petersen listens to the translation.

and shows it to Tracy, several feet away behind his judge's bench. "I want that you tell me—was she feeble-minded—my mother? Was she!" he implores Tracy. In the few minutes he is on screen, Clift takes *Judgment at Nuremberg* out of the realm of the star-studded epic and makes it a small, personal drama.

Unfortunately, moments like this happen too seldom in the film, which is afflicted with a kind of moralistic elephantiasis, the result of scriptwriter Abby Mann's desire to get every morsel of encyclopedic documentation on the screen. There are other isolated and effective scenes and performances, notably Schell's fervent defense of his countrymen (in a role for which he won an Academy Award) and Tracy's foxy grandpa of a judge. Judy Garland has a role almost as small as Clift's, that of a German Hausfrau whose Jewish friend had involved her in a case of "racial contamination" in the thirties. Clift hung around the set after his appearance and observed the other actors. Stanley Kramer recalls: "Once he

watched Judy Garland do a scene and he huddled in a corner like a puppy dog, weeping. When it was over he came up to me and said, 'She didn't do it right!' "

Clift had difficulty remembering his lines, but Tracy told him to play just to him; forget the lines and "Do it into my eyes and you'll be magnificent." When Clift had gotten through the last of four takes—each one different—Tracy hurried over from the bench and embraced Clift, praising him for his profound artistry. Clift received an Oscar nomination as best supporting actor for that performance. It was his fourth, and the last one he ever got.

The critics were divided on the issue of whether or not *Judgment at Nuremberg* had merit. Bosley Crowther of *The New York Times* admired the film and its performers: Tracy acted "superbly"; Garland made Irene Hoffman "amazingly real"; Schell performed "masterfully"; only Lancaster "played weakly." "They have one German witness," Crowther said,

Clift rehearses in the witness box.

Rudolf Petersen implores the judge, "I want that you tell me—was she feeble-minded—my mother?"

"played touchingly by Montgomery Clift, testify to his sterilization on the order of one of the judges on trial."

Time's reviewer was more critical: "Director Kramer . . . has crudely mismanaged both actors and camera and has carelessly permitted several reels of fat to accumulate around the movie's middle. *Judgment* is on the whole just one more courtroom meller and an awful long meller at that."

The *Show* critic said: "Montgomery Clift and Judy Garland, as two of the witnesses, and Burt Lancaster, as a defendant, far surpass anything I have seen them do before."

Dilys Powell, writing in the *London Sunday Times*, reported: "I am not forgetting all the other fine performances when I say that Montgomery Clift's portrait of this sad, simple, vulnerable human being is the highlight of the film."

Sigmund Freud (Montgomery Clift) observes an experiment in hypnosis.

Sigmund Freud hypnotizes Carl von Schlosser (David McCallum).

FREUD

1962

Universal-International. *Directed by* John Huston. *Produced by* Wolfgang Reinhardt. *Associate producer:* George Golitzin. *Screenplay:* Charles Kaufman, Wolfgang Reinhardt, *story by* Charles Kaufman. *Music:* Jerry Goldsmith. *Music supervision:* Joseph Gershenson. *Electronic music sequence:* Henk Badings. *Director of photography:* Douglas Slocombe. *Film editor:* Ralph Kemplen. *Art director:* Stephen B. Grimes. *Title background and forward paintings:* James Leong. *Sound engineers:* Basil Fenton-Smith and Renato Cadueri. *Dubbing editor:* Gerald Hambling. *Assistant directors:* Ray Gosnell, Jr. and Laci von Ronay. *Production manager:* C.O. Erickson. *Costume designer:* Doris Langley Moore.

Makeup: Robert Schiffer and Raimund Stangl. *Technical consultant:* Earl A. Loomis, Jr., M.D. *Medical consultant:* David Stafford-Clark. *Camera operator:* Desmond Davis. *Script supervisor:* Angela Allen. *Casting consultant:* Robert Lennard. *Cooperation:* Musée Massena, Nice, France. *Locations:* Munich and Vienna. 139 minutes.

CAST

Sigmund Freud, Montgomery Clift; *Cecily Koertner,* Susannah York; *Dr. Joseph Breuer,* Larry Parks; *Martha Freud,* Susan Kohner; *Dr. Theodore Meynert,* Eric Portman; *Frau Ida Koertner,* Eileen Herlie; *Professor Charcot,* Fernand Le-

Freud's first attempt to hypnotize Cecily. Dr. Breuer looks on.

Dr. Breuer (Larry Parks) explains his theories of hypnosis to Freud.

doux; *Carl von Schlosser*, David McCallum; *Frau Freud*, Rosalie Crutchley; *Jacob Freud*, David Kossoff; *Jacob Koertner*, Joseph Fürst; *Babinsky*, Alexander Mango; *Brouhardier*, Leonard Sachs; *Wilkie*, Allan Cuthbertson; *Nora Wimmer*, Moira Redmond; *Magda*, Maria Perschy; *Frau Bernays*, Elizabeth Neumann-Viertel; *Mitzi Freud*, Ursula Lyn; *Dr. Guber*, Victor Beaumont; *Student doctor*, Manfred Andrea; *Bit players:* Anita Gutwell, Charles Regnier, P.V. Pollnitz, Hr. Rabb, Friedrich V. Lederbur, J. Swarbrick, M.V. Eden, M. Haufler, A. Vanderhyde, F. Moyne, M. Herbst, Voigt, Vogel, E. Roth, Ol Abdou, J. Holzleitner, U. Emmer, S. Brecht, Y. Maralon, A.V. Loeben, Dr. Ohrenstein, E. Lenkers, Cutty, A.P. Wolff, B. Taubenberger, M. Schanauer, Stefan Schnabel, Mrs. Marks, M. Freeman, G. Woodfine.

During World War II, director John Huston made a short film for the Army about soldiers who had broken down under fire, called *Let There Be Light.* He had never forgotten his experience with the psychically crippled veterans, and in 1957 Jean-Paul Sartre had signed to write a screenplay about the father of modern psychoanalysis, Sigmund Freud. The lengthy script that Sartre turned in was unusable as far as Huston was concerned; it was much too concerned with Freud's theories on sex and perversion.

The plot (taken from Sartre's work by the film's producer, Wolfgang Reinhardt, and Charles Kaufman) compresses the many years it took Freud to evolve his psychoanalytic theories into what seems like a few months. Almost every neurotic symptom imaginable conveniently manifests itself in one (composite) patient, Cecily Koertner. She is sexually repressed, hysterical, and fixated on her father. And so Freud goes to work, developing one hypothesis after another. An early case, written so clumsily that it disguises the fact that the patient is a homosexual, involves Carl von Schlosser, who covers a female dressmaker's dummy with his father's Hussar's tunic. Little is seen of Freud's home life with his wife, Martha, whom he alternately discusses his theories with and patronizes, saying, when she

Freud tries to relieve Cecily Koertner's (Susannah York) hysterical symptoms.

reads one of his papers: "Martha, that's not for your eyes." The film is interrupted by Huston's voice, ponderously narrating what is already evident on screen, and by a few of Freud's dreams, which graphically depict the secrets of the unconscious. He awakens from these formulating new doctrines with the speed of a patent medicine man selling snake oil: "Reversal, yes!" or "Could it be that dreams are ideas escaping from repression in disguise?" *Freud* is a conscientious attempt to understand both the man and his ideas, but the theme is too complicated and the film, which is nothing but a succession of one-to-one consultations between doctor and patient (which do not lend themselves to illustration) is ultimately too dull.

Clift was suffering from a thyroid condition when he agreed to make *Freud*; he had difficulty remembering his lines, and an accident on the set revealed the fact that he was suffering from cataracts. But he was too much of a pro to let his private agony affect his portrayal. His Freud is even more restrained than his usual style of underplaying permits. And, paradoxically, the one aspect of his performance that Huston empha-

Freud tries to remember his own past with the help of his mother's snake bracelet.

Freud searches for the causes of the Oedipus complex using his child's toy train to jog his memory.

sizes is his eyes. Cinematographer Douglas Slocombe has carefully lit Clift's eyes to help him show his concern, his compassion, and his burning intensity over the revelations that come to him as he formulates his theories. Freud was thirty when the action covered here took place. Clift is forty-one; his hair is thinning and his beard is flecked with gray. But Freud's beard is effective makeup for Clift's somewhat damaged looks. And he was, at last, stepping into the character roles he had so long wanted to do.

Clift was enthusiastic about the role, declaring: "It is a very long part and one which might have become wearying if I lost hold of it. I have to give it electricity all the time. I try to hold Freud in focus as much as possible."

The spirit of truth may shine from Clift's face, but the words he speaks are too glib. "There must be sexuality in childhood, even in infancy!" he exclaims after an encounter with Susannah York, who plays Cecily. The audience is even

Martha tries to understand her husband's theories.

Freud discusses his work with his wife Martha (Susan Kohner).

treated to the first Freudian slip as Cecily substitutes "prostitute" for "Protestant," and we see Freud working his way through his own neurosis as he acknowledges his former Oedipal feelings toward his mother. Through all of this, Clift works hard to let the essence of Freud's search for enlightenment emerge, using his eloquent hands in economical but expressive gestures and regarding his patients intently, as though willing them to unfold their secrets to him.

Susannah York is admirably controlled considering the hysterical causes of the symptoms she must embody. Susan Kohner is warmly sympathetic in the small role of Martha, and Larry Parks is staunch and supportive as Freud's mentor, Dr. Joseph Breuer.

Clift believed he would be nominated for an Oscar for this performance. He told his brother, Brooks: "I hope I get the Academy Award. I've never won. I've been nominated four times. One always wants it 'cause it increases your salary or

something. But this time I want it. I'd *love* it." He was not even nominated.

The critics were divided on the subject of *Freud,* subtitled *The Secret Passion* at the time of its release to give it box office appeal.

The New Yorker reviewer called the casting of Clift as Freud a "fatal misstep. That sombre young Viennese Jew of the eighteen-eighties . . . has simply nothing to do with a nice young American of the nineteen-sixties. Despite the black-beard and fancy dress he has donned, Mr. Clift is a boyish Yankee. . . ."

Penelope Gilliatt, writing in the *London Observer,* said: "Montgomery Clift as Freud, tapping his teeth with a pencil as he bounds swiftly through the work of a life-time and stomping about on short strolls while he sorts out the Oedipal business, belongs here only because he has a pair of freezing basilisk eyes, which is what commercial filmmakers feel visionaries should have."

Bosley Crowther, in *The New York Times,*

Freud conquers his fear of entering the Jewish cemetery where his father is buried.

stated: "Montgomery Clift . . . is a bit too dependent on a stark look and an attitude of reluctance to be a literal representation of Freud, but he does get across a burning notion of a sensitive, emotionally anguished man."

Freud's daughter Anna, writing from London, repudiated the film: "In our opinion neither historic nor scientific truth about the person, Sigmund Freud, or his work, can be or is conveyed by the film, contrary to the pretensions made by its producers."

CIA agent Adam (Roddy McDowall) recruits Professor
James Bower (Montgomery Clift).

THE DEFECTOR

1966
Warner Bros.-Seven Arts. *Directed and produced by* Raoul Levy. *Executive producer:* Julien Derode. *Screenplay:* Robert Guenette, Raoul Lévy, Lewis Gannet and Peter Franke, *based on* The Spy *by* Paul Thomas. *Adaptation:* Jean Clouzot and Raoul Lévy. *Director of photography:* Raoul Coutard. *Music:* Serge Gainsbourg. *Art directors:* Pierre Guffroy, Jürgen Kiebach and Ernst Schomer. *Film editors:* Albert Jürgenson and Roger Dwyre. *Sound engineer:* Joseph de Bretagne. *Assistant director:* Thomas Grimm. *Production managers:* Hans Sommer and Jean-Paul Delamotte. *Production director:* Hans Seitz. *German production director:* Heinrich Moll. *Production*

secretary: Madeleine von Crobath. *Cost accountant:* Ingeborg Wilfert. *Makeup:* Raimund Stangl. *Locations:* Munich, Elbe River, Germany. Eastmancolor. 106 minutes.

CAST

Prof. James Bower, Montgomery Clift; *Peter Heinzman,* Hardy Kruger; *CIA agent Adam,* Roddy McDowall; *Frieda Hoffman,* Macha Méril; *Orlovsky,* David Opatoshu; *Ingrid,* Christine Delaroche; *Dr. Saltzer,* Hannes Messemer; *The Major,* Karl Lieffen; *Orlovsky's friend,* Jean-Luc Godard; Uta Levka.

Bower has a drink with his contact's nurse (Macha Méril).

Bower escapes from East Germany with the workers.

In October 1965, the writer Salka Viertel recommended Clift to producer/director Raoul Lévy. Lévy had written a spy thriller which could be done cheaply, a sort of poor man's *Spy Who Came in From the Cold* called *The Defector*, based on a Paul Thomas novel. Clift deemed the script abominable, but wanted to do it to prove he could work again; it was four years after *Freud* and he still had not made a film. It would be a kind of preparation for *Reflections in a Golden Eye*, proof to the world (and to Warner Bros.-Seven Arts who were producing both films) that he could still act.

But for now there were problems getting a leading lady. First Leslie Caron was set, then Simone Signoret, Monica Vitti, and Nicole Courcel each considered the part of the nurse. Finally the role of Frieda Hoffman went to Macha Méril.

Then there was the script, which Monty worked on first with Caron, then with Mira Rostova, who was again coaching him (for the first time since the early days of *From Here to Eternity*). The screenplay was impossible to conquer; it was shallow, silly, confused, and of no interest—except, of course, that Clift was acting in it. *The Defector* concerns an American scientist, James Bower, who is urged to spy for the CIA while ostensibly vacationing in East Germany. He is to make contact with a Dr. Saltzer who will help him acquire a strip of microfilm prepared by a Soviet scientist and bring it back to the West. Bower is hounded by Peter Heinzman, an OGPU operative, who has divined his purpose and is determined that he will not succeed. When Bower does get his hands on the microfilm it proves worthless. Bower is afraid he will not be able to return to the West and the doctor's nurse, Frieda, helps him escape in the back of a van. He bicycles to the border with a group of farm workers and makes a mad dash for the border, undergoing a harrowing series of narrow escapes. But Heinzman is not finished with him and, pretending to be a defector, escapes to the West, where he is mysteriously run down by a truck. There is some indication that his death was caused by the CIA, and on that enigmatic note *The Defector* ends.

The Montgomery Clift who appears on the

screen here is a far cry even from the Montgomery Clift of *Freud* four years earlier. He is thin to the point of emaciation; his mouth is strained; he is older, tired looking; his hair is graying and there are deep creases at his eyes. It's a good thing his romantic sequences with Macha Méril are kept to a minimum as this Clift is a character actor, not a romantic leading man, and he can no longer employ the passionate flirtatiousness that he used so assuredly and effectively in films like *The Heiress* and *Indiscretion of an American Wife.* Nevertheless, his brief *amour* with Méril is one of the few pleasures *The Defector* has to offer. They are light and happy with one another in

contrast to all the murky, heavy-handed doings the rest of the film entails.

There were also problems during the filming with Méril, who did not want to play a bed scene —fully clothed—with Clift. As she reported the misunderstanding, Clift disapproved of her suggestion that the sequence be cut: "Did he think I was attacking his acting? Next day he was like stone. Something had gone out of him. I think Monty felt that the *part* needed this scene, and that *he* did, where he is shown seducing a healthy young girl. Like the later scene where he dives into the Elbe, and he wants to do it himself. So Raoul saw how much he wanted those scenes,

The professor attempts a daring daylight escape.

In the safety of West Germany: Bower, Adam, and Peter Heinzman, the defector (Hardy Kruger).

Waiting to cross the river.

and put them back in. And, in fact, I guess he was quite right. Because they come off very well.'' She ended by admiring Clift tremendously, saying: "I think Monty is better now than he ever was. Monty was getting older. He was almost too *beautiful* before. We did our parting scene—my last scene—and when we were discussing it, he had been over it so often, so hard, that just talking about it there were tears in his eyes.''

The scene Méril refers to, in which Clift jumps into the Elbe, was his way of demonstrating that he could undertake the rigors of an action film. Although Lévy could easily have used a double, Clift insisted on inflicting great corporeal punishment on himself by suspending himself underneath a bridge, climbing at night up another bridge, swimming in the Elbe's fast-moving current, crawling through barbed wire, stealing a boat, and jumping into the river just before the boat hits a mine. It was grueling and Clift could not always withstand the strain.

Lévy, who complicated the filming by carrying on a romance with his married script girl, worried about his star: "I hope he gets through the next two weeks.'' Mira Rostova, for her part, felt that Lévy was barely adequate. "He was no director,'' she said, "he was a joke.''

212

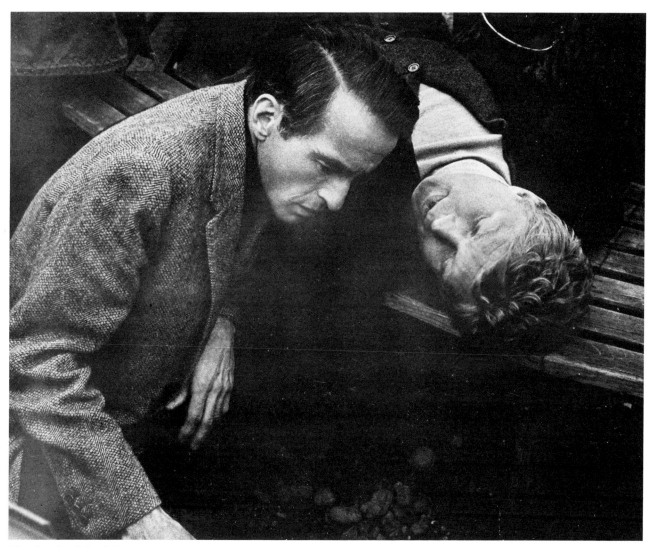

The death of the defector.

And *The Defector* bears her out. It is a film Clift would not have considered a few years previously, and, sadly, it is his last.

The critics agreed that *The Defector* was a deplorable final film for a star as luminous as Clift. *Time*'s reviewer said: "Aside from some radiant color photography by Raoul Coutard, Clift is the only interesting thing in this sluggish and somewhat muddled movie. But the interest in Clift, who died of a heart attack soon after this picture was completed, will be mostly morbid. Suffice it to say that his acting, though competent, is less striking than his appearance. He looks like a man who knows he is in bad health—and in a bad picture. It provides an undistinguished conclusion to a distinguished career."

Joseph Gelmis, writing in *Newsday*, reported: "Despite its weaknesses, *The Defector* is worth seeing for Clift's performance. It is sad and fascinating and full of grief. And the terrible fact is, the man wasn't pretending. He was sick, probably dying, when he made the film, his first since *Freud*, four years ago."

Bosley Crowther of *The New York Times* felt that ". . . Mr. Clift is apt in his last film—lonely, bewildered, courageous."

But the best remembrance was provided by Arthur Knight in *Saturday Review:* "Montgomery Clift's last film before his untimely death is a sad epitaph to the tragedy-strewn career of a young man who was once one of our most promising and interesting new stars."

THEATER

Thomas Mitchell, Georgette McKee (Andrea King),
and Montgomery Clift in Fly Away Home.

AS HUSBANDS GO

By Rachel Crothers. Amateur production, Sarasota, Florida, March 30, 1933.

FLY AWAY HOME

By Dorothy Bennett and Irving White. *Directed by* Thomas Mitchell. *Sets:* Raymond Sovey. *Produced by* Theron Bamberger and Warner Bros. 48th Street Theatre, New York, January 15, 1935.

CAST

Harmer Masters, Montgomery Clift; *Buff Masters*, Georgette McKee (Andrea King); *Linda Masters*, Joan Tompkins; *Corey Masters*, Edwin Philips; *Penny*, Clare Woodbury; *Tinka Collingsby*, Lili Zehner; *Johnny Heming*, Philip Faversham; *James Masters*, Thomas Mitchell; *Armand Sloan*, Albert Van Dekker; *Maria*, Geraldine Kay; *Gabriel*, Sheldon Leonard; *Taxi Driver*, Elmer Brown; *Nan Masters*, Ann Mason.

JUBILEE

Book by Moss Hart. *Music by* Cole Porter. *Staged and lit by* Hassard Short. *Dialogue directed by* Monty Woolley. *Costumes:* Irene Sharaff. *Orchestra conducted by* Frank Tours. *Orchestrations:* Russell Bennett. *Dance Arrangements:* Albertina Rasch. *Scenery:* Jo Mielziner. *Produced by* Sam Harris and Max Gordon. Imperial Theatre, New York, October 12, 1935.

CAST

The King, Melville Cooper; *The Queen*, Mary Boland; *Prince James*, Charles Walters; *Princess Diana*, Mar-

Georgette McKee (Andrea King), Edwin Phillips, Mary Wickes, Monty, and Betty Field in the summer stock production of Fly Away Home.

garet Adams; *Prince Peter*, Montgomery Clift; *Prince Rudolph*, Jackie Kelk; *Lord Wyndham*, Richie Ling; *Eric Dare*, Derek Williams; *Karen O'Kane*, June Knight; *Eva Standing*, May Boley; *Charles Rausmiller (Mowgli)*, Mark Plant; *Mrs. Watkins*, Jane Evans; *Laura Fitzgerald*, Olive Reeves-Smith; *Sandwich Man*, Charles Brokaw; *Professor Rexford*, Ralph Sumpter; *Beach Widow*, Dorothy Fox; *Cabinet Minister*, Leo Chalzel; *Cabinet Minister*, Charles Brokaw; *Lifeguard*, Don Douglas; *Announcer*, Albert Amato; *Master of Ceremonies*, Harold Murray; *Drunk*, Jack Edwards; *Usher*, Ted Fetter; *Zoo Keeper*, Leo Chalzel.

YR. OBEDIENT HUSBAND

By Horace Jackson. *Staged by* John Cromwell. *Sets:* Jo Mielziner. *Produced by* Maxwell Productions. Broadhurst Theatre, New York, January 10, 1938.

CAST

Mrs. Scurlock, Dame May Whitty; *Mistress Binns*, Brenda Forbes; *Prue*, Florence Eldridge; *Podd*, Frieda Altman; *Richard Steele*, Fredric March; *Joseph Addison*, J.W. Austin; *Partridge*, Martin Wolfson; *Elizabeth*, Marilyn Jolie; *Patrick*, Harold Thomas; *Silas Pennyfield*, Walter Jones; *Lady Envil*, Helena Glenn; *Lord Envil*, Leslie Austen; *John Gay*, John Pickard; *Mrs. Howe*, Ethel Morrison; *Thomas Howe, M.P.*, A.J. Herbert; *Lady Warwick (Mrs. Addison)*, Katherine Stewart; *Lord Finch*, Montgomery Clift.

EYE ON THE SPARROW

By Maxwell Selser. *Staged by* John M. Worth (pseudonym for Antoinette Perry, according to Burns Mantle). *Produced by* Girvan G. Higginson. Vanderbilt Theatre, New York, May 3, 1938.

CAST

Philip Thomas, Montgomery Clift; *Nancy Thomas*, Katherine Deane; *Freeman*, Edgar Stehli; *Roger Sanford*, Barry Sullivan; *Ted Strong*, Philip Ober; *Barbara Thomas*, Catharine Doucet; *Fejac Strode*, Leslie King; *Jim Wright*, Perce Benton; *Rostican*, Stiano Braggiotti; *Florence Augden*, Dorothy Francis; *O'Mara*, Francesca Lenni; *Thomas Hosea*, Edward Fielding; *Rent Collector*, Ernest Woodward; *Moving Man*, Lester Damon; *Rug Man*, Sandy Strouse.

Jackie Kelk and Monty in Jubilee.

Monty, Lois Hall, and Morgan James in Dame Nature.

THE WIND AND THE RAIN

By Merton Hodge. *Directed by* Charles J. Parsons. Millbrook Theatre, Millbrook, Conn. July 25–30, 1938.

CAST

Mrs. McPhe, Shirley DeMe; *Gilbert Raymond,* Lex Lindsay; *John Williams,* James Gregory; *Charles Tritton,* Montgomery Clift; *Dr. Paul Duhamel,* Allan Tower; *Anne Hargreaves,* Evelyn Evers; *Jill Manning,* Celeste Holm; *Roger Cole,* Jeffrey (William Clark); *Pete Morgan,* Robin Clapp.

DAME NATURE

By André Birabeau, *derived from the French by* Patricia Collinge. *Staged by* Worthington Miner. *Sets:* Norris Houghton. *Production supervision:* Theresa Helburn, Lawrence Langner and Worthington Miner. *Produced by* the Theatre Guild. Booth Theatre, New York, September 26, 1938.

CAST

Max, Thomas Coffin Cooke; *Beer, a Schoolboy,* Charles Bellin; *Second Schoolboy,* Frederick Bradlee; *Third Schoolboy,* Edwin Mills; *Concièrge,* Edwin Cooper; *Doctor Faridet,* Harry Irvine; *Leonie Perrot,* Lois Hall; *André Brisac,* Montgomery Clift; *Batton,* Morgan James; *Fourth Schoolboy,* Peter Miner; *Nanine,* Kathryn Grill; *Marie,* Grace Matthews; *Madame Brisac,* Jessie Royce Landis; *Uncle Lucien,* Forrest Orr; *Paul Marachal,* Wilton Graff.

THE MOTHER

By Paul Selver and Miles Malleson, *from the play by* Karel Capek. *Staged by* Miles Malleson. *Sets:* Lester Polakov. *Produced by* Victor Payne-Jennings *in association with* Kathleen Robinson. Lyceum Theatre, New York, April 25, 1939.

CAST

The Mother, Alla Nazimova; *The Father*, Reginald Bach; *Andrew*, Stephen Ker Appleby; *George*, Carl Norval; *Christopher*, Alan Brixley; *Peter*, Tom Palmer; *Tony*, Montgomery Clift; *Old Man*, Edward Broadley.

THERE SHALL BE NO NIGHT

By Robert E. Sherwood. *Staged by* Alfred Lunt. *Sets:* Richard Whorf. *Costumes:* Valentina. *Produced by* the Playwrights Company and the Theatre Guild. Alvin Theatre, New York, April 29, 1940.

CAST

Dr. Kaarlo Valkonen, Alfred Lunt; *Miranda Valkonen*, Lynn Fontanne; *Dave Corween*, Richard Whorf; *Uncle Waldemar*, Sydney Greenstreet; *Gus Shuman*, Brooks West; *Erik Valkonen*, Montgomery Clift; *Kaatri Alquist*, Elisabeth Fraser; *Dr. Ziemssen*, Maurice Coulbourne; *Major Rutkowski*, Edward Raquello; *Joe Burnett*, Charles Ansley; *Ben Gichner*, Thomas Gomez; *Frank Olmstead*, William Le Massena; *Sergeant Gosden*, Claude Horton; *Lempi*, Phyllis Thaxter; *Ilma*, Charva Chester; *Photographer*, Ralph Nelson; *Photographer*, Robert Downing.

OUT OF THE FRYING PAN

By Francis Swann. *Directed by* Sanford Meisner, *assisted by* David Pressman. *Sets by* Richard Burns. *Produced by* Jean Muir and Mr. Meisner. The County Theatre, Suffern, New York, week of August 4, 1941.

CAST

George Bodell, Michael Strong; *Norman Reese*, Kenneth Tobey; *Mrs. Garnet*, Mabel Paige; *Tony Dennison*, Montgomery Clift; *Muriel Foster*, Florence Mc-Michael; *Kate Ault*, Peggy Meyer; *Marge Benson*, Sally Gracie; *Dottie Coburn*, Gertrude Beach; *Mr. Coburn*, Harry Antrim; *Mr. Kenny*, Percy Kilbride; *Mac*, Tony Manning; *Joe*, Henry Lawson.

There Shall Be No Night: *Lynn Fontanne, Monty, and Alfred Lunt.*

Frances Heflin, Florence Eldridge, Fredric March, and Monty in The Skin of Our Teeth.

219

A portrait from Foxhole in the Parlor.

MEXICAN MURAL

By Raymon Naya. *Staged and produced by* Robert Lewis. *Scenery:* Herbert Andrews. *Lighting:* Wil-Washcoe. Chanin Auditorium, New York, April 26, 1942.

CAST

First Panel: Vera Cruz Interior
Rumbero, Wallace House; *Comparsas,* Priscilla Newton; Robert Lander; *Didi Ruiz,* Perry Wilson; *Dona Alex,* Kathryn Grill; *Lalo Brito,* Montgomery Clift; *Luisa,* Eda Reiss.
Second Panel: Miracle Painting
Celestina Ruiz, Libby Holman; *Chelina,* Terry Dicks; *Doctor Brito,* Spencer James; *Morena,* Gertrude Gilpin; *Petra,* Henrietta Lovelace; *Verbena,* Mira Rosovskaya (Mira Rostova); *Lady,* Norma Chambers;
Third Panel: Moonlight Scene
Mariano Ruiz, Kevin McCarthy; *Miguel Ruiz,* Owen Jordon; *Troubadours,* Wallace House; Spencer James; *Mata Hari,* David Opatoshu; *Gold Shirts,* Larry Hugo; William Le Massena; Morton Amster; *People of Vera Cruz,* Tom Barry, Viola Kates, Priscilla Newton, Robert Lander;
Fourth Panel: Patio with Flamingo
Redhead, Kenneth Tobey; *Juliana,* Norma Chambers; *Maria Chris,* Viola Kates.

THE SKIN OF OUR TEETH

By Thornton Wilder. *Staged by* Elia Kazan. *Sets:* Albert Johnson. *Costumes:* Mary Perry Schenck. *Produced by* Michael Myerberg. Plymouth Theatre, New York, November 18, 1942.

CAST

Announcer, Morton DaCosta; *Sabina,* Tallulah Bankhead; *Mr. Fitzpatrick,* E.G. Marshall; *Mrs. Antrobus,* Florence Eldridge; *Dinosaur,* Remo Buffano; *Mammoth,* Andrew Ratousheff; *Telegraph Boy,* Dickie Van Patten; *Gladys,* Frances Heflin; *Henry,* Montgomery Clift; *Mr. Antrobus,* Fredric March; *Doctor,* Arthur Griffin; *Professor,* Ralph Kellard; *Judge,* Joseph Smiley; *Homer,* Ralph Cullinan; *Miss E. Muse,* Edith Faversham; *Miss T. Muse,* Emily Lorraine; *Miss M. Muse,* Eva Mudge Nelson; *Ushers,* Stanley Prager, Harry Clark; *Girls,* Elizabeth Scott, Patricia Riordan; *Fortune Teller,* Florence Reed; *Chair Pushers,* Early Sydnor, Carroll Clark; *Conveners,* Stanley Weede, Seumas Flynn, Aubrey Fasset, Stanley Prager, Harry Clark, Stephan Cole; *Broadcast Official,* Morton DaCosta; *Defeated Candidate,* Joseph Smiley; *Mr. Tremayne,* Ralph Kellard; *Hester,* Eulabelle Moore; *Ivy,* Viola Dean; *Fred Bailey,* Stanley Prager.

Marianne Stewart and Monty in You Touched Me!

OUR TOWN

By Thornton Wilder. *Staged by* Jed Harris *and* Wesley McKee. *Revived by* Jed Harris. City Center, New York, January 10, 1944.

CAST

Stage Manager, Marc Connelly; *Dr. Gibbs*, Curtis Cooksey; *Joe Crowell*, Richard Dalton; *Howie Newsome*, Donald Keyes; *Mrs. Gibbs*, Evelyn Varden; *Mrs. Webb*, Ethel Remey; *George Gibbs*, Montgomery Clift; *Rebecca Gibbs*, Carolyn Hummel; *Wally Webb*, Teddy Rose; *Emily Webb*, Martha Scott; *Professor Willard*, Arthur Allen; *Mr. Webb*, Parker Fennelly; *Woman in Balcony*, Alice Hill; *Man in Auditorium*, John Paul; *Lady in Box*, Frederica Going; *Simon Stimson*, William Swetland; *Mrs. Soames*, Doro Merande; *Constable Warren*, Owen Coll; *Si Crowell*, Roy Robson; *Baseball Players*, Alfred Porter, Charles Wiley, Jr., Henry Michaels; *Sam Craig*, Jay Velie; *Joe Stoddard*, John Ravold; *Mr. Carter*, Walter O. Hill.

THE SEARCHING WIND

By Lillian Hellman. Staged and produced by Herman Shumlin. Sets: Howard Bay. Costumes: Aline Bernstein. Fulton Theatre, New York, April 12, 1944.

CAST

Moses Taney, Dudley Digges; *Samuel Hazen,* Montgomery Clift; *Ponette,* Alfred Hesse; *Sophronia,* Mercedes Gilbert; *Emily Hazen,* Cornelia Otis Skinner; *Alexander Hazen,* Dennis King; *First Waiter,* Edgar Andrews; *Second Waiter,* Joseph de Santis; *Catherine Bowman,* Barbara O'Neil; *Hotel Manager,* Walter Kohler; *Eppler,* William E. Schoeller; *Edward Halsey,* Eric Latham; *James Sears,* Eugene Earl; *Count Max von Stammer,* Arnold Korff.

FOXHOLE IN THE PARLOR

By Elsa Shelley. *Directed by* John Haggott. *Sets:* Lee Simonson. *Produced by* Harry Bloomfield. Booth Theatre, New York, May 23, 1945.

CAST

Leroy, Reginald Beane; *Tom Austen,* Russell Hardie; *Vicki King,* Ann Lincoln; *Ann Austen,* Flora Campbell; *Senator Bowen,* Raymond Greenleaf; *Dennis Patterson,* Montgomery Clift; *Kate Mitchell,* Grace Coppin.

YOU TOUCHED ME!

By Tennessee Williams and Donald Windham, *from a D. H. Lawrence short story. Staged by* Guthrie McClintic *in association with* Lee Shubert. *Sets:* Motley. Booth Theatre, New York, September 25, 1945.

CAST

Matilda Rockley, Marianne Stewart; *Emmie Rockley,* Catherine Willard; *Phoebe,* Norah Howard; *Hadrian,* Montgomery Clift; *Cornelius Rockley,* Edmund Gwenn; *Rev. Guilford Melton,* Neil Fitzgerald; *Policeman,* Freeman Hammond.

THE SEAGULL

By Anton Chekov, *adapted by* Mira Rostova, Kevin McCarthy and Montgomery Clift. *Staged by* Norris Houghton. *Music arranged by* Max Marlin. *Sets:* Duane McKinney. *Costumes:* Alvin Colt. *Lighting:* Klaus Holm. Phoenix Theatre, New York, May 11, 1954.

CAST

Mme. Irina Arkadina, Judith Evelyn; *Constantin Treplev,* Montgomery Clift; *Peter Sorin,* Sam Jaffe; *Nina Zarechnaya,* Mira Rostova; *Shamrayev,* Will Geer; *Paulina,* June Walker; *Masha,* Maureen Stapleton; *Boris Trigorin,* Kevin McCarthy; *Dr. Dorn,* George Voskovec; *Medvedenko,* John Fiedler; *Yakov,* Karl Light; *Cook,* Lou Polan; *Housemaid,* Sarah Marshall.

As Constantin Treplev in The Sea Gull.